Investigating Science
with Dinosaurs

INVESTIGATING SCIENCE
WITH DINOSAURS

CRAIG A. MUNSART

TEACHER IDEAS PRESS
A Division of
Libraries Unlimited, Inc.
Englewood, Colorado
1993

TEACHER IDEAS PRESS
A Division of
Libraries Unlimited, Inc.
P.O. Box 6633
Englewood, CO 80155-6633

Library of Congress Cataloging-in-Publication Data

Munsart, Craig A.
    Investigating science with dinosaurs / Craig A. Munsart.
    xiii, 249 p. 22x28 cm.
    Includes bibliographical references and index.
    ISBN 1-56308-008-7
    1. Science--Study and teaching (Elementary)--United States.
2. Teaching--Aids and devices. 3. Dinosaurs. 4. Activity programs
in education--United States.   I. Title.
LB1585.3.M86   1993
372.3'5'044-dc20   92-41785
                                                            CIP

This book is dedicated
to the memory of

Dr. Walter S. Newman

whose contagious enthusiasm
made geology come alive for me,

and to students like

Brian G.,

who would rather study
science and dinosaurs
than anything else in school.

CONTENTS

**Part 3
Investigating Dinosaur Worlds**

PREFACE

It is difficult for anyone to view a museum's dinosaur skeleton and not be awestruck by the enormity, power, and uniqueness of the assembled collection of inanimate bones. There is a magic about standing in the shadow of the remains of an extinct creature, remains that tower over humbled, human spectators. I was fortunate enough to have spent the first 30 years of my life in New York City, where I experienced many such magical hours gazing at the collection of dinosaurs in the American Museum of Natural History.

Wonder is defined as "something that arouses awe, astonishment, surprise, or admiration; marvel." Students often miss the wonder in a large dinosaur skeleton and casually observe, "Oh yeah, that's *Triceratops*," without considering where it came from, how it lived (and died), what it can tell us about the earth or how we know what we know about it. Students easily memorize names and dimensions of dinosaurs but often learn little about the science that surrounds these creatures; the wonder is lost in the process. Scientific analysis, however, has its own drawbacks: it is much like a magic trick in that once the secret behind the mystery is revealed, the wonder can be destroyed. As Henry Drummond says in *Inherit the Wind* (Lawrence and Lee 1955, 83), "Mister, you may conquer the air; but the birds will lose their wonder."

As a geologist I learned to understand and appreciate the processes that occur in the world around me. That understanding heightened, rather than diminished, the "wow" I felt when seeing Grand Teton, Yosemite, and Hawaii Volcanoes national parks. I am hoping this book will have that same effect upon both teachers and students. Understanding how science and dinosaurs interact will hopefully heighten the appreciation and sense of wonder for both.

In *Bully for Brontosaurus* Stephen J. Gould (1991, 99) writes:

> I survey the dinosaur craze and wonder why science suffers so badly within our schools.... Kids love science so long as fine teaching and good material grace the presentation. If the dinosaur craze of pop culture has been adequately subverted for educational ends, why can't we capitalize on this benevolent spin-off? Why can't we sustain the interest rather than letting it wither like the flower of grass, as soon as a child moves on to his next stage? Why can't we infuse some of this excitement into our schools and use it to boost and expand interest in all of science?

In some small way I hope this book can nurture and expand a student's interest in all of science, using dinosaurs as a springboard.

Today, dinosaurs are perhaps more highly visible than they ever were during their 165-million-year reign over the animal kingdom. When Sextus Propertius claimed that "absence makes the heart grow fonder" in (circa) A.D. 30, it is unlikely he was referring to dinosaurs. The fact remains, however, that since their extinction more than 60 million years ago, dinosaurs have never been regarded more fondly than they are today. They appear as cookies, cake icing designs, gummy candies, and breakfast cereals, and on student lunch boxes, rental trucks, postage stamps, and T-shirts; they even have a weekly, prime-time, television series.

Their popularity with children is particularly difficult to explain. Winnie the Pooh is adorable and cuddly; it is easy to have sympathy for Dumbo; and children can identify with Snoopy. *Allosaurus* and *Tyrannosaurus rex* have none of their charm—dinosaurs are generally large and intimidating. Thinking of dinosaurs as lovable should be improbable at best. Yet people want to like dinosaurs. Despite their often fearsome appearance, dinosaurs have often been portrayed as cute and lovable ever since "Gertie" the apatosaur first appeared in movies in 1912. Cartoons such as the "Flintstones," "B.C.," and "Alley Oop" (inaccurately) portray early man coexisting with dinosaurs as household pets or denizens of the same environment.

From preschool to college, students enjoy learning about dinosaurs because of their mystery, their uniqueness, and their sheer size. Announcing to students that "we are going to learn about dinosaurs" will usually elicit an enthusiastic response. A similar announcement about learning science is generally less well received. This book will attempt to demonstrate that the two subjects are not mutually exclusive. Many excellent books exist that cover state-of-the-art knowledge and controversies about dinosaurs in great detail. This book will build upon that knowledge base. For the teacher this book will provide a group of classroom-tested activities leading students through the discovery process of science, data acquisition and manipulation, and scientific applications. Activities within each chapter will introduce students to the principles of science, explain how those principles were applied in the past, and apply those principles to exercises involving experiential learning of physics, earth science, and mathematics. For students, this book will build upon their enthusiasm for dinosaurs and allow them to become scientists. Students will have the opportunity to learn how scientists know what they know, or what they *think* they know. A knowledge of how science works will provide an understanding of the continuing evolution of the discovery and analytical processes that lead to the facts (as they are known today).

This book is designed to be "user friendly" for teachers. Chapters contain both explanations of the subject matter and activities to be performed by students. Time required, materials needed, student grouping, and step-by-step instructions are provided for each activity, as are extension activities for advanced students or students in upper grades. Activities integrate reading and library skills as much as possible. In many cases, illustrations are designed to be used as overhead transparencies. The activities have been tested by both teachers and students in grades 4 through 12. Some that require mathematics may be more appropriate for secondary students only. Skill levels of your students will ultimately determine grade-level compatibility. Supplementary material at the end of the book includes a summary of activities and the skills they require, explanations of fossils and geologic time, a glossary of scientific terms, a pronunciation guide to dinosaur names, and a comprehensive bibliography of all titles mentioned in text.

It is important for students (and teachers) to realize that science is a tapestry woven of threads from individual disciplines. As you will see in the pages that follow, the study of dinosaurs involves mechanics, chemistry, paleontology, geology, nuclear physics, biology, and, of course, mathematics.

A company lawyer I knew had a sign that read, "OBSCURE OBFUSCATION." It was an explanation of "legalese," the language that lawyers use that only lawyers could possibly understand. All specializations require a unique vocabulary, or jargon. Preparing a recipe, playing baseball, piloting the space shuttle, even teaching a class all require vocabulary that is unique to the task. Vocabulary is important, but only as a tool for the completion of the task. I remember observing a science class where the students were constantly drilled on vocabulary words about trees. At the conclusion of the study of trees the students knew that a stoma was the pore in a leaf but did not have the faintest idea of how a tree functioned or why the stoma was important. I have made a strong effort to minimize the use of paleontological jargon, not in an effort to trivialize the content, but to make the text more accessible to a broader audience; in short, to avoid obfuscation.

REFERENCES

Gould, Stephen J. 1991. *Bully for Brontosaurus*. New York: W. W. Norton.

Lawrence, Jerome, and Robert E. Lee. 1955. *Inherit the Wind*. New York: Bantam Books.

ACKNOWLEDGMENTS

This book owes a great deal to dinosaur experts, both past and present. the early pioneers such as Dr. Gideon Mantell, Sir Richard Owen, Baron Georges Cuvier, Edward Drinker Cope, Othniel Charles Marsh, Roy Chapman Andrews, and Barnum Brown and the new pioneers such as Edwin Colbert, John Ostrom, Martin Lockley, Richard Thulborn, John Horner, and Robert Bakker. The science of paleontology also owes a great debt to those thousands whose names are lost to history who labored as field crews under the direction of those more familiar names. I must also thank the students and faculty of Kyffin and Red Rocks Elementary, Drake Junior High, and Green Mountain Senior High schools in Jefferson County, Colorado, for their help in evaluating and improving many of the activities. Thanks to my supporters from the Friends of Dinosaur Ridge, especially Bob Reynolds, Joe Tempel, and Pete Modreski. Many teachers in the Denver metropolitan area participated in teacher-training workshops for the Dinosaur Ridge resource area west of Denver and, in doing so, became guinea pigs for the activities in this book; there are too many to thank individually, but you know who you are. M. Susann W. Powers, librarian with the U.S. Geological Survey and custodian of the GEO Center in Denver, was an exceptional resource. Dr. Martin Lockley, associate professor of geology at the University of Colorado at Denver, critically reviewed the manuscript and provided valuable technical expertise. You would not be reading this now were it not for the staff of Libraries Unlimited in Englewood, Colorado. David Loertscher was an ardent fan of this book when it was merely a glimmer and remained a steadfast supporter and helpful critic during its growth. Dr. Richard Scott was an exceptional resource and sounding board for much of the book's development. After shocking me with a "medium edit," Deborah Korte ultimately made this a much better book; I was truly impressed, and I thank her. Dr. Suzanne Barchers, my former boss and now editor and friend, kept me on track and provided educational expertise and constant support. Any good things that happen to this book can, in no small way, be credited to Suzanne. And thanks especially to Rosalyn Munsart, who as an elementary teacher tried many of these activities in her class and became my sounding board, and as my wife quietly tolerated (most of the time) the mess around the house as I worked on this project.

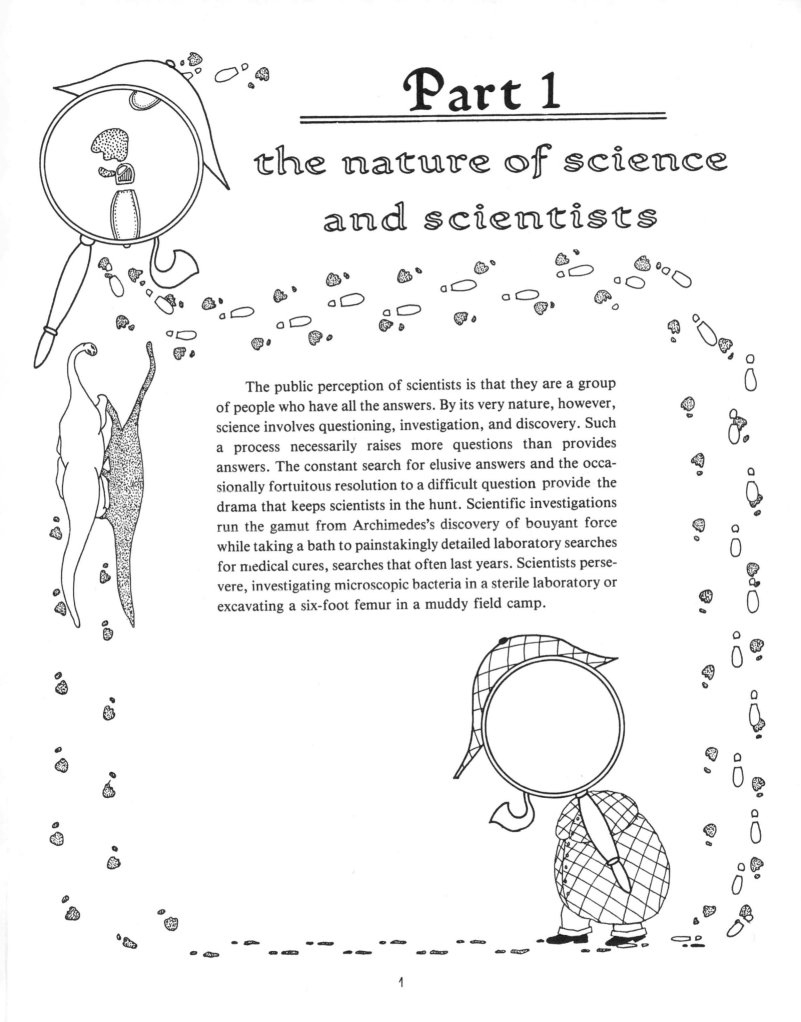

Part 1

the nature of science and scientists

The public perception of scientists is that they are a group of people who have all the answers. By its very nature, however, science involves questioning, investigation, and discovery. Such a process necessarily raises more questions than provides answers. The constant search for elusive answers and the occasionally fortuitous resolution to a difficult question provide the drama that keeps scientists in the hunt. Scientific investigations run the gamut from Archimedes's discovery of bouyant force while taking a bath to painstakingly detailed laboratory searches for medical cures, searches that often last years. Scientists persevere, investigating microscopic bacteria in a sterile laboratory or excavating a six-foot femur in a muddy field camp.

1

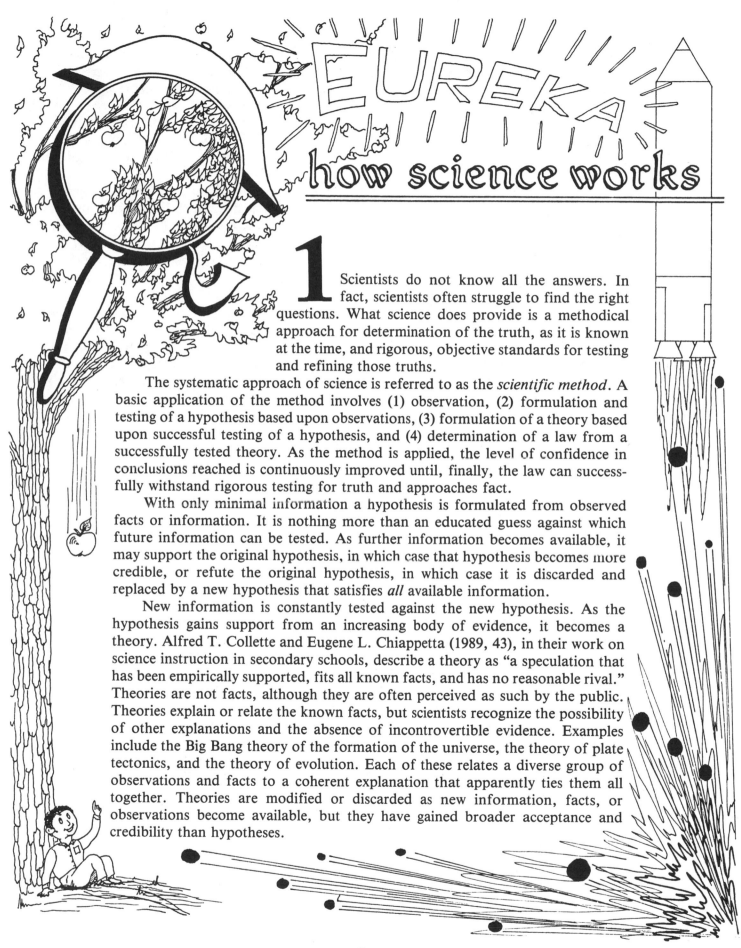

EUREKA
how science works

1 Scientists do not know all the answers. In fact, scientists often struggle to find the right questions. What science does provide is a methodical approach for determination of the truth, as it is known at the time, and rigorous, objective standards for testing and refining those truths.

The systematic approach of science is referred to as the *scientific method*. A basic application of the method involves (1) observation, (2) formulation and testing of a hypothesis based upon observations, (3) formulation of a theory based upon successful testing of a hypothesis, and (4) determination of a law from a successfully tested theory. As the method is applied, the level of confidence in conclusions reached is continuously improved until, finally, the law can successfully withstand rigorous testing for truth and approaches fact.

With only minimal information a hypothesis is formulated from observed facts or information. It is nothing more than an educated guess against which future information can be tested. As further information becomes available, it may support the original hypothesis, in which case that hypothesis becomes more credible, or refute the original hypothesis, in which case it is discarded and replaced by a new hypothesis that satisfies *all* available information.

New information is constantly tested against the new hypothesis. As the hypothesis gains support from an increasing body of evidence, it becomes a theory. Alfred T. Collette and Eugene L. Chiappetta (1989, 43), in their work on science instruction in secondary schools, describe a theory as "a speculation that has been empirically supported, fits all known facts, and has no reasonable rival." Theories are not facts, although they are often perceived as such by the public. Theories explain or relate the known facts, but scientists recognize the possibility of other explanations and the absence of incontrovertible evidence. Examples include the Big Bang theory of the formation of the universe, the theory of plate tectonics, and the theory of evolution. Each of these relates a diverse group of observations and facts to a coherent explanation that apparently ties them all together. Theories are modified or discarded as new information, facts, or observations become available, but they have gained broader acceptance and credibility than hypotheses.

When the preponderance of evidence overwhelmingly supports a theory, that theory may be considered a law. The law is the closest member of the hierarchy of scientific method to truth. The universal law of gravitation and Newton's law of motion are examples. Laws may satisfy *almost* all conditions and still be accepted. From among the many possible explanations or hypotheses of a single event or observation, a single law emerges that can be broadly and correctly applied to a wide diversity of related facts. In an ideal case that law will satisfy all related facts (Newton's first law of motion); in a close-to-ideal case the law satisfies all but certain unique conditions (Boyle's law, which predicts the behavior of gases when changing their volume or pressure—at high pressures many gases differ from Boyle's predictions).

A description of the scientific method is, unfortunately, often the first introduction for many people to the nature of science. Although accurate, it ignores much of the spontaneity and excitement that motivates most scientists. It creates the impression that science is a dull, plodding, by-the-numbers process at which almost anyone can succeed if he or she is willing to apply thought processes in a linear, left-brain, noncreative mode. Such a perception of science clearly destroys the wonder of discovery and understandably causes the aversion to science seen in many children. Happily, science also involves dramatic, exciting, spontaneous discoveries: the "Eureka!" of Archimedes in the bathtub, the minor headache of Isaac Newton sitting under the apple tree, and the serendipitous discovery of the principle of Velcro™ by a Swiss mountaineer removing burrs from his socks after walking through a field.

I have chosen dinosaurs as a vehicle for introducing children to science precisely because their discoveries have rarely followed slow, logical progressions. The history of our knowledge of dinosaurs is a detective story (hence the Sherlock Holmes decorative motif in the chapter openings that follow), full of tantalizing clues, mysterious footprints, fragmentary evidence, and surprise discoveries. The scientist-detectives were, and still are, intensely excitable people who thrilled to the hunt for knowledge, became both rivals and friends, concocted imaginative explanations for their discoveries, made mistakes, and corrected them. In short, they are real human beings who found challenge, stimulation, and fulfillment—not dull, dry accumulations of facts—in the mysteries of science.

A common bond among scientists is their willingness to organize and publicly share their information and their interpretations. Much as evidence gathered to solve a crime is subjected to public scrutiny in a courtroom, data gathered as a result of scientific investigation are put on public view to be tested, improved, or rejected. Basic characteristics of the scientist are honesty and a willingness to admit mistakes and move ahead to refine knowledge. Scientists readily accept that being wrong is as much a part of the process as the ultimate solution. For each correct solution many unsuccessful trials were conducted, each revealing some new bit of information that ultimately led to triumph. Students should be encouraged to experiment; any failure should be viewed not as a dead end, but as a step up the ladder to the correct solution. During this age of instant gratification, it is difficult to get students to persevere to solve problems; that is, perhaps, the greatest challenge of science education.

Learning about the nature of science through dinosaurs offers several advantages. Young people are already "hooked" on dinosaurs: Their interest exists at the outset. Many types of science—mathematics, physics, chemistry, geology—are involved, not as the study of the discipline, but as tools used in our search for information. The combination of action and analysis present in the real-world digging and interpretation of dinosaurs can be paralleled in presenting science to children. Also, dinosaur science allows many projects to be tailored to various levels of difficulty, by age level or learning ability.

Many elements of creativity in science were recognized by scientists of the past. If these can be instilled in our students—scientists of the future—we can all congratulate one another. The following aphorisms may help:

> Try many things.
> Learn from the masters.
> Action creates results.
> One cannot possess a useless talent or skill.
> Do what makes your heart leap.

Think big.

Dare to explore where there is no light.

Find a contradiction between theory and data.

Be sloppy enough that something unexpected happens, but not so sloppy that you can't
tell what happened.

Turn it on its head.

Seek beauty and simplicity.

Science does not succeed because of those who accept things as they are. On the contrary, scientific success is generated by those who look to improve upon what exists and by those who seek to create where nothing exists. The essence of such thinking has been captured by Robert Scott Root-Bernstein (1991, 420) in his poem "The Trick to Being a Maverick":

Train broadly. Think big. Proceed by leap and fill.
> Nothing ventured, nothing gained. Intuition: logic kill.
Embrace ignorance. Change fields. Become an autodidact.
> Dare to err. Dumb questions air. Eschew the true and tried act.
Act childlike. Think simple. Turn it head o'er tails.
> Always try it. Don't deny it. Push it till it fails.
Speculate. Correlate. Curiosity appease.
> Ya gotta have themata—aesthetically they please.
Be a maverick. Challenge dogma. Try impossible things.
> Dream well. Imagine better. Build a theory that sings.
Predict events. Experiment, but never deputize.
> Court precision and skepticism. It's good to criticize.
Play act. Abstract. Form patterns and recognize.
> Model it. Feel it. Metaphor and analogize.
Heuristics, stochastics—these guide you in the void.
> Insistence. Persistence. Don't be paranoid.
Haziness. Craziness. Goal: implausibility.
> Laughter first. Misunderstandings. Last respectability.
Joy in work. Research fun. Covet independency.
> Freedom seek. Self satisfy. Court irresponsibility.
Do these things and you shall find surprises unexpected.
> Detours left which turn out right, old dogmas now corrected.
So do us all a favor: Start thinking good thoughts now.
> Discovering and inventing: There's no better life I vow.

REFERENCES

Collette, Alfred T., and Eugene L. Chiappetta. 1989. *Science Instruction in the Middle and Secondary Schools*. Columbus, Ohio: Merrill.

Root-Bernstein, Robert Scott. 1991. *Discovering*. Cambridge, Mass.: First Harvard University Press.

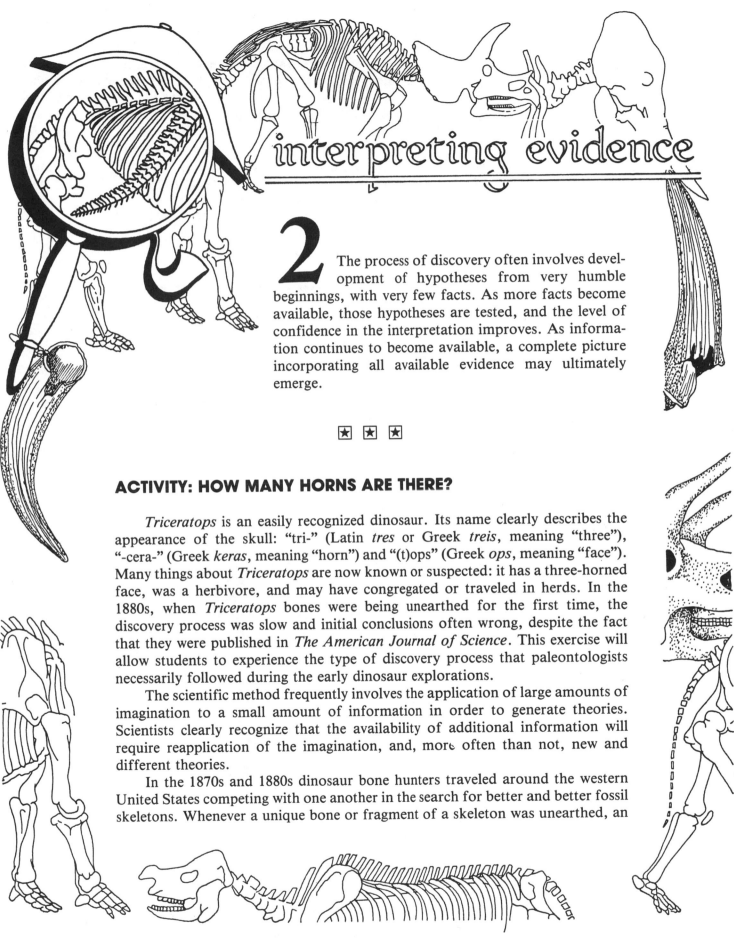

interpreting evidence

2

The process of discovery often involves development of hypotheses from very humble beginnings, with very few facts. As more facts become available, those hypotheses are tested, and the level of confidence in the interpretation improves. As information continues to become available, a complete picture incorporating all available evidence may ultimately emerge.

★ ★ ★

ACTIVITY: HOW MANY HORNS ARE THERE?

Triceratops is an easily recognized dinosaur. Its name clearly describes the appearance of the skull: "tri-" (Latin *tres* or Greek *treis*, meaning "three"), "-cera-" (Greek *keras*, meaning "horn") and "(t)ops" (Greek *ops*, meaning "face"). Many things about *Triceratops* are now known or suspected: it has a three-horned face, was a herbivore, and may have congregated or traveled in herds. In the 1880s, when *Triceratops* bones were being unearthed for the first time, the discovery process was slow and initial conclusions often wrong, despite the fact that they were published in *The American Journal of Science*. This exercise will allow students to experience the type of discovery process that paleontologists necessarily followed during the early dinosaur explorations.

The scientific method frequently involves the application of large amounts of imagination to a small amount of information in order to generate theories. Scientists clearly recognize that the availability of additional information will require reapplication of the imagination, and, more often than not, new and different theories.

In the 1870s and 1880s dinosaur bone hunters traveled around the western United States competing with one another in the search for better and better fossil skeletons. Whenever a unique bone or fragment of a skeleton was unearthed, an attempt was made to describe the entire animal, especially if a case could be made for its being a new species. There are four parts to this exercise. In each part more "facts" will be revealed, and students will be asked to draw conclusions based upon those facts. During this progressive discovery activity, more and more parts of a *Triceratops* are unearthed. As increasing information becomes available, the nature of the find becomes more readily identifiable. It is important for the students to recognize that all conclusions are valid which do not violate the available information. At the beginning of each part, read the story aloud to the class (any drawings may be shown on an overhead projector or distributed to the students). The story in part 1 is fictitious. Other parts are factual or based upon facts. Refer to the map in figure 2.1 during the discussions. *Teacher's note: It is important during this exercise to avoid using the words* dinosaur *and* Triceratops. *Allow students to draw their own conclusions—which they will!*

Fig. 2.1. Map showing area of interest in *Triceratops* discoveries.

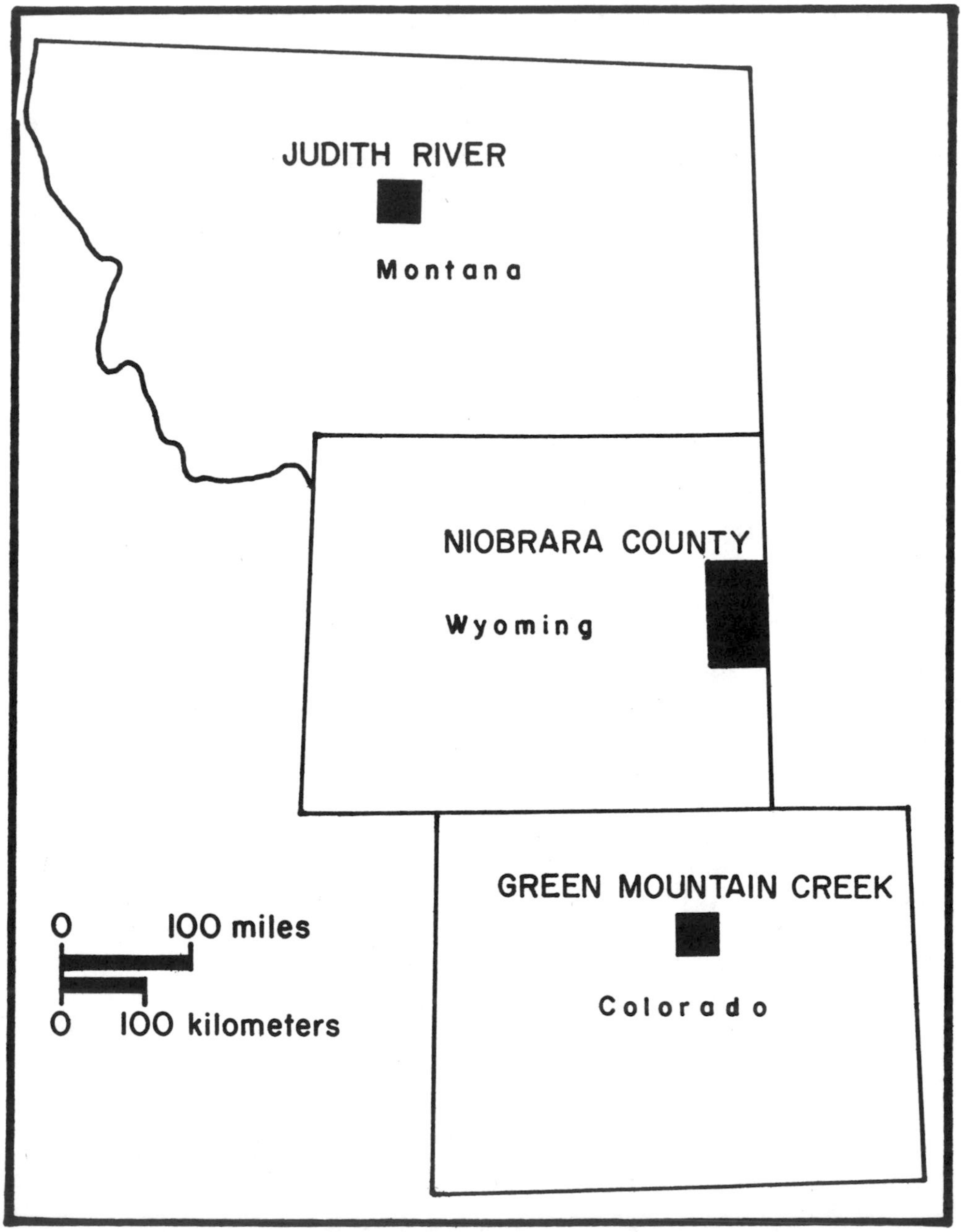

REQUIREMENTS

Time

Approximately 3 hours total (minimum) divided into four equal periods of 45 minutes

Materials

- Figures 2.1 through 2.4 as overhead transparencies
- Drawing materials for students

Grouping

Whole class and individuals

DIRECTIONS

Part 1. It was late in the afternoon on a hot, dusty hillside in Montana (see fig. 2.1, page 8) in June of 1887. The scientists had been looking for bones all day with no success, but just as they were about to return to camp, the 10-year-old daughter of the expedition leader tripped over something on the way back to the wagons. She looked down and found a pointed object that caught her shoe. When her father came to see whether she was hurt, she showed him the object. He called two men over to start digging. What they found looked like a large single horn, approximately 30 centimeters (12 inches) long. Even after further digging they could find nothing else. The object they found looked like the drawing in figure 2.2. As they sat around the campfire that night, they talked about what the animal might have looked like. They also talked about the kind of animal it might have been. Was the bone from a bison (or buffalo) or some other animal they saw on the hillsides, or could it have been from something older, maybe even something extinct? They could not tell from the object they found.

At this point students can make use of library resources to research the kinds of animals, modern or extinct, that might have died in Montana, producing similar horn fossils. Cattle, antelope, bison, or rhinoceros might be good examples.

Ask the students to draw a picture of what they think the animal may have looked like, reminding them the only evidence they have is the one pointed object that looks like a horn. When they have all completed the drawings, show each drawing to the class and discuss whether these drawings are reasonable based on the one fact presented so far. Discuss what other facts they would need to support the drawings.

Fig. 2.2. One horn, such as might have been discovered in Montana.

Part 2.   In an apparently unrelated incident several weeks later, the following article was published by Othniel C. Marsh of Yale University, one of the great dinosaur hunters of the time, in the July 1887 issue of the *American Journal of Science* (323-324):

> This species of Bison is represented by various remains, the most important of which is the portion of a skull, figured below [see fig. 2.3]. This specimen which may be regarded as the type, indicates one of [the] largest of American bovines, and one differing widely from those already described. The horn-cores, instead of being short and transverse [sticking out to the side], as in the existing bisons, are long and elevated [sticking up in the air], with slender, pointed ends. They have large cavities [holes] in the base, but in the upper two-thirds are nearly, or quite, solid.... The locality of the type specimen is on the banks of Green Mountain Creek, near Denver, Colorado.

Fig. 2.3. Twin horns described by Marsh in 1887 after discovery in Colorado. Based on original drawing by O. C. Marsh.

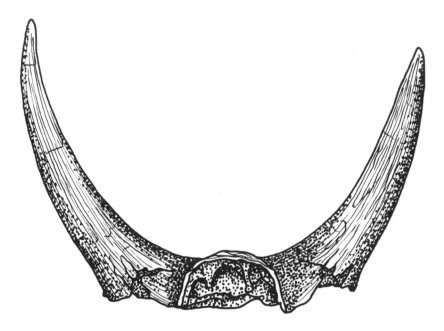

Using this new information, ask students to draw what they think the animal might have looked like. Repeat the discussion and analysis that was done in part 1. Once again, allow the students to display their interpretations to the class and have them discuss how the interpretations have changed with the additional information.

Part 3. In 1888 in Niobrara County, Wyoming, a large skull was found. The shape of this skull led scientists to firmly believe that what was found was quite different than a bison, because the skull weighed more than one ton. It was described as having "horns as long as a hoe handle and eye holes as big as your hat!" (Plate 1964, 196). The skull not only had the two large horns (similar to the skull found outside Denver) but also had a third horn, much like a rhinoceros (see fig. 2.4). Both the size and shape of the skull made it clear to scientists they had found something new. They still did not know what the rest of the animal looked like.

Once again ask students to draw a picture of what they think the whole animal might have looked like. Ask students what other clues about the animal the skull might provide. (Hint: teeth might provide information about diet, and the attachment of the neck might tell whether the animal stood up like a giraffe. With such a large, heavy head, would the animal have had a long skinny neck or a short, stout neck?)

Fig. 2.4. Three-horned skull discovered in Wyoming.

Part 4. Between 1889 and 1882, collectors in eastern Wyoming found what they thought was a complete skeleton, so they were able to determine how many bones the animal had. The big problem was that they were not sure which bones went where. Because the soft parts of the animal, such as muscles and skin, were not preserved, they did not know what the living animal looked like or what kind of noises it made. (Animal noises are produced by both soft and hard body parts—humans, for example, use larynx, lips, mouth, and tongue. Without the soft parts discussions about sounds produced by dinosaurs are speculative.) By looking at large modern horned animals like the elephant or rhinoceros, they tried to reconstruct, or make a picture of, what the living animal might have looked like. A drawing of the skeleton as they assembled it appears in figure 2.5, page 12. How does it differ from an elephant skeleton (fig. 2.6, p. 12) or that of a rhinoceros (fig. 2.7, p. 13)? How is it similar?

Fig. 2.5. Assembled *Triceratops* skeleton.

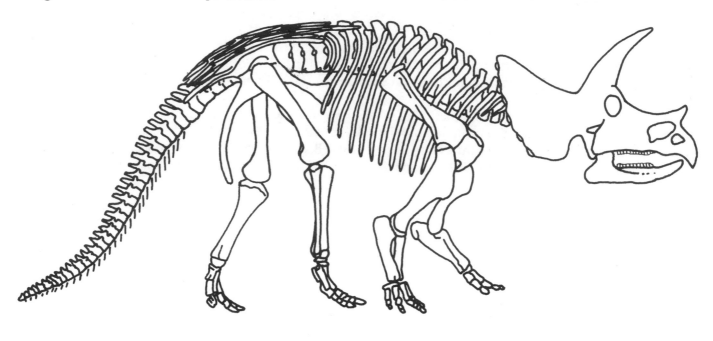

Fig. 2.6. Modern elephant skeleton.

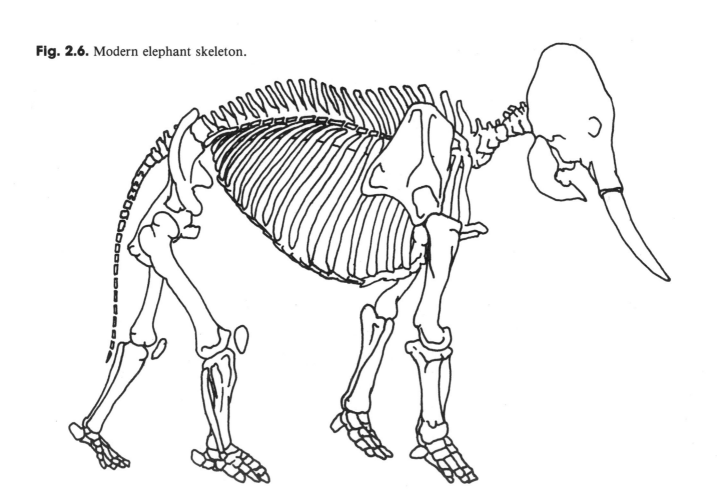

Fig. 2.7. Modern rhinoceros skeleton.

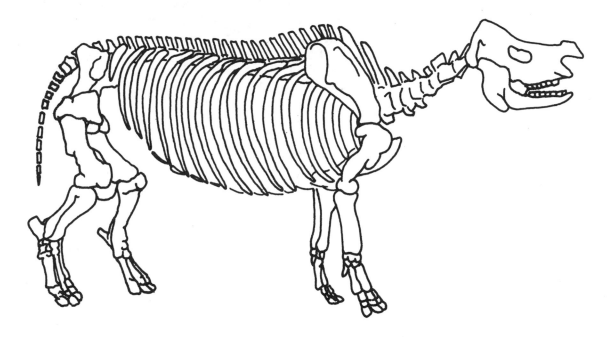

Have your students try to draw the living animal by putting meat and skin onto the skeleton (by this point, it should be clear to students that the animal discovered was *Triceratops*). For practice, a visit to the library and zoo might familiarize students with the relationships between skeletons and living animals. Did the unknown animal have a trunk? What color was it? Were its front legs skinny or fat? Did it have big ears? Did it have a long tongue? Because only the hard parts of the animal (such as bones and teeth) were preserved, scientists must make educated guesses (hypotheses). As many of these things are not well known, the interpretations of your students may be just as valid as the interpretations published in the many books about dinosaurs.

Summary.   The scientific method involves much trial and error based upon the facts as they are known *at the time*. As more information becomes available, theories change and the entire process evolves. Science is not static. Today, as information is becoming available at ever-increasing rates, it is more important than ever for students to think beyond the mere facts. It is important for them to learn that what we know today does not provide limits; what we know today provides the foundation for what we do tomorrow.

EXTENSIONS

1. Present the following questions: What if scientists found a fourth horn? Where might it be placed on the animal? Could it be from another animal? What might have been its use? Hold a class discussion or have students draw their interpretations on the board or at their seats.

2. Skeletons can provide information about an animal's environment as well as about the animal itself: The long neck of a giraffe skeleton, for instance, indicates the presence of tall trees, and the presence of flippers instead of feet on other skeletons indicates an aquatic environment. (For a discussion of what skeletons can reveal about the environment, see Alfred Sherwood Romer's *Vertebrate Paleontology*. Have students provide their interpretation of the discovered animal's surroundings. Did it live in the jungle, the ocean, or the desert? How and what did it eat? What evidence do they have? Have students perform library work to see how animals adapt to specific climates (for example, the desert heat or the arctic cold).

⊠ ⊠ ⊠

ACTIVITY: WHAT IS IT? (*STEGOSAURUS*)

Stegosaurus is one of the most easily recognized of all dinosaurs, yet the first description of its appearance bore little resemblance to the common interpretation of *Stegosaurus* today. As any magician will tell you, things are not always as they seem. What holds true for magic is equally true of vertebrate paleontology. In this activity, students will interpret the initial description of a fossil find and realize that scientists must often stretch their imaginations to describe what lies before them.

REQUIREMENTS

Time

One class period

Materials

- Drawing materials for each student
- Overhead projector (optional)
- Dinosaur description prepared as a transparency or handout

Grouping

Individuals

DIRECTIONS

1. The following description is taken from the initial 1877 announcement of the discovery of a new order of extinct reptile from the Rocky Mountains by O. C. Marsh in the *American Journal of Science* (513):

> The Museum of Yale College has recently received the greater portion of the skeleton of a huge reptile, which proves to be one of the most remarkable animals yet discovered.... The limb bones indicate an aquatic life. The body was long, and protected by large bony dermal plates, somewhat like those of [a turtle]. One of the large dermal plates was over three feet (one meter) in length. The present species was probably thirty feet long, and moved mainly by swimming.

In 1879, Arthur Lakes (who discovered the actual bones) wrote, "This monster was ... part dinosaur, part plesiosaur, and part turtle, at least he seemed related to them all. It was the ... warrior of the lakes and ponds" (735). Prepare an overhead transparency of these descriptions.

2. Tell the class you are going to read these descriptions of a newly found dinosaur. Ask them to listen carefully.

3. Ask the class to draw a picture of the new dinosaur based upon the descriptions. Read the descriptions once more and then project the transparency so the students may use it as a reference as they draw.

4. At the end of the period have students present their drawings individually to the class or display them all at once as an art show and have the students describe their drawings.

5. Now tell the students the description was of *Stegosaurus*. Show the students a picture of *Stegosaurus* and discuss with them how *Stegosaurus* differs from the pictures they drew based on the description.

6. Discuss with students what new evidence needed to be found to change the original ideas of *Stegosaurus* to the *Stegosaurus* as it is seen today.

EXTENSION

Ask students to prepare a one-half-page description of something based upon its component parts, animate or inanimate, without naming the object. Then have them read their descriptions to the class for the class to guess what the object is. Tell students the idea is to make it as difficult as possible. For instance, an airplane sitting at an airport might be described as "a long, shiny tube with two large, flat things sticking out to the side in the front, two small, flat things sticking out to the side in the back. A flat tall thing sticks up in the back. It makes a very loud roar when it starts to move."

★ ★ ★

During the discovery process, scientists attempt to form a complete picture from only a few facts, which can lead to some embarrassing moments. One of the great feuds in the history of dinosaur discoveries took place between two of the most prolific bone hunters in the United States, Othniel C. Marsh and Edward D. Cope. In part, the feud was precipitated by the highly competitive nature of their work. Each was trying to outdo the other in quantity of dinosaur skeletons and dinosaur species discovered. In the rapid search for quantity, quality suffered. In 1869 Cope restored a marine reptile (a plesiosaur, not a dinosaur) that was subsequently displayed in the Philadelphia Academy of Natural Sciences. An argument between Cope and Marsh ensued when Marsh happily pointed out to Cope that the head was placed on the wrong end of the animal. (Both the neck and tail of a plesiosaur are long and narrow, so the error is not as strange as it first seems. The particular specimen reconstructed was, in fact, called *Elasmosaurus*, or "plated reptile," because it looks like a long, thin metal plate.) Cope was displeased with Marsh for even suggesting he was wrong and for making the apparent error public. Despite Cope's protestations that the reconstruction was correct, an examination of the vertebrae proved he had indeed put the head at the end of the tail. The two bone hunters were enemies from then on. The feud had profound effects on the lives of both men (Lanham 1973, 170-184; Plate 1964, 94-98; Wilford 1985, 118-129).

Marsh was not immune to such errors either. In the 1870s there was a tremendous rush in the western United States (backed by money from eastern museums) to discover as many dinosaurs as possible, as quickly as possible. O. C. Marsh had a staff of collectors searching for dinosaur bones. The collectors unearthed two skeletons of a so-called "*Brontosaurus*" in Wyoming in the 1870s; unfortunately neither one had a skull. Marsh took remedial action and found two skulls, one 6, and the other 650, kilometers away. In the rush to complete the skeletons Marsh overlooked a small detail; the skulls belonged to a different dinosaur, *Camarasaurus*—not *Brontosaurus*. The one completed skeleton was mounted in the Carnegie Museum in Pittsburgh. In 1915, after a complete *Brontosaurus* skeleton was excavated in Utah, a museum collector noticed that the head was different from the one mounted by Marsh. Despite the desire to correct the mistake by replacing the skull, no one wanted to contradict Marsh, even 40 years after the fact. The compromise reached was to remove the head from the original skeleton. In 1979 subsequent review determined the museum collector had been right in 1915, and, finally, after more than 100 years, the correct head was placed on the museum skeleton.

Despite their errors, Cope and Marsh were incredibly successful dinosaur hunters. Prior to their competition, only nine dinosaur species were known from North America. The two scientists discovered 136 additional species.

REFERENCES

Lakes, Arthur. "The Dinosaurs of the Rocky Mountains." *Kansas City Review of Science* 2 (1879): 731-735.

Lanham, Url. 1973. *The Bone Hunters*. New York: Columbia University Press.

Marsh, O. C. 1877. "A New Order of Extinct Reptilia (*Stegosauria*) from the Jurassic of the Rocky Mountains." *American Journal of Science*, 3d series, 14, no. 84: 513-514.

Marsh, O. C. 1887. "Notice of New Fossil Mammals." *American Journal of Science*, 3d series, 34, no. 202: 323-324.

Plate, Robert. 1964. *The Dinosaur Hunters: Othniel C. Marsh and Edward D. Cope*. New York: David McKay.

Romer, Alfred Sherwood. 1945. *Vertebrate Paleontology*. Chicago: University of Chicago Press.

Wilford, John Noble. 1985. *The Riddle of the Dinosaur*. New York: Vintage Books.

SUGGESTED READING

Dixon, Dougal. *The Illustrated Dinosaur Encyclopedia*. New York: Gallery Books, 1988.

Norman, David. *The Illustrated Encyclopedia of Dinosaurs*. New York: Crown, 1985.

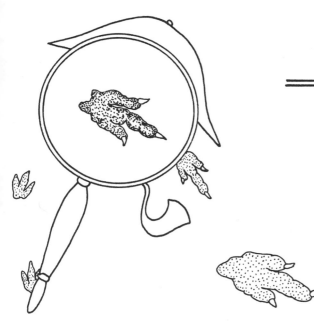

Part 2

investigating dinosaurs

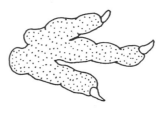

By their very nature, dinosaurs are mysterious creatures. The combination of their tremendous size and unique appearance and the fact that they are creatures of the distant past create a sense of mystery far more pervasive than that found in most popular fiction. How big were they? How fast could they run? How did they support their tremendous weight? In short, how do we know what we know about these animals? Investigating details of the dinosaur is like trying to assemble a large jigsaw puzzle, but with several complicating factors: There is no picture on the box; scientists do not know how many pieces exist; and they don't know where the pieces can be found. Of the many footprints that were made by the animals, only a small percentage was preserved as fossils. Only a minute percentage of those has been exposed where they can be studied. The many thousands of different dinosaur species that roamed the earth for 165 million years are today represented by skeletons that number only in the hundreds. Many species have been identified merely from bone fragments. It should not be surprising that so much remains to be discovered about dinosaurs; it should instead be surprising that we have learned as much as we have.

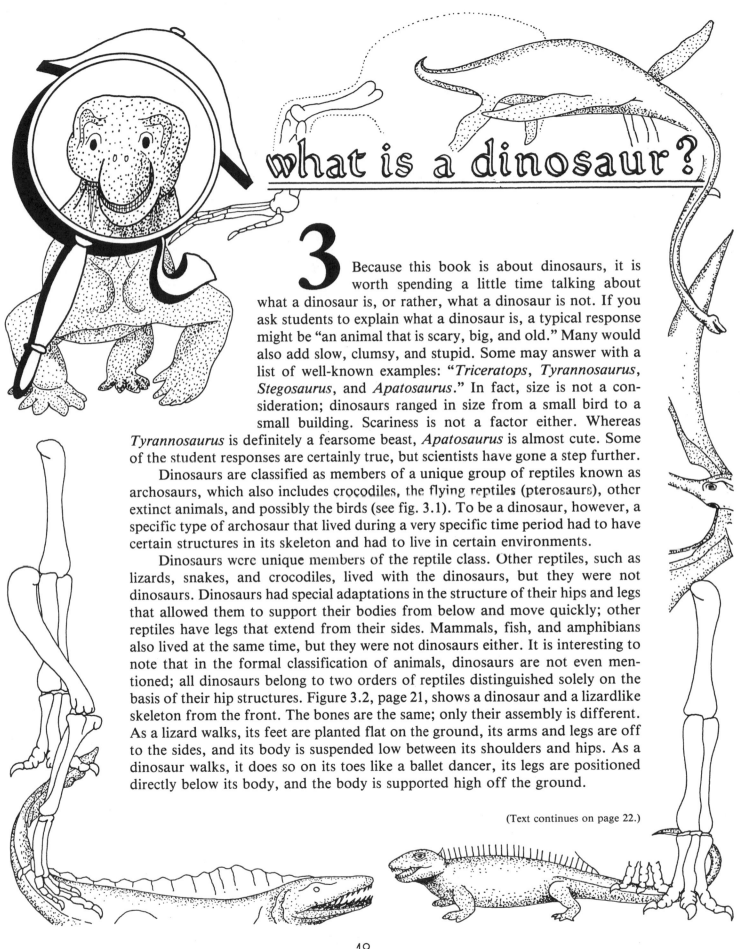

what is a dinosaur?

3 Because this book is about dinosaurs, it is worth spending a little time talking about what a dinosaur is, or rather, what a dinosaur is not. If you ask students to explain what a dinosaur is, a typical response might be "an animal that is scary, big, and old." Many would also add slow, clumsy, and stupid. Some may answer with a list of well-known examples: "*Triceratops*, *Tyrannosaurus*, *Stegosaurus*, and *Apatosaurus*." In fact, size is not a consideration; dinosaurs ranged in size from a small bird to a small building. Scariness is not a factor either. Whereas *Tyrannosaurus* is definitely a fearsome beast, *Apatosaurus* is almost cute. Some of the student responses are certainly true, but scientists have gone a step further.

Dinosaurs are classified as members of a unique group of reptiles known as archosaurs, which also includes crocodiles, the flying reptiles (pterosaurs), other extinct animals, and possibly the birds (see fig. 3.1). To be a dinosaur, however, a specific type of archosaur that lived during a very specific time period had to have certain structures in its skeleton and had to live in certain environments.

Dinosaurs were unique members of the reptile class. Other reptiles, such as lizards, snakes, and crocodiles, lived with the dinosaurs, but they were not dinosaurs. Dinosaurs had special adaptations in the structure of their hips and legs that allowed them to support their bodies from below and move quickly; other reptiles have legs that extend from their sides. Mammals, fish, and amphibians also lived at the same time, but they were not dinosaurs either. It is interesting to note that in the formal classification of animals, dinosaurs are not even mentioned; all dinosaurs belong to two orders of reptiles distinguished solely on the basis of their hip structures. Figure 3.2, page 21, shows a dinosaur and a lizardlike skeleton from the front. The bones are the same; only their assembly is different. As a lizard walks, its feet are planted flat on the ground, its arms and legs are off to the sides, and its body is suspended low between its shoulders and hips. As a dinosaur walks, it does so on its toes like a ballet dancer, its legs are positioned directly below its body, and the body is supported high off the ground.

(Text continues on page 22.)

Fig. 3.1. The dinosaur family tree.

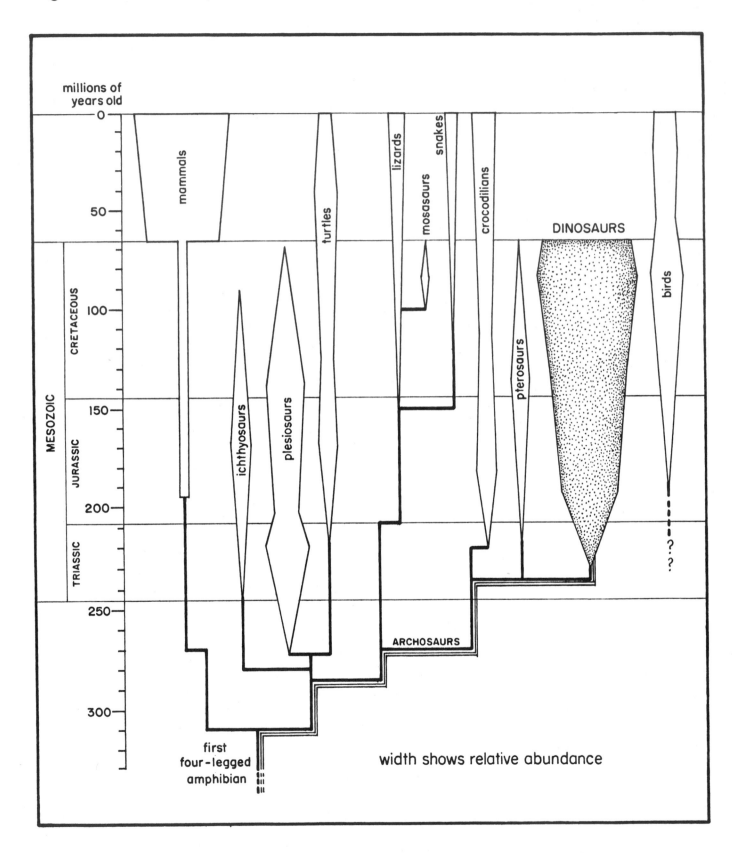

Fig. 3.2. Comparison of skeleton and posture of dinosaurs (top) and nondinosaurian reptiles such as lizards (bottom).

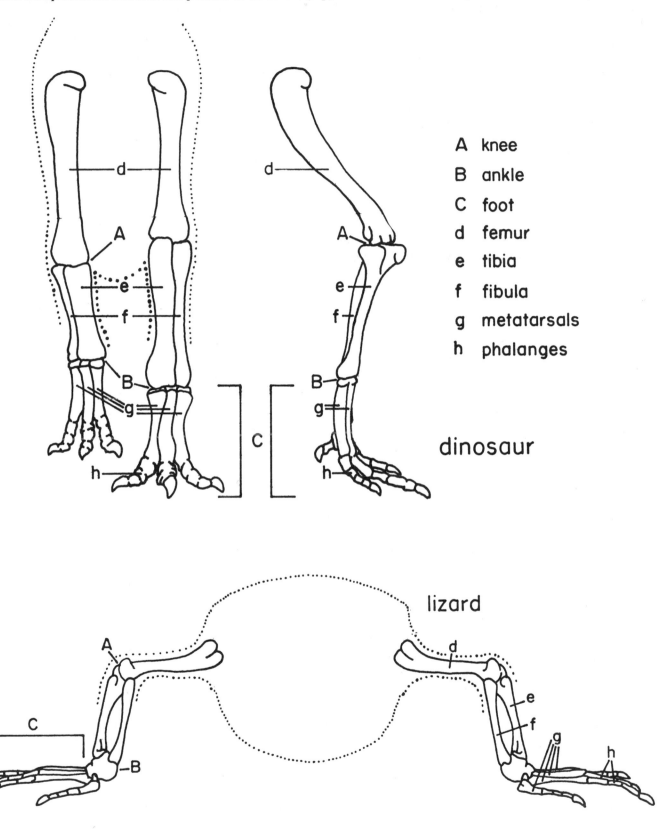

A knee
B ankle
C foot
d femur
e tibia
f fibula
g metatarsals
h phalanges

dinosaur

lizard

Dinosaurs are known from only a very specific portion of earth history, the Mesozoic era (230-66 million years ago) (see appendix C, "Geologic Time"). Although this is known as the Age of Dinosaurs, dinosaurs from the earliest Mesozoic (Early or Middle Triassic period, 245 million years ago) are not known. Many animals often considered to be dinosaurs not only are structurally different from dinosaurs but lived before or after the dinosaurs. *Dimetrodon* (see fig. 3.3), often found in dinosaur books, lived during the Permian period of the Paleozoic era (286-245 million years ago); it is older than the dinosaurs. Animals like the woolly mammoth were "scary, big, and old," but they lived "only" tens of thousands of years ago, much younger than the dinosaurs. Fossil evidence indicates that human ancestors are no older than 2 or 3 million years. Clearly, the dinosaurs had vanished from the earth more than 60 million years before the earliest humans existed. People and dinosaurs did not live contemporaneously. For the sake of this discussion, birds are not considered as dinosaurs (see chapter 17, "Where Are They Now?").

★ ★ ★

ACTIVITY: WHICH IS MORE EFFICIENT?

REQUIREMENTS

Time

15-20 minutes

Materials

- Pencil and paper
- Figure 3.2 as overhead transparency or handouts

Grouping

Whole class, then individuals

DIRECTIONS

1. Show students the overhead transparency of figure 3.2 and discuss the differences in how dinosaurs and lizards walk.

2. Have students compare the bones of the two skeletons with the bones in their own bodies.

3. Tell students they will be walking like both animals. Ask them to remember how it feels, because afterwards they will have to write about it.

4. Have students get on the floor in a crawling position.

5. Have them place their arms directly under their shoulders, with their hands arched up so only their fingers touch the floor. Their palms should not be touching the floor. They are now like dinosaurs.

6. Ask them to place as much weight as possible on their arms to see how it feels.

7. Have them hold this position for a count of 10 (you may need to count fast).

8. Now ask them to crawl in this position.

Fig. 3.3. Various animals often considered to be dinosaurs (none are dinosaurs): (A) *Pteranodon*, (B) mosasaur, (C) *Moschops*, (D) *Dimetrodon*, (E) plesiosaur.

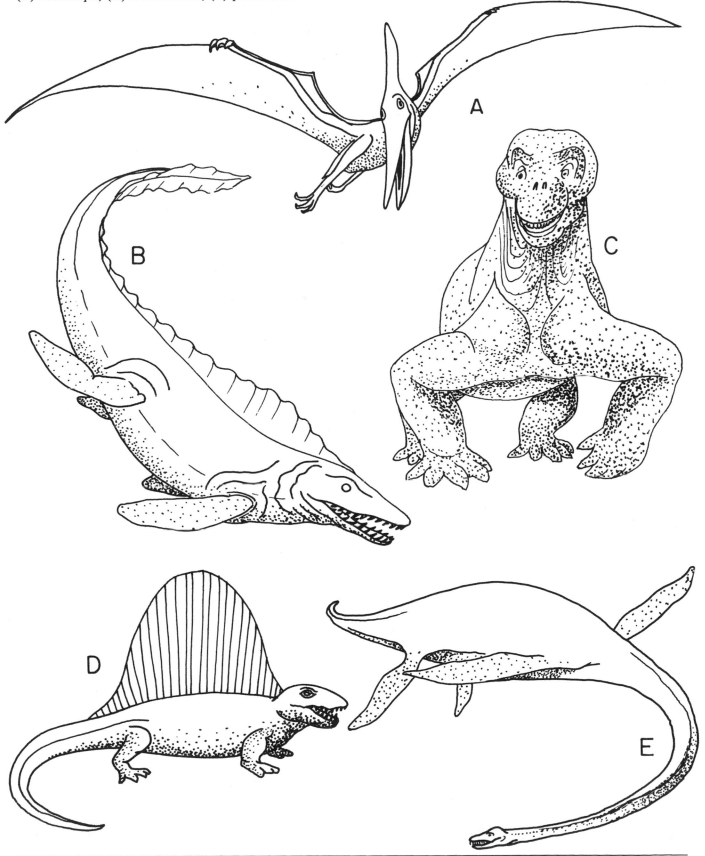

9. Keeping their body and feet in the same position, have them hold their upper arms and elbows out to their sides (as in the lizardlike skeleton in fig. 3.2, p. 21), with their palms flat and hands turned out. They are now like lizards.

10. Again, ask them to shift their weight forward on their arms.

11. Ask them to crawl forward in the sprawling, lizardlike position.

12. Ask them to return to their seats and describe the differences in a paragraph. You may wish to have students read the paragraphs to the class. (They should observe that crawling like a dinosaur was much easier, faster, and more comfortable. Moving like the lizard was very awkward. More observant students might notice the body had to wriggle and twist while walking in the sprawling position, much as lizards do.)

★ ★ ★

The term *dinosaurs* is not recognized in the formal classification of these animals. From kingdom to species, the grouping of animals becomes smaller and smaller based on unique characteristics. Despite their uniqueness, dinosaurs do not have their own classification. An example of the formal taxonomic classification of two dinosaurs follows:

CLASSIFICATION	*TRICERATOPS*	*TYRANNOSAURUS*
Kingdom	*Animalia*	*Animalia*
Phylum	*Chordata*	*Chordata*
Class	*Reptilia*	*Reptilia*
Subclass	*Diapsida*	*Diapsida*
Superorder	*Archosauria*	*Archosauria*
Order	*Ornithischia*	*Saurischia*
Suborder	*Ceratopsia*	*Theropoda*
Family	*Ceratopsidae*	*Tyrannosauridae*
Genus	*Triceratops*	*Tyrannosaurus*
Species	*Triceratops horridus*	*Tyrannosaurus rex*

It was only logical to classify dinosaurs, along with the lizards, as reptiles. After all, *dinosaur* means "terrible lizard," or reptile. The irony is that even as Sir Richard Owen was proposing the name dinosaur for the new fossil finds in 1841, much of the evidence he submitted suggested the animals were nonreptilian and may have been more like mammals. Two of the nonreptilian features he described are massive (rather than long-and-skinny) body size and body elevated above the ground. Since then, evidence for even more nonreptilian features has been found, including the ability to sustain speed, mammal-like predator-to-prey ratios, possible warm-bloodedness, and mammalian bone structure.

The saying is often heard, "If it walks like a duck, sounds like a duck, and looks like a duck, then it's a duck!" The obverse should hold true for dinosaurs: "It doesn't walk like a reptile, isn't built like a reptile, and doesn't have bones like a reptile ...," but it's classified as a reptile. It has been suggested that dinosaurs be removed from the class *Reptilia* and given their own class, *Dinosauria* (which, incidentally, is closer to birds than to other reptiles).

Dinosaurs lived on land. They were able to spend some time in water, much as people can wade or swim in lakes and oceans, but the dinosaurs, like humans today, were creatures of the land. Animals that were primarily fliers (pteranodons) (birds are, arguably, dinosaur descendants) or lived in the ocean (mosasaurs, plesiosaurs, and ichthyosaurs) were not dinosaurs.

Use an overhead transparency or handouts of figure 3.3 to discuss with students why the following animals are not dinosaurs:

1.   Mosasaur (lived in the ocean)

2.   *Dimetrodon* (wrong body structure, older than dinosaurs)

3.   *Pteranodon* (primarily a flying reptile)

4.   Plesiosaur (lived in the ocean)

5.   *Moschops* (legs not under its body)

★ ★ ★

ACTIVITY: CHARTING THE DINOSAURS

A method of graphically analyzing relationships among many different aspects of a problem is *semantic feature analysis*. The method allows students to develop vocabulary, categorization, and classification skills and to identify relationships. Students will fill in a prepared grid displaying both general topics or categories and specific features and characteristics to determine whether an animal is a dinosaur. Figure 3.4, page 26, is a sample grid for this activity. The general topics or categories are shown on the left side (in this case animal names), and the features or characteristics are shown across the top. Figure 3.5, page 27, is a blank grid that can be used as a handout or as an overhead transparency. If the characteristics are present in the category, the grid space is filled in with a plus (+); if it is not present, the space receives a minus (−). For example, *Dimetrodon* (see fig. 3.4) is older than 230 million years and had legs to the side; the two grid spaces for those characteristics are filled in with pluses, and the remaining spaces (where characteristics are absent) are minuses. Any animal that has pluses is not a dinosaur. This is merely one example of how to use semantic feature analysis. Any group of characteristics can be shown.

REQUIREMENTS

Time

Variable; can be done as a one-period library visit or can be done as an ongoing project during a dinosaur unit.

Materials

• Nonfiction dinosaur books in libraries (school or public) or in students' homes.

• Pencil and paper for students

• Large wall chart (optional)

• Figure 3.4 as an overhead transparency or handouts

Grouping

Individuals or small groups (2-3)

DIRECTIONS

1. Hold a class discussion based upon the information given above and select animals and identify characteristics to be used in a chart like the one in figure 3.4. The chart can be prepared positively or nega-
tively. That is, nondinosaur characteristics can be shown and any pluses mean the animal is not a
dinosaur (as in fig. 3.4), or the converse can be prepared.

2. Prepare the chart on the board or as an overhead transparency and have students copy it, or once the
grid is completed, prepare it as handouts for the students.

3. Review the procedures for completing the chart so the students feel confident about doing it.

Fig. 3.4. Example of a semantic feature analysis chart used to catalog nondinosaur features.

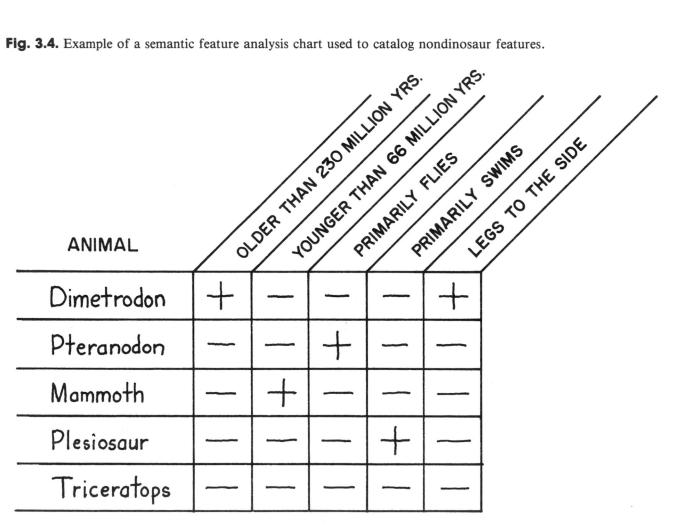

ANIMAL	OLDER THAN 230 MILLION YRS.	YOUNGER THAN 66 MILLION YRS.	PRIMARILY FLIES	PRIMARILY SWIMS	LEGS TO THE SIDE
Dimetrodon	+	−	−	−	+
Pteranodon	−	−	+	−	−
Mammoth	−	+	−	−	−
Plesiosaur	−	−	−	+	−
Triceratops	−	−	−	−	−

Fig. 3.5. Blank grid for use during semantic feature analysis.

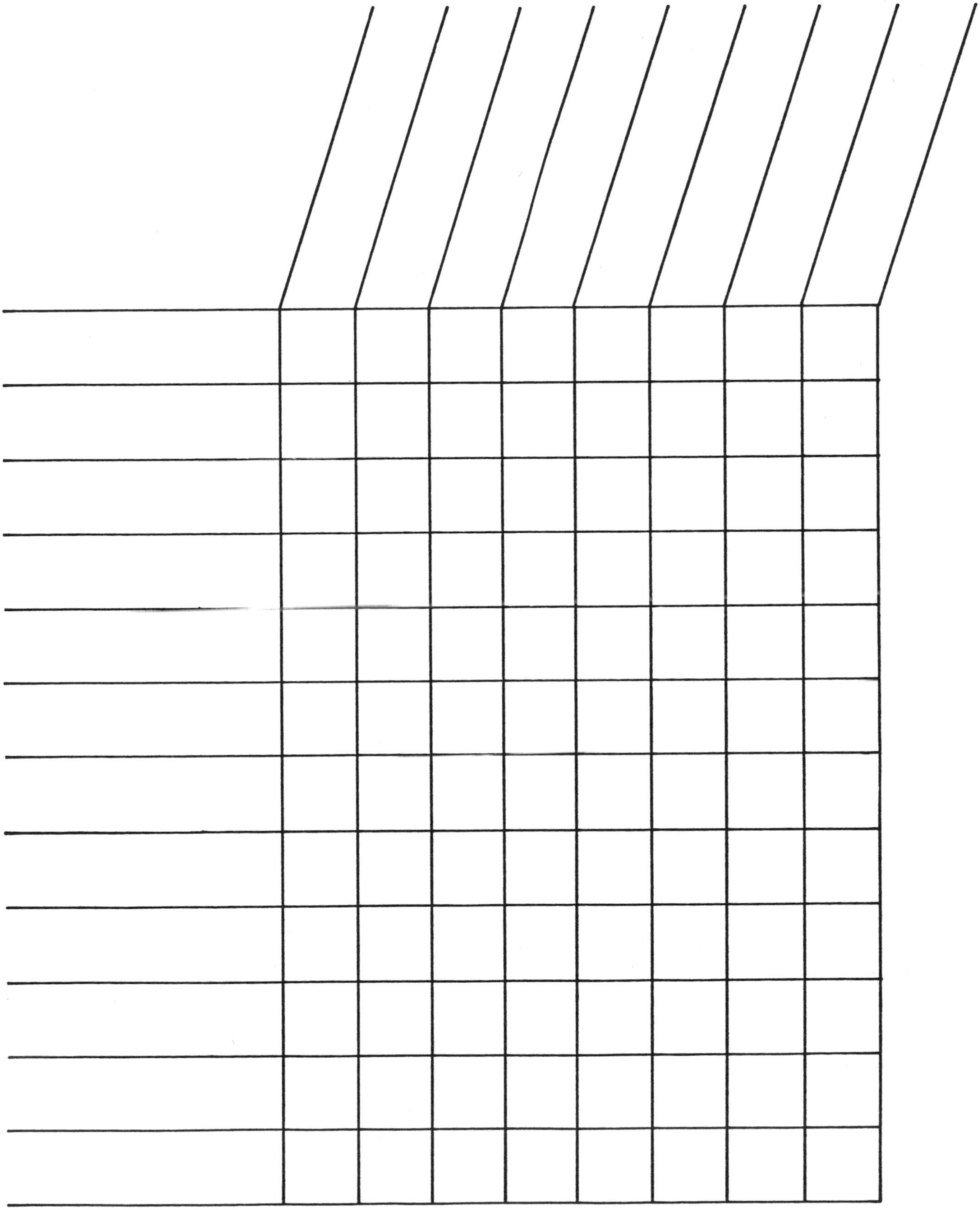

4. As students review books that discuss animals considered dinosaurs, have them fill in the grid you have created.

5. Grids can be prepared individually or in small groups, or a large wall-size grid can be made for use by the entire class.

EXTENSION

Similar grids can be prepared to relate other dinosaur characteristics: carnivorous/herbivorous, bipedal/quadripedal, horned/not horned, grazer/browser, size, time period during which it lived, continent(s) where it was found. There are myriad possibilities for a master chart that can be used as a wall reference chart of dinosaurs during a complete unit. It may be completed as a project in itself or completed as students do research on other areas during the unit.

★ ★ ★

ACTIVITY: BOOKS CAN BE WRONG

Armed with the above knowledge of dinosaurs, students can search through the many books about dinosaurs in the library to discover inaccuracies. Many otherwise excellent children's books about dinosaurs are marred by including animals that are not dinosaurs or by erroneously showing dinosaurs interacting with prehistoric man. This is often done in an effort to make a book more entertaining; what it also does is perpetuate fallacies such as the coexistence of humans and dinosaurs.

REQUIREMENTS

Time

Variable; can be done as a one-period library visit or can be done as an ongoing project during a dinosaur unit

Materials

- Dinosaur books in libraries (school or public), or in students' homes
- Pencil and paper for students
- Large wall chart (optional)

Grouping

Individuals or small groups (2-3)

DIRECTIONS

Students can report the results of the library search either as a presentation to the class or as a written report to be submitted for grading. Tabulation of all the found errors on a large wall chart can reinforce the large numbers of errors in the books and reinforce nondinosaurs to the students. Be careful to avoid duplications. The chart could include headings as follows: title of the book, author of the book, problem with the book (would contain entries such as "people with dinosaurs," "animal lived in the sea"), name (if a nondinosaur was considered a dinosaur, the student should be specific about the name), and student or team finding the errors.

The search can be turned into a contest; the group finding the most errors wins.

The semantic feature analysis chart described on page 25 can be used to examine the information contained in the books (see fig. 3.6). The chart can be prepared listing the books and authors as topics and details about dinosaurs as characteristics, making it a useful reference that can be maintained during the year. A single wall chart may be prepared for the entire class to complete, or charts may be assigned individually or in small groups. When completed, the chart can be used to provide quick evaluations. For instance, in figure 3.6, the more plus signs a book has, the less accurate it is. The chart allows students to use characteristics they personally select or characteristics selected during class discussions. It also permits students to focus their attention on diagnostic features.

EXTENSIONS

1. Have students write publishers about their findings, either as endorsements or criticisms of the scientific accuracy.

2. As student knowledge of dinosaurs increases, the level of complexity of the characteristics evaluated can also increase. Did certain dinosaurs actually coexist? Did certain plant or animal species coexist with specific dinosaurs? Did dinosaurs actually populate the area shown in the book?

3. Books may seem to be in error merely because certain facts were not available at the time they were written. As an example, information gained from recent Voyager and Magellan space probes has refuted "facts" in astronomy books published only five years ago. Students might investigate books written over a long time span to see how they differ.

Fig. 3.6. Example of a semantic feature analysis chart for use in analyzing dinosaur literature.

AUTHOR / TITLE	YOUNGER THAN KNOWN DINOSAURS	OLDER THAN KNOWN DINOSAURS	ANIMALS THAT FLY	ANIMALS THAT SWIM	DINOSAURS AND PEOPLE	DINOSAURS TALKING	DINOSAURS PLAYING GAMES	STRANGE DINOSAUR BEHAVIOR
SHEEHAN / STEGOSAURUS	−	+	−	−	−	−	−	−
WATSON / DINOSAURS	−	−	+	+	−	−	−	−
YORINKS / UGH	−	−	−	−	+	−	+	−
MOORE / DINOSAURS &, K-1	−	−	+	+	+	−	−	+

⊠ ⊠ ⊠

SUGGESTED READING

Bakker, Robert. *The Dinosaur Heresies*. New York: Zebra Books, 1986.

Black Hills Institute of Geological Research. *What Is a Dinosaur?* Hill City, S. Dak.: Black Hills Institute of Geological Research, 1990.

Charig, Alan. *A New Look at the Dinosaurs*. New York: Facts on File, 1983.

dePaola, Tomie. *Little Grunt and the Big Egg*. New York: Holiday House, 1990.

Lambert, David. *Collins Guide to Dinosaurs*. London: William Collins and Sons, 1983.

Lambert, David. *The Dinosaur Data Book*. New York: Avon Books, 1990.

Manetti, William. *Dinosaurs in Your Backyard*. New York: Atheneum, 1982.

Moore, Jo Ellen. *Dinosaurs and Other Prehistoric Animals, K-1*. Monterey, Calif.: Evan-Moore, 1991.

Norman, David. *The Illustrated Encyclopedia of Dinosaurs*. New York: Crown, 1985.

Pittelman, Susan D., Joan E. Heimlich, Roberta L. Berglund, and Michael P. French. *Semantic Feature Analysis*. Newark, Del.: International Reading Association, 1991.

Sheehan, Angela. *Dinosaurs*. Windermere, Fla.: Ray Rourke, 1981.

Sheehan, Angela. *Stegosaurus*. Windermere, Fla.: Ray Rourke, 1981.

Swinton, W. E. *Dinosaurs*. London: British Museum of Natural History, 1962.

Watson, Jane Werner. *Dinosaurs*. Racine, Wis.: Western, 1959.

Wilford, John Noble. *The Riddle of the Dinosaur*. New York: Vintage Books, 1985.

Yorinks, Arthur. *Ugh*. New York: Farrar, Straus & Giroux, 1990.

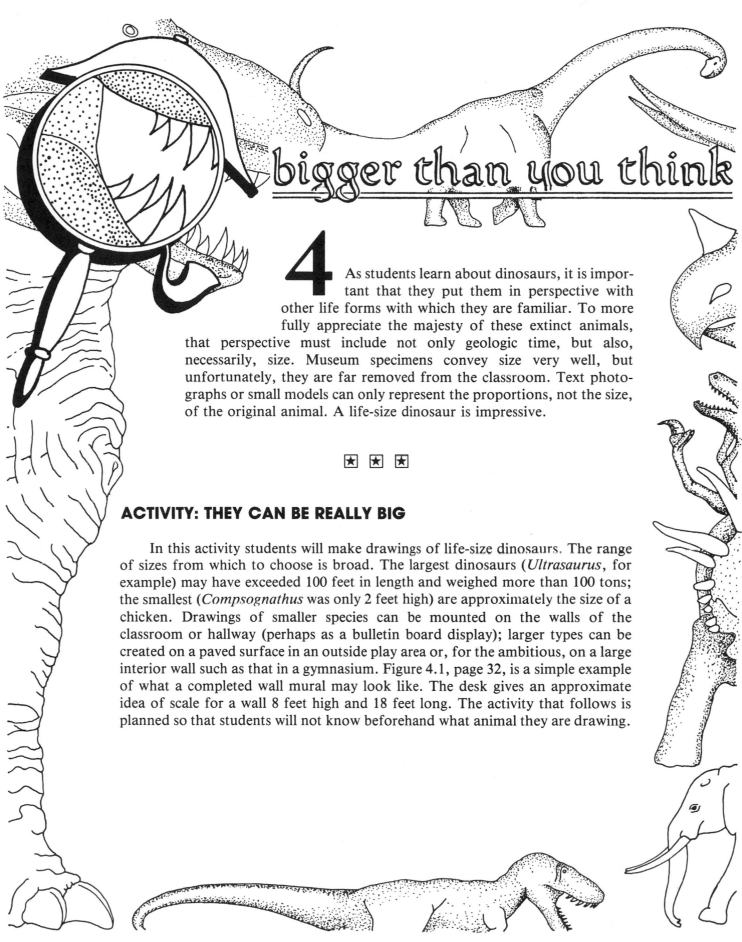

bigger than you think

4 As students learn about dinosaurs, it is important that they put them in perspective with other life forms with which they are familiar. To more fully appreciate the majesty of these extinct animals, that perspective must include not only geologic time, but also, necessarily, size. Museum specimens convey size very well, but unfortunately, they are far removed from the classroom. Text photographs or small models can only represent the proportions, not the size, of the original animal. A life-size dinosaur is impressive.

★ ★ ★

ACTIVITY: THEY CAN BE REALLY BIG

In this activity students will make drawings of life-size dinosaurs. The range of sizes from which to choose is broad. The largest dinosaurs (*Ultrasaurus*, for example) may have exceeded 100 feet in length and weighed more than 100 tons; the smallest (*Compsognathus* was only 2 feet high) are approximately the size of a chicken. Drawings of smaller species can be mounted on the walls of the classroom or hallway (perhaps as a bulletin board display); larger types can be created on a paved surface in an outside play area or, for the ambitious, on a large interior wall such as that in a gymnasium. Figure 4.1, page 32, is a simple example of what a completed wall mural may look like. The desk gives an approximate idea of scale for a wall 8 feet high and 18 feet long. The activity that follows is planned so that students will not know beforehand what animal they are drawing.

Fig. 4.1. Example of wall mural (Note: *Tyrannosaurus* head is an opposed image [see text] of that in fig. 4.5).

REQUIREMENTS

Time

Minimum one class period; may be longer depending upon project selected

Materials

- Staples to attach to wall; push pins or thumbtacks will also work, but these can fall to the floor, creating a student hazard, and are not recommended.
- Clear, cellophane tape to attach pieces to one another
- Large wall (dimensions depend upon dinosaur selected)
- Drawing selected from the figures that follow

For an indoors project, one of the following per student:

- Pencil and eraser
- Large sheet of paper (12" × 12" or 24" × 24", depending upon dinosaur selected). Newsprint pads are relatively inexpensive and are available in large sizes (24" × 36").
- Wide black marker

For an outdoors project:

- At least one large piece of chalk per student (have lots of extra—some surfaces are very abrasive)
- Precut 4' string or yardstick for measuring for each student
- Paved area, traffic-free during activity
- Long (30' to 40') string or rope

Grouping

A progression: individuals, then overlapping small groups, and finally the entire class

The table below summarizes the animals presented in this activity. If animals are to be combined on a mural, only those animals that actually coexisted should be drawn together. For instance, it would be paleontologically incorrect to show *Plateosaurus* being eaten by *Tyrannosaurus*; the former became extinct 100 million years before the latter appeared (see "Extensions"). It is possible to regrid the dinosaurs for 8½" × 11" paper; this makes the paper supply easier to obtain but increases the number of grid pieces by about 50 percent. The increase complicates assembly as well as student drawing because each student will need to prepare more grid pieces.

Summary Table

Dinosaur Name	Overall Size (Feet)	Number of Squares	Size of Square (Feet)
Brachiosaurus	67 × 27	48	4 × 4
Stegosaurus	27½ × 13	62	2 × 2
Tyrannosaurus	32 × 14	51	2 × 2
Tyrannosaurus head	8 × 6	42	1 × 1
Camptosaurus	18 × 7½	20	1 × 1
Deinonychus	7¾ × 3¾	20	1 × 1
Velociraptor	8 × 3	17	1 × 1
Protoceratops	8 × 2¾	20	1 × 1
Plateosaurus	20 × 7	26	2 × 2
Styracosaurus	6 × 7½	42	1 × 1
Triceratops head	9 × 6	50	1 × 1

DIRECTIONS

1. Select a dinosaur from figures 4.2 through 4.12, pages 34-39, based upon wall space available and number of students.

2. To create an opposed image (the dinosaur faces in the opposite direction), make an enlarged copy of the desired figure (to any workable size). Trace over the image and grid lines on the back side of the copy (use a light table or hold it up against a window). The picture and grid will now be reversed.

3. Create a two-column list with grid space number on the left column and student name on the right. Assign students their grid spaces by number.

4. Give students a copy of their own grid squares. (The drawing can be enlarged slightly so the grid space given to each student might be easier to copy. Then cut the drawing apart along grid lines.)

(Directions continue on page 40.)

Fig. 4.2. *Brachiosaurus*. Actual size 67' × 27'. Grid size 48" × 48".

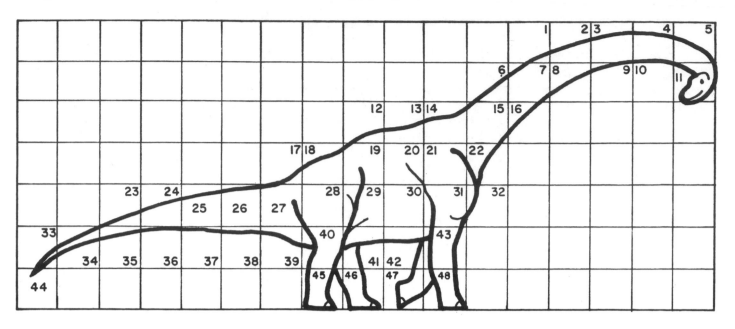

Fig. 4.3. *Stegosaurus*. Actual size 27'6" × 13'. Grid size 24" × 24".

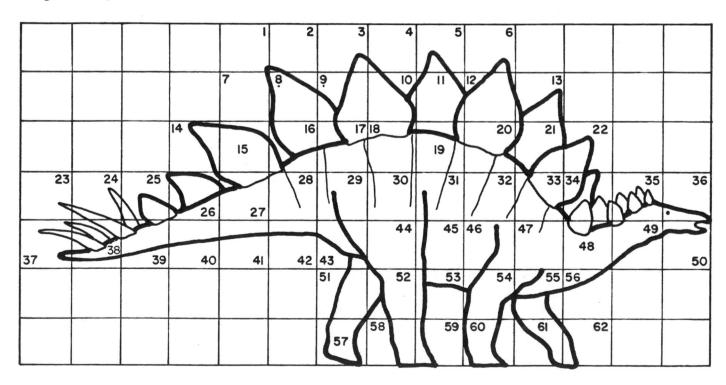

Fig. 4.4. *Tyrannosaurus*. Actual size 32' × 14'. Grid size 24" × 24".

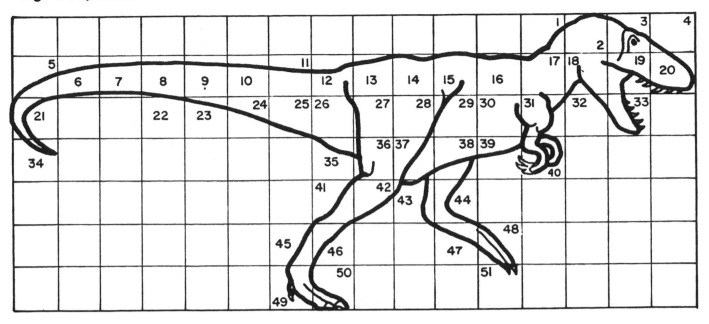

Fig. 4.5. *Tyrannosaurus* head. Actual size 8' × 6'. Grid size 12" × 12".

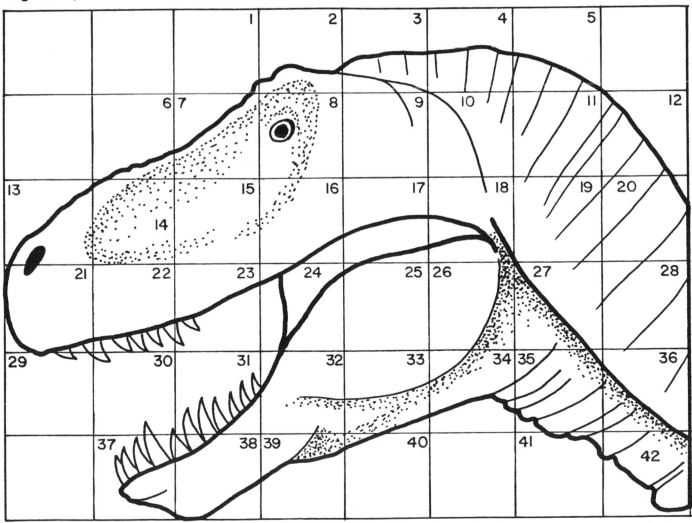

From *Investigating Science with Dinosaurs*, copyright 1993, Teacher Ideas Press, P.O. Box 6633, Englewood, CO 80155-6633

Fig. 4.6. *Camptosaurus*. Actual size 18' × 7'6". Grid size 12" × 12".

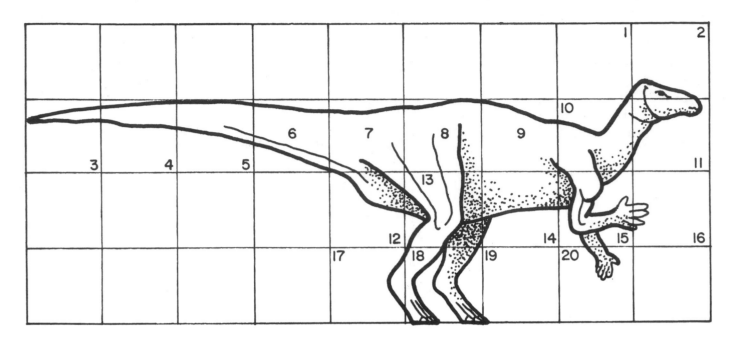

Fig. 4.7. *Deinonychus*. Actual size 7'10" × 3'9". Grid size 12" × 12".

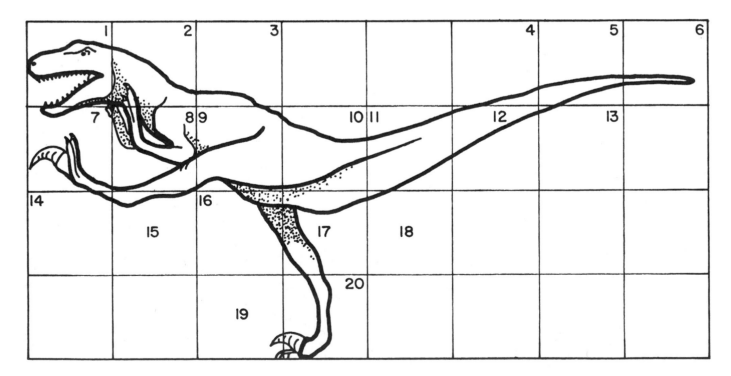

Fig. 4.8. *Velociraptor*. Actual size 8' × 3'. Grid size 12" × 12".

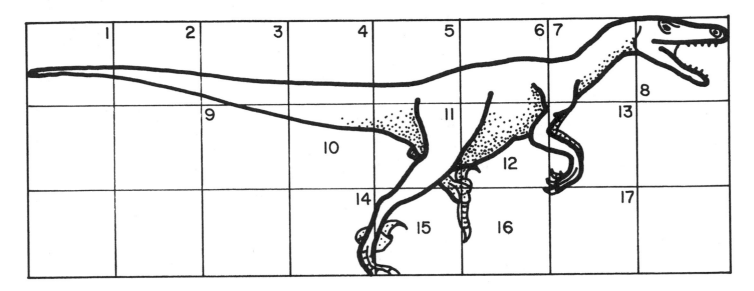

Fig. 4.9. *Protoceratops*. Actual size 7'11" × 2'7". Grid size 12" × 12".

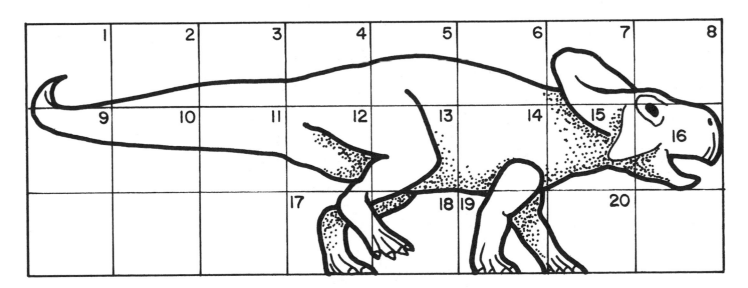

Fig. 4.10. *Plateosaurus*. Actual size 20' × 7'. Grid size 24" × 24".

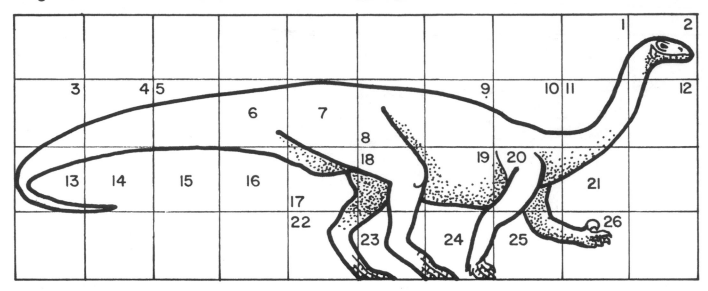

Fig. 4.11. *Styracosaurus*. Actual size 6'2" × 7'6". Grid size 12" × 12".

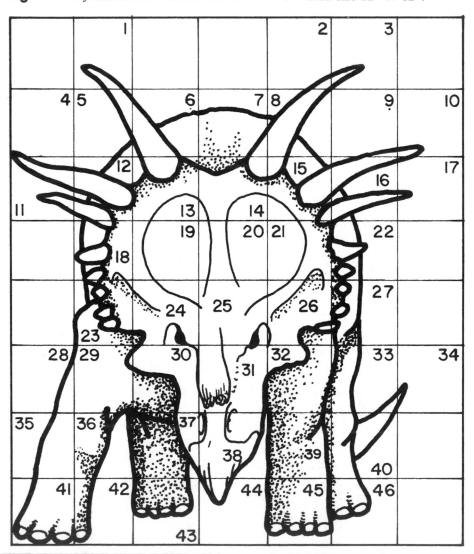

Fig. 4.12. *Triceratops* head. Actual size 9' × 6'. Grid size 12" × 12".

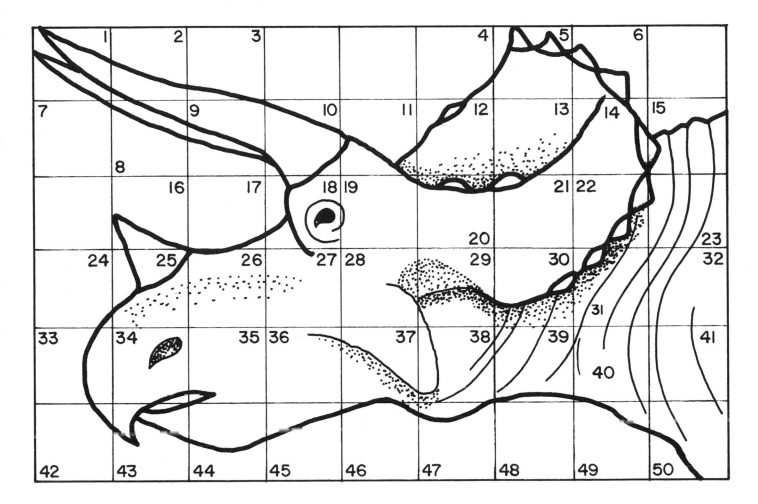

5. Give each student an appropriately sized piece of blank paper (12" × 12" or 24" × 24") to match the grid size for the animal selected (grid sizes are indicated in figure captions).

6. Instruct students to enlarge the drawing in their assigned small grid square to fill the large piece of blank paper they have been given. (Important: instruct students that the drawing must go all the way to the edge of the paper; they must not leave any margins.) This should be done in class using pencil; if given as homework, the risk of missing grid spaces is increased. As a first step they should place a small mark in the top right corner of both the small grid and the blank piece of paper as a reference point.

7. Once students have completed their enlarged grid spaces, they must check the drawings of the adjoining grid spaces to be certain all lines connect. The two-column list prepared in step 3 must be made available so that students can determine which students' work will adjoin theirs. The entire class will be behaving as a network to ensure all grid-space drawings are continuous. A small, page-size grid showing the location of the grid numbers only (not the dinosaur drawing!) is helpful and can be placed where students can use it as a reference.

8. Once all grid connections have been satisfactorily completed, the pencil lines should be gone over with black marker to improve visibility.

9. The grid squares can now be assembled on the preselected wall to complete the enlarged dinosaur.

10. For outdoor drawing, give students chalk and guide them as they measure and draw the grid of the entire animal on the paved area. Use the long piece of string or rope to establish a base for the grid.

11. All grid spaces should be identified with small numbers in the upper right-hand corner.

12. Prepare a grid number/student name list as in step 3; assign grid numbers to students.

13. Give small grid squares to students as in step 4. (Alternatively, students can select grid squares from a container. Three or four students at a time can then draw their selected grid spaces. This can be done as a team competition as well—many variations are possible.)

14. Follow sequence given in steps 5 through 8 (assembly is not required).

15. When the drawing is completed, have students identify the animal using classroom or library resources.

The completed animal drawing will allow students to appreciate the awesome size of the creatures that they are studying. More important, however, is the appreciation for size the student will gain by drawing the small segment of the grid; the animal's foot or hand, or a small portion of the teeth and jaw.

EXTENSIONS

1. Drawing the mural can be combined with library research on the animal to determine its habitat and other animals that coexisted with it. Wall murals can be enhanced by drawing appropriate plants. Students may be required to use library sources to document all elements of the mural for authenticity. Paleontologists might be invited to class as judges or advisors. A sense of depth can be created by drawing footprints on the floor of the classroom, leading up to the wall, or by constructing a small portion of the animal or plants as a three-dimensional model projecting from the wall.

2. Students can be asked to color the dinosaur when completed. Dinosaur skin coloration is not preserved in the fossil record. If camouflage were critical to the animal's survival (as for lions and deer), earth tones would be used. If, on the other hand, colors functioned much as they do for birds (vivid coloring helps attract mates), very bright, visually attractive colors might be used. Students can research animal color schemes to find one they consider appropriate.

3. Similar procedures can be used for anything being studied to create a classroom environment; tipis for Native Americans, elephants for African wildlife, a small airplane or a schoolbus for transportation.

4. Large animals, such as *Brachiosaurus* or *Allosaurus*, will not fit on a classroom wall. For comparison, however, their lower legs or skulls can be shown among the smaller animals.

★ ★ ★

SUGGESTED READING

Lambert, David. *The Dinosaur Data Book*. New York: Avon Books, 1990.

Norman, David. *The Illustrated Encyclopedia of Dinosaurs*. New York: Crown, 1985.

Peters, David. *A Gallery of Dinosaurs and Other Early Reptiles*. New York: Alfred A. Knopf, 1989.

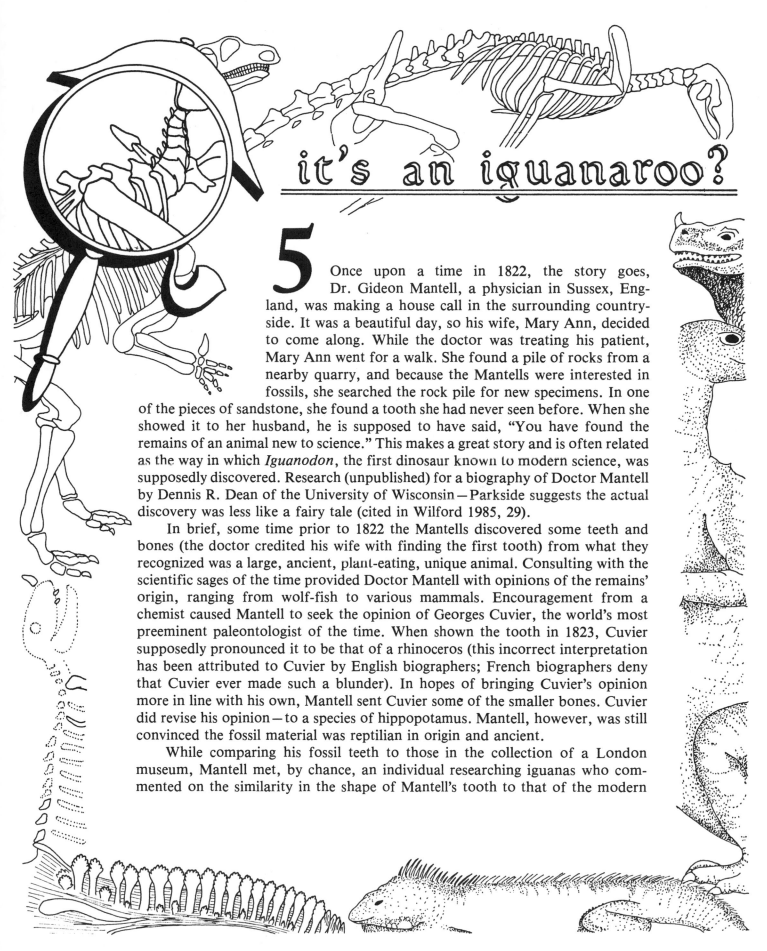

it's an iguanaroo?

5 Once upon a time in 1822, the story goes, Dr. Gideon Mantell, a physician in Sussex, England, was making a house call in the surrounding countryside. It was a beautiful day, so his wife, Mary Ann, decided to come along. While the doctor was treating his patient, Mary Ann went for a walk. She found a pile of rocks from a nearby quarry, and because the Mantells were interested in fossils, she searched the rock pile for new specimens. In one of the pieces of sandstone, she found a tooth she had never seen before. When she showed it to her husband, he is supposed to have said, "You have found the remains of an animal new to science." This makes a great story and is often related as the way in which *Iguanodon*, the first dinosaur known to modern science, was supposedly discovered. Research (unpublished) for a biography of Doctor Mantell by Dennis R. Dean of the University of Wisconsin—Parkside suggests the actual discovery was less like a fairy tale (cited in Wilford 1985, 29).

In brief, some time prior to 1822 the Mantells discovered some teeth and bones (the doctor credited his wife with finding the first tooth) from what they recognized was a large, ancient, plant-eating, unique animal. Consulting with the scientific sages of the time provided Doctor Mantell with opinions of the remains' origin, ranging from wolf-fish to various mammals. Encouragement from a chemist caused Mantell to seek the opinion of Georges Cuvier, the world's most preeminent paleontologist of the time. When shown the tooth in 1823, Cuvier supposedly pronounced it to be that of a rhinoceros (this incorrect interpretation has been attributed to Cuvier by English biographers; French biographers deny that Cuvier ever made such a blunder). In hopes of bringing Cuvier's opinion more in line with his own, Mantell sent Cuvier some of the smaller bones. Cuvier did revise his opinion—to a species of hippopotamus. Mantell, however, was still convinced the fossil material was reptilian in origin and ancient.

While comparing his fossil teeth to those in the collection of a London museum, Mantell met, by chance, an individual researching iguanas who commented on the similarity in the shape of Mantell's tooth to that of the modern iguana. This was all the encouragement Mantell needed. In 1825 he gave a full report of the giant (18-meter) ancient reptile he named *Iguanodon* ("iguana tooth") to the Royal Society of London. On the basis of the rather skimpy evidence he had collected indicating a large reptile with teeth like an iguana's, Mantell represented the animal as a large iguana. One of the bones he found appeared to be a horn, so, perhaps following Cuvier's purported erroneous rhinoceros analysis, Mantell placed a horn on the nose of his *Iguanodon*.

☆ ☆ ☆

ACTIVITY: WHY DID HE THINK IT WAS SO BIG?

To determine how big his ancient reptile might have been, Mantell had very few clues—only a few teeth and bones. For lack of a better idea, Mantell figured that if the fossil tooth was a certain enlargement of the modern tooth, then the fossil animal was a comparable enlargement of the modern animal. Although it seems reasonable, his line of thinking was imperfect. In 1841 the British paleontologist Richard Owen (who first named such fossils dinosaurs) described the possible problems (1841, 142-143):

> [D]imensions of 100 feet in length [were] arrived at by a comparison of the teeth and clavicle of the *Iguanodon* with the *Iguana*, of 75 feet from a similar comparison of their femora [thighbones], and of 80 feet from that of the claw-bone, which, if founded upon the largest specimen from Horsham, instead of the one compared by Dr. Mantell, would yield a result of upwards of 200 feet for the total length of the *Iguanodon*.

Estimates for the size of *Iguanodon* based upon such methods ranged from 60 to 200 feet. Comparisons, such as the one used by Mantell, may have been the best method available at the time, but they were far from exact. However imprecise the method may have been, Mantell's procedure can easily be duplicated by students.

REQUIREMENTS

Time

Half of a class period

Materials

- Copies of figure 5.1 for each student
- Small metric rulers

Grouping

Individuals

DIRECTIONS

1. Distribute copies of figure 5.1 to students. Explain what the drawings are and that representations are actual size.

2. Tell students that they are paleontologists who have just found a single, large fossil tooth that resembles that of an iguana, and they need to determine how large the fossil animal was. Show them figure 5.2, page 46, so they can see what an iguana looks like.

3. The jaw of the iguana shown in figure 5.1 is from an iguana approximately 1.5 meters long.

4. The students should not need additional instruction. Allow the class to discuss the problem among themselves to see how they might solve it. Only if they seem to be hopelessly lost give them the idea of ratios. One way might be to show them the following ratio:

$$\frac{\text{iguana size}}{\text{iguana tooth size}} = \frac{\textit{Iguanodon} \text{ size}}{\textit{Iguanodon} \text{ tooth size}}$$

5. When they determine an answer, have them write the answer on a piece of paper.

6. When all students have completed the activity, discuss the various sizes determined. These answers may vary considerably, depending upon the way the students measure the teeth and which teeth they measure. Discuss possible variations in size. What if the *Iguanodon* tooth was actually from a baby? How big would an adult have been?

7. Show them figure 5.3, page 46, indicating the bones Mantell found and explain that they have just completed the same exercise Mantell did in the early 1820s.

8. Read Owen's quote discussing problems with the method.

Fig. 5.1. *Iguanodon* tooth (left) and jaw of a modern-day iguana (right), both shown actual size. Modified from Benton.

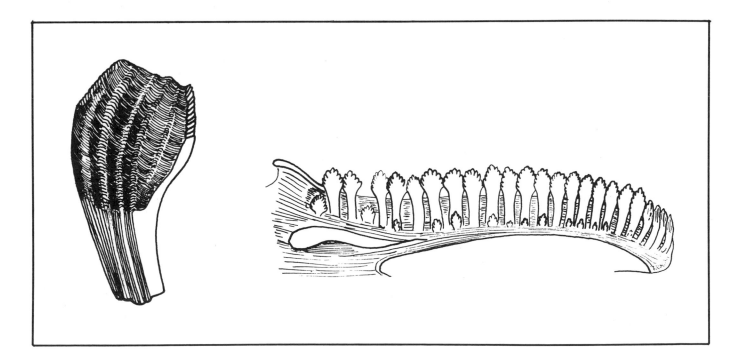

Fig. 5.2. Modern iguana. Actual length approximately 1.5 meters. Modified from Charig.

Fig. 5.3. Doctor Mantell's original interpretation of the skeleton of his *Iguanodon* as published in 1825 in *Philosophical Transactions of the Royal Society, London*, 115. The bones and teeth he and his wife found are shown with solid lines. Modified from Mantell.

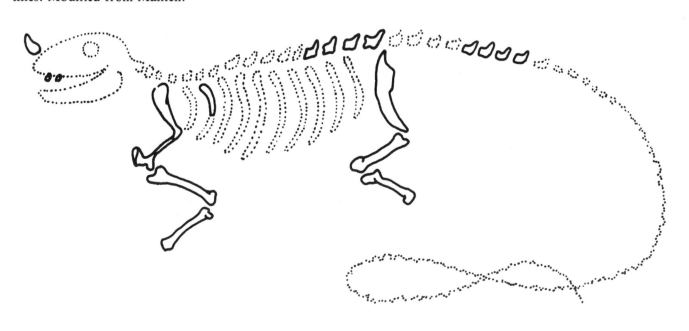

EXTENSIONS

1. Have students select a skeleton to study after a trip to the library. Each student can select a different animal, or they can work in teams. Their job is to determine the ratio of different parts of the animal to the total length or height. For example, for a specific skeleton, the femur may be one third the total height, and the tibia may be one fifth the total height. Have students list the various ratios they determine. When completed, have them calculate the height or length of this animal, using the ratios for each of the bones they measured, as if each bone were the only one found. This will demonstrate the problems inherent in using only one part of an animal to determine the size of the whole. It is now known that *Iguanodon* had very short front legs and long back legs (it was originally thought that *Iguanodon* walked on four legs). Its projected size would have depended upon whether the front or rear leg bones were found and measured.

2. Students can create a time line using the dates and data available on the discovery of *Iguanodon*, illustrating it with the appropriate interpretation of *Iguanodon*'s appearance as it was perceived at the time.

☒ ☒ ☒

In 1846 large, three-toed footprints were found in southern England and identified as large birds on the basis of similar interpretations of three-toed tracks known from North America. Only later were they considered to be those of *Iguanodon*.

In 1854 a world exposition was held in London, and the opportunity was perfect for England's scientific community to display its dinosaur discoveries to the world (by then four dinosaurs, including *Iguanodon*, had been identified). Life-size sculptures of the dinosaurs were made (which can still be seen today). Interestingly enough, *Iguanodon* was represented as a squat, scaly, rhinoceroslike quadruped (see fig. 5.4) completely different from Mantell's drawing but quite like Cuvier's erroneous assessment, which he had recanted some 30 years earlier (if you believe the British version of events).

Fig. 5.4. *Iguanodon* model built for the 1854 World Exposition in London. Modified from Benton.

In 1858 Joseph Leidy of the Academy of Natural Sciences in Philadelphia examined a dinosaur skeleton in New Jersey and, based upon the teeth, considered it related to the *Iguanodons* of England, suggesting that these extinct animals may have wandered across the planet. One of Leidy's major contributions to the improvement of *Iguanodon* restoration was his analysis of the limbs: the front limbs were half the length of the hind limbs. The models built in England for the fair had been in error. To Leidy the animal had to have been more like a kangaroo, supporting itself upright on its two large hind legs and its tail (see fig. 5.5).

Fig. 5.5. Leidy's interpretation of *Iguanodon* based upon his discovery of 1858. Modified from Benton.

Historic pictures of Leidy's laboratory show kangaroo and bird skeletons beside the hadrosaur (*Iguanodon* relative) reconstruction. Reviewing Leidy's findings, Thomas Henry Huxley, the famous ally of Charles Darwin, reexamined Mantell's original interpretation and concluded the animal in question had birdlike hindquarters and must have walked or hopped on two rear legs; the new model was indeed a significant improvement.

In 1862 more three-toed tracks were discovered in southern England; this time they were attributed to *Iguanodon* and helped confirm an upright, birdlike posture and locomotion. In 1877-1878, in a coal mine almost 1,000 feet below the city of Bernissart, Belgium, the most dramatic discovery in the recreation of *Iguanodon* was occurring. Ultimately, 31 *Iguanodons* were recovered from the coal mine; 11 skeletons were mounted standing, 20 more, many complete, are lying down in the museum in Brussels where they are exhibited. This superabundance of skeletal data removed most doubts about the appearance of *Iguanodon*.

☒ ☒ ☒

ACTIVITY: KANGAROO?

Leidy's description of the dinosaur seems strange today, but 100 years ago, with only a little information available, it seemed a reasonable guess. Figure 5.6, page 50, shows drawings of a kangaroo skeleton and a modern interpretation of what *Iguanodon* probably looked like.

REQUIREMENTS

Time

One or two class periods

Materials

A copy of figure 5.6 for each student

Grouping

Individuals

DIRECTIONS

1. Distribute a copy of figure 5.6 to each student.

2. Tell students they are members of a museum staff. Someone has just told them that the extinct animal shown at the bottom of figure 5.6 is like a kangaroo. Their job is to examine the skeletons of the two animals and determine whether the extinct creature is indeed like a kangaroo (for instance, does it walk, run, or live like a kangaroo).

3. Students must complete a report to the director of the museum detailing the reasons they believe the animal was or was not like a kangaroo.

4. Library or homework time can be used for students to obtain more detailed information about the habits and lifestyles of kangaroos.

☒ ☒ ☒

Fig. 5.6. Skeletons of *Iguanodon* (bottom) and kangaroo (top). Modified from Casier.

The emergence of track analysis in the latter twentieth century has yielded even more new information about *Iguanodon* posture and locomotion. Specifically, tail marks are not found, indicating the tail was supported above the ground as the animal moved, and small handprints are often found in the trackways, indicating that at least for some of the time, *Iguanodon* and its close relatives were capable of quadrupedal behavior.

Later evidence has proved some of Mantell's conclusions incorrect, but the significance of the discovery, his recognition of its meaning, and his persistence to have the scientific community recognize the discovery are all important. By the time Mantell's report was published, Cuvier had come to agree with Mantell's assessment that the skeleton belonged to a large, ancient, reptilian herbivore.

Although Mantell's find marked the first recognition of a unique, extinct fossil reptile, it was not the first time the bones of these extinct creatures had been unearthed, nor the first time such remains had been misinterpreted. Many nondocumented finds of dinosaur bones were probably made by the ancient peoples of the world, but these finds were unlikely to have been recognized as ancient life forms in the paleontological sense and, in any case, were never recorded. Native Americans apparently believed dinosaur bones were the remains of giants slain on ancient battlegrounds. In 1676 a book published a drawing of what was described as a human thigh bone from Oxfordshire, England. It was thought to be from giant men but was probably part of the thigh bone from a *Megalosaurus*. In 1809 a section of the leg bone of a large animal was found in England by William Smith, the "Father of English Geology," who had no idea what it was. It was not until the 1970s, approximately 160 years after its discovery, that it was identified as belonging to *Iguanodon*. These discoveries are not discussed here to lessen the importance of Mantell's achievements but merely to show that scientific process involves a constant progression of evaluation as new information becomes available. Mantell made a giant leap forward, but it was part of a long journey. It has taken approximately 180 years to create the picture of *Iguanodon* that now exists.

An excellent children's book about the development of *Iguanodon* is Aliki's *Dinosaur Bones* (New York: Thomas Y. Crowell, 1988).

REFERENCES

Owen, Richard. 1841. "Report on British Fossil Reptiles." *Report of the 11th Meeting of the British Association for the Advancement of Science*: 142-143.

Wilford, John Noble. 1985. *The Riddle of the Dinosaur*. New York: Vintage Books.

SUGGESTED READING

Batory, R. Dana, and William A. S. Sarjeant. "Sussex Iguanodon Footprints and the Writing of *The Lost World*." In *Dinosaur Tracks and Traces*, edited by David M. Gillette and Martin G. Lockley. Cambridge: Cambridge University Press, 1989.

Benton, Michael J. *On the Trail of the Dinosaurs*. New York: Crown, 1989.

Casier, Edgar. *Les Iguanodons de Bernissart*. Brussels: Institut Royal des Sciences Naturelles de Belgique, 1960.

Charig, Alan. *A New Look at the Dinosaurs*. New York: Facts on File, 1983.

Desmond, Adrian J. *The Hot-Blooded Dinosaurs*. New York: Dial Press, 1976.

Hsu, Kenneth J. *The Great Dying*. San Diego, Calif.: Harcourt Brace Jovanovich, 1986.

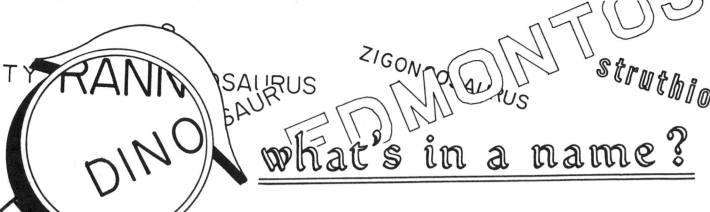

what's in a name?

6 At first glance, it is easy to believe that paleontologists concocted dinosaur names merely to confuse and confound the general public. A simple exercise is all it will take to demonstrate that just the opposite is true. Show the students a picture of *Triceratops*. Ask them to tell you its name. Without fail they will say, "*Triceratops*."
Ask them how they know it is *Triceratops*, and they will say, "because it has three horns on its head." They already know precisely what the name means (literally translated, it means "three-horned face")—they just don't realize it!

Almost 1,500 years before Darwin, the Greek philosopher Aristotle examined the natural world that surrounded him. Aristotle wrote in his native tongue, but 1,000 years later a great number of his works were translated into Latin, the language of choice of a Renaissance world emerging from the Dark Ages. Latin became the international language of science and so continues to this day. In the mid-eighteenth century Swedish physician and botanist Carolus Linnaeus believed that all life on earth was created according to some divine master plan, and he set out to organize life forms within that plan. Linnaeus developed a system to categorize and name (in Latin) the new biological discoveries of the time, significantly improving the earlier work of Aristotle (*Historia Animalium*). As new scientific discoveries are made, be they botanical, geological, zoological, or astronomical, they undoubtedly will receive names that are Latin or derived from Latin.

As developed by Linnaeus, the scientific labels of plants and animals consist of a two-part Latin name (binomial). The first name is the genus and the second is the species. A species is a group of organisms whose members have similar anatomical characteristics and the ability to interbreed. Genera are groups of similar species. For example, the common dog is *Canis familiaris*, and the wolf is *Canis lupus*. *Canis* is the genus, or larger group, followed by the species name. In general these names are somehow descriptive of the organism: where it was found or some characteristic feature or habit. Occasionally they are derived from the names of people or places associated with the discovery. Scientific names can be more frivolous than one might think; one paleontologist named many species of marine invertebrates after beautiful women he had known.

Dinosaur names are often chosen on the basis of these three categories: (1) place of discovery, (2) name of the discoverer or some expert in the field, or (3) description of the animal or some feature of its anatomy. The lists that follow are not intended to be all-inclusive. They merely provide examples of these three types of names.

The naming of a dinosaur after a place is very straightforward. The actual name of a site associated with the discovery is included in the name of the animal:

Albertosaurus	Alberta, Canada
Bactrosaurus	Bactria, Mongolia
Edmontosaurus	Edmonton, Alberta, Canada
Nemegtosaurus	Nemegtu, Mongolia
Zigongosaurus	Zigong, China

Infrequently, a discovery is named for a person, either a paleontologist or a benefactor of the discovery:

Lambeosaurus	for Lawrence Lambe, paleontologist with the Geological Survey of Canada
Diplodocus carnegii	for Andrew Carnegie, who financed the expedition to discover a dinosaur for the Carnegie Museum in Pittsburgh, Pennsylvania
Hadrosaurus foulkii	for William Parker Foulk, who excavated the specimen

By far the greatest number of dinosaur names are descriptive, revealing the shape, analogy to a modern animal, behavior, size, or some other anatomical feature of the animal:

Ar/rhino/cera/tops	no/nose/horned/face
Corytho/saurus	Corinthian helmet/reptile
Iguano/don	iguana/tooth
Lyco/rhinus	wolf/snout
Maia/saurus	good mother/reptile
Pro/compso/gnathus	before/pretty/jaw
Stego/saurus	roofed/reptile
Tyranno/saurus rex	tyrannical/reptile king

The names seem convoluted at first, but like so many words in the English language, they are composed of a string of Greek or Latin roots. Once those roots are known, the name of virtually any dinosaur becomes an interpretive label. Table 6.1 lists many of the roots (prefixes, suffixes, and combining forms) from which dinosaur names are created:

Table 6.1.
Greek and Latin Descriptors

a, ar, an	no, not	**mimus**	mimic
acro	top	**mono**	single
allo	strange	**morpho**	shaped
alti	tall, high	**mucro**	pointed
angusti	sharp	**nano**	dwarf
apato	deceptive	**nodo**	lumpy
baro	heavy, pressure	**nycho**	clawed
bi	two	**ornitho**	bird
brachio	arm	**pachy**	thick
brachy	short	**ped, pod, pes**	foot
bronto	thunder	**penta**	five
canthus	spiked, spined	**phalangia**	toes
cera	horned	**phobo**	fearsome
coelo	hollow	**placo, plateo**	flat
compso	pretty	**pola, poly**	many
dactyl	finger	**preno**	sloping
deino	terrible	**ptero**	winged
derm	skin	**quadri**	four
di	two	**raptor**	thief
don, den	tooth	**rex**	king
dromaeo	running	**rhino**	nose
drypto	wounding	**saurus**	reptile, lizard
echino	spiked	**segno**	slow
elasmo	plated	**stego**	roofed
elmi	foot	**steneo**	narrow
gnathus	jaw	**stenotes**	finger
hetero	mixed	**stereo**	twin
lana	wooly	**struthio**	ostrich
lepto	slender	**tarbo**	alarming
lestes	robber	**tetra**	four
lopho	ridged	**thero**	beast
luro	tail	**top**	head, face
macro	large	**tri**	three
maia	good mother	**tyranno**	tyrant
mega	huge	**velox, veloci**	speedy, fast
metro	measured		

⊠ ⊠ ⊠

ACTIVITY: WHAT DOES IT LOOK LIKE?

Because a dinosaur name is largely descriptive, once the name is known, it should be possible to describe the animal, audibly and visibly.

REQUIREMENTS

Time

45-90 minutes

Materials

- Small pieces of paper with one of the Greek or Latin descriptors in table 6.1 written on each piece (79 total)

- Container to hold the pieces

- Drawing supplies for each student (paper, pencil, materials for coloring: markers, colored pencils)

- Handouts of the list of descriptors on page 55 for each student or pair

Grouping

Individuals or pairs, depending upon class size

DIRECTIONS

1. Before class, write one root and its definition on a small piece of paper and place it in a container, one for nouns, one for modifiers. Repeat the process until all 79 roots are in the appropriate containers.

2. Discuss dinosaur names and some of the roots with students until they are familiar with how the name is used as a descriptor.

3. Distribute drawing materials to the students.

4. If the class size is less than or equal to 26, have students work individually. Each student will draw two modifiers and one noun from the containers. If the class size is 27 or more, students will work in teams of 2 and each team will draw a noun and three modifiers from the containers.

5. Have the students write the roots and definitions they have selected on the back of the drawing paper and return the slips of paper to the container.

6. Their task is to design a dinosaur based upon the roots they selected. They must draw it in its surroundings in a size large enough so it can be seen by the entire class.

7. Caution them to draw it carefully in pencil first until it satisfies all requirements, then color it.

8. After completion students will present and explain their dinosaurs to the class. The presenters will write their roots and definitions on the board before the presentation. The audience will (in their notebooks) write down the roots and definitions of all presenters. The presentations do not need to be elaborate as long as the presenters make clear how their design satisfies the roots selected.

EXTENSIONS

1. Students can be asked to discover the uses of roots in other branches of science: astronomy, biology, botany, medicine. Methods of investigation can be library resources or phone calls to scientists.

2. Students can be asked to do a library search for names of other animals using similar roots (the roots are not unique to dinosaurs). The modern animals listed below all have names incorporating some of the same roots:

acanthocinus	(beetle) "long antennae"
acanthogobius	(fish) "spiny tail fin"
Carcharhinus	(shark) "jagged nose"
ceratophyrs	"horned toads"
diodontidae	(fish) "two kinds of teeth"
diplospinus	(fish) "double forked tail fin"
echinoderm	(spiky animals like sea urchins) "spiny skin"
heterodontiformes	(shark) "mixed kinds of teeth"
pachyderm	(classification of elephants, rhinoceros and hippopotamus) "thick skin"
pentaceros	(fish) "many head spines"
platyrrhines	(lemur) "flat, broad nose"
pterocera	(snail) "wing-shaped horns"
rhinobatus	(fish) "long, pointed snout"
Rhinoceros	"nose horn"
Trachysaurus	"stump-tailed lizard"

3. Students can investigate how a name is registered and becomes official. Propose to students that they have discovered what they think is a new species of animal or plant. Have them learn how to find out whether it is new and if so, how to register its new name. In one actual case the name *Stereocephalus* was proposed for a newly discovered dinosaur. Unfortunately, that name was already used for an insect, so the newly found dinosaur was named *Euoplocephalus*.

★ ★ ★

ACTIVITY: DICTIONARY SEARCH

Words in many languages have their roots in Latin or Greek. Using many of the prefixes, roots, and suffixes given in table 6.1, page 55, it is possible to understand the meaning of words in other languages such as English, French, Spanish, and Italian. In this activity students will discover that the roots are used not only in science. As part of this activity the librarian can be requested to teach a dictionary skill lesson explaining (1) how roots are given in the definition and (2) dictionaries that have root tracking.

REQUIREMENTS

Time

45-90 minutes of library time, or library assignment over a weekend

Materials

- Pencil and paper for each student
- Copy of table 6.1 for each student

Grouping

Individuals

DIRECTIONS

1. Give each student a copy of table 6.1.

2. Students will be required to find as many words as possible using these roots. Encourage students to use English or one of the Romance languages.

3. Students should submit a list of the words they found, the definitions of those words, and the roots incorporated in the word.

EXTENSIONS

If there are students with other language or cultural backgrounds, encourage them to do research about dinosaur names in their own countries or languages. They may be able to provide interesting insights.

⊠ ⊠ ⊠

SUGGESTED READING

Eschmeyer, William N., Earl S. Herald, and Howard Hammann. *A Field Guide to Pacific Coast Fishes of North America*. Boston: Houghton Mifflin, 1983.

Norman, David. *The Illustrated Encyclopedia of Dinosaurs*. New York: Crown, 1985.

Sarton, George. *A History of Science*. New York: John Wiley and Sons, 1952.

Stanek, V. J. *The Pictorial Encyclopedia of the Animal Kingdom*. New York: Crown, 1962.

Wilford, John Noble. *The Riddle of the Dinosaur*. New York: Vintage Books, 1985.

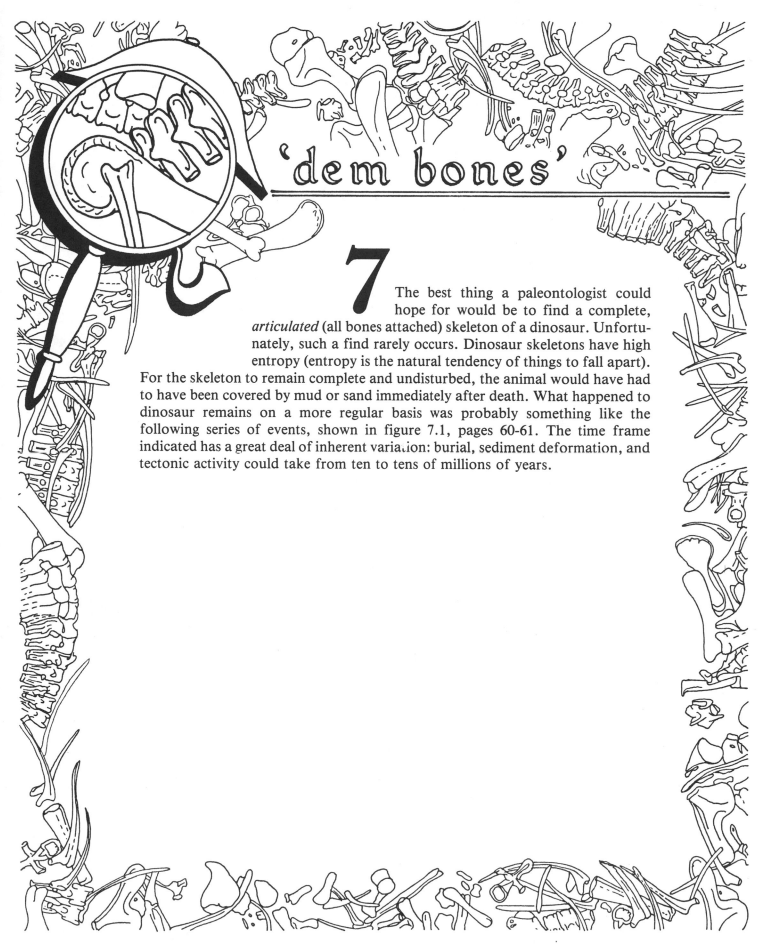

'dem bones

7

The best thing a paleontologist could hope for would be to find a complete, *articulated* (all bones attached) skeleton of a dinosaur. Unfortunately, such a find rarely occurs. Dinosaur skeletons have high entropy (entropy is the natural tendency of things to fall apart). For the skeleton to remain complete and undisturbed, the animal would have had to have been covered by mud or sand immediately after death. What happened to dinosaur remains on a more regular basis was probably something like the following series of events, shown in figure 7.1, pages 60-61. The time frame indicated has a great deal of inherent variation: burial, sediment deformation, and tectonic activity could take from ten to tens of millions of years.

Fig. 7.1. Sequential diagram of bone-site formation, burial, and exposure.

1. A solitary, perhaps injured or sick, animal was tracked by predators (fig. 7.1a).

2. The animal was attacked, in much the same way a pack of wolves attacks a moose (fig. 7.1b).

3. (Minutes to hours later) Cruelly, even as the prey was dying, the gorging and dismembering by the attackers began. Eventually the carcass was completely torn apart, and some bones were carried away from the killing site (fig. 7.1c).

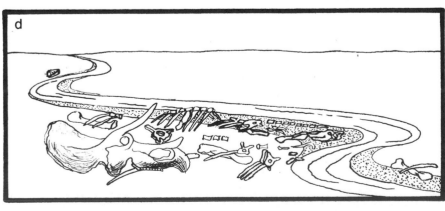

4. (Days or weeks after the kill) As the skeletal remains lay exposed on the surface, they were assaulted by the weather, and the bones were further disturbed. Bones were washed away by streams or heavy rains, and new bones, from other kills, were carried into the site by streams (fig. 7.1d).

Fig. 7.1. — *Continued*

5. (Weeks or months after the kill) Rivers that carried bones to the original site also transported sand and mud, which buried the bones. In some places, windblown sand covered the skeletal remains with thick layers of sediment (fig. 7.1e).

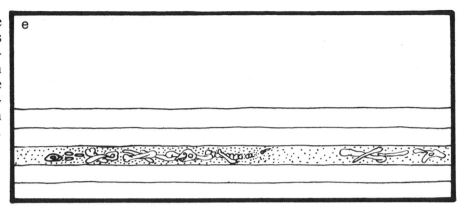

6. (Thousands or millions of years after the kill) Over time, additional sand and mud layers further buried and compressed the bones and the earlier sediments, turning the sediments into rock and possibly deforming the bones (fig. 7.1f).

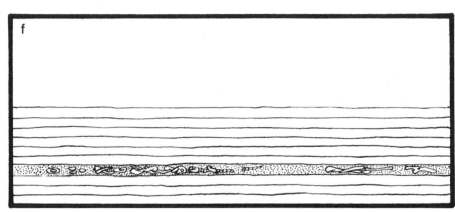

7. (Tens of millions of years after the kill) Tectonic activity (deformation of the earth's crust) tilted and uplifted the previously buried layers and exposed the bone layer at the surface (fig. 7.1g).

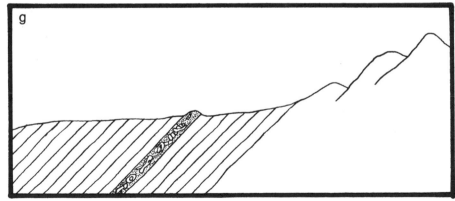

8. (Tens of millions of years after the kill) Weathering and erosion removed some of the enclosing rock material partially separating the bones from the materials in which they were encased during burial. Careful collection will recover as much of the original material as possible. In the excitement of the moment, however, casual collectors might take a single bone without even thinking other bones might be nearby, further dispersing the remains (fig. 7.1h).

In short, all the processes at work operate to separate and disperse the bones of the original skeleton.

Imagine a group picnic. Two families are gathered around the picnic table. Over a large fire, chickens, a side of beef, and several freshly caught fish are being cooked. Everyone takes some of each for dinner. When dinner is over, one of the paper plates has a chicken drumstick, a fish tail, and two beef rib bones. Another has bones from two chicken wings, the fish backbone, and some steak bones. Others have similar assortments. Someone has even thrown a plate of bones into the trash. Suddenly, there's a furious storm. The wind and heavy rain scatter and mix all the bones into a single pile on the ground. Some time later, you wander onto the picnic site and find these bones. You have never seen a chicken, a cow, or a fish, but you have been asked to reconstruct the original animals from the bone pile. The modern paleontologist faces the same problem. As paleontologists go about their work at a bone site, they are usually working with scattered bones. The scientist has no idea how many animals, or even how many different kinds of animals, are represented.

One of the major dinosaur quarries in the United States, Como Bluff, Wyoming, was described by one of its early workers, Samuel W. Williston (1878, 44):

> By far the most commonly, extensive
> deposits, or "quarries," are found
> containing remains of numerous individuals
> mingled together in the most inextricable
> co..fusion, and in every conceivable
> position, with connected limb bones standing
> nearly upright, connected vertebrae
> describing vertical curves, etc., precisely
> as though in some ancient mud holes these
> huge monsters had become mired and died, and
> succeeding generations had trodden their
> bones down, and then left their own to
> mingle with them.

Figure 7.2 shows a small portion of a large dinosaur bone site in Wyoming. The scale key on the drawing gives some idea of how large the bones are. Assembling a complete skeleton from such a collection is not just a herculean effort, it is a tribute to those involved that it is ever accomplished. Any fully mounted museum skeleton should be viewed with great respect because of the efforts required to obtain and assemble it.

Fig. 7.2. A portion of the Howe Bone Quarry in Wyoming. These Jurassic dinosaur bones cover an area approximately 65' × 55'. Modified from Czerkas and Czerkas.

★ ★ ★

ACTIVITY: BONE ASSEMBLY

In this activity students will gain a sense of the effort required to unravel the mysteries of a bone site. Although the process is simplified, some of the frustrations and uncertainties of an actual site will become clear to students.

REQUIREMENTS

Time

90-135 minutes minimum; flexible

Materials

- Handouts of skeleton drawings (figures 7.3-7.12)
- Scissors
- Clear tape or glue sticks
- Large envelopes (8½" × 11")
- Large sheets of blank paper (at least 11" × 17")

Grouping

Pairs

DIRECTIONS

Part 1

1. Divide students into pairs and distribute copies of figures 7.3 to 7.12, pages 65 to 74, to the class, three figures per pair. Each pair of students will ultimately have three skeletons to reassemble. Different pairs may have the same skeletons.

2. Give each student a pair of scissors.

3. Have the students cut around the parts of the skeleton on the page. Remind them to leave a small border around the bone cutouts to reduce the chances of damaging the bones.

4. Collect the cut skeleton sections from the students, placing all the pieces from one pair of students in a single envelope and labeling it with their names. Some envelopes may have duplicate skeletons.

5. Discard all scrap paper and collect the scissors.

6. At this point students will know that each envelope contains three complete skeletons. You now have the option of complicating this activity by removing or adding bones from selected envelopes, without the students' knowledge. A significant complicating factor is removal of the skull, because the students then will not know how many animal skeletons are represented.

(Text continues on page 75.)

Fig. 7.3. *Deinonychus* skeleton. Modified from Norman.

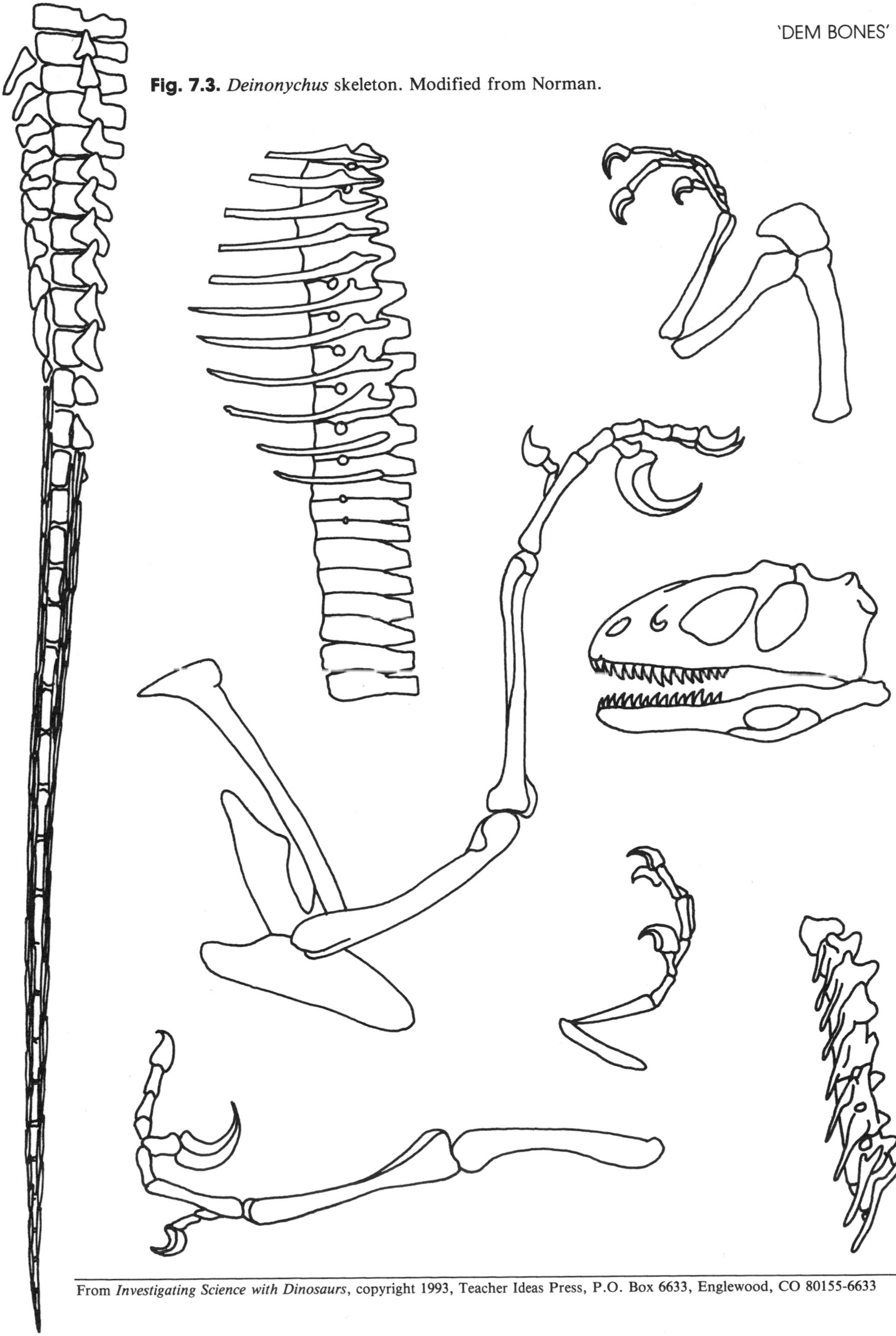

Fig. 7.4. *Ouranosaurus* skeleton. Modified from Norman.

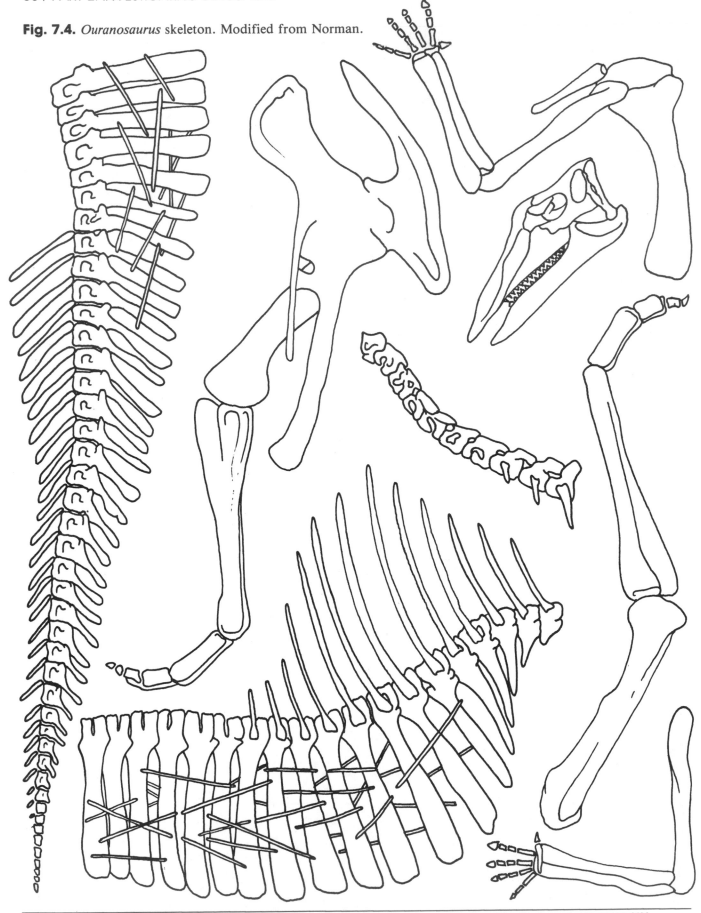

Fig. 7.5. *Tyrannosaurus* skeleton. Modified from Norman.

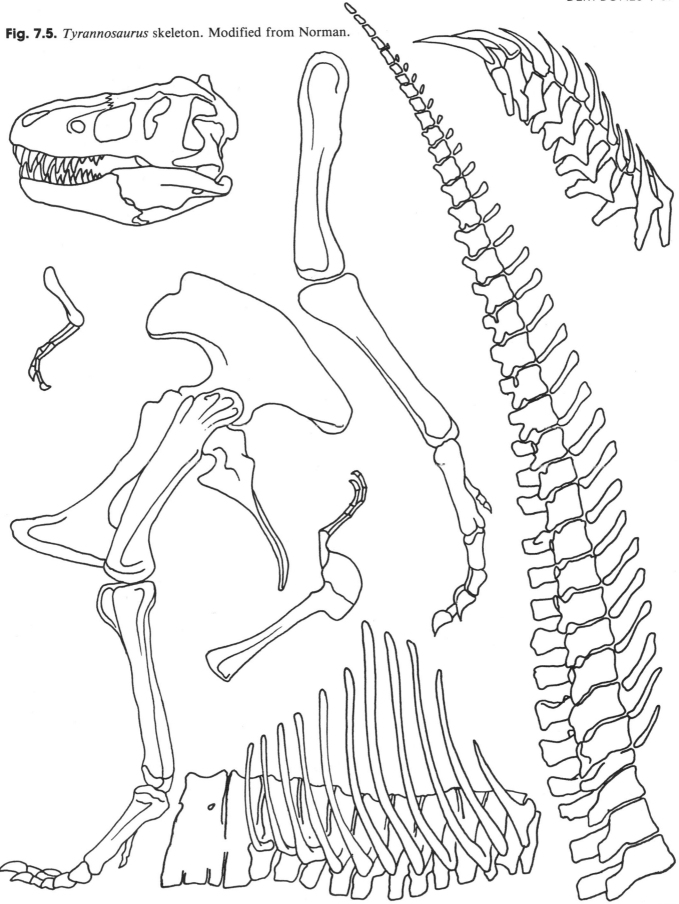

Fig. 7.6. *Tenontosaurus* skeleton. Modified from Czerkas and Czerkas.

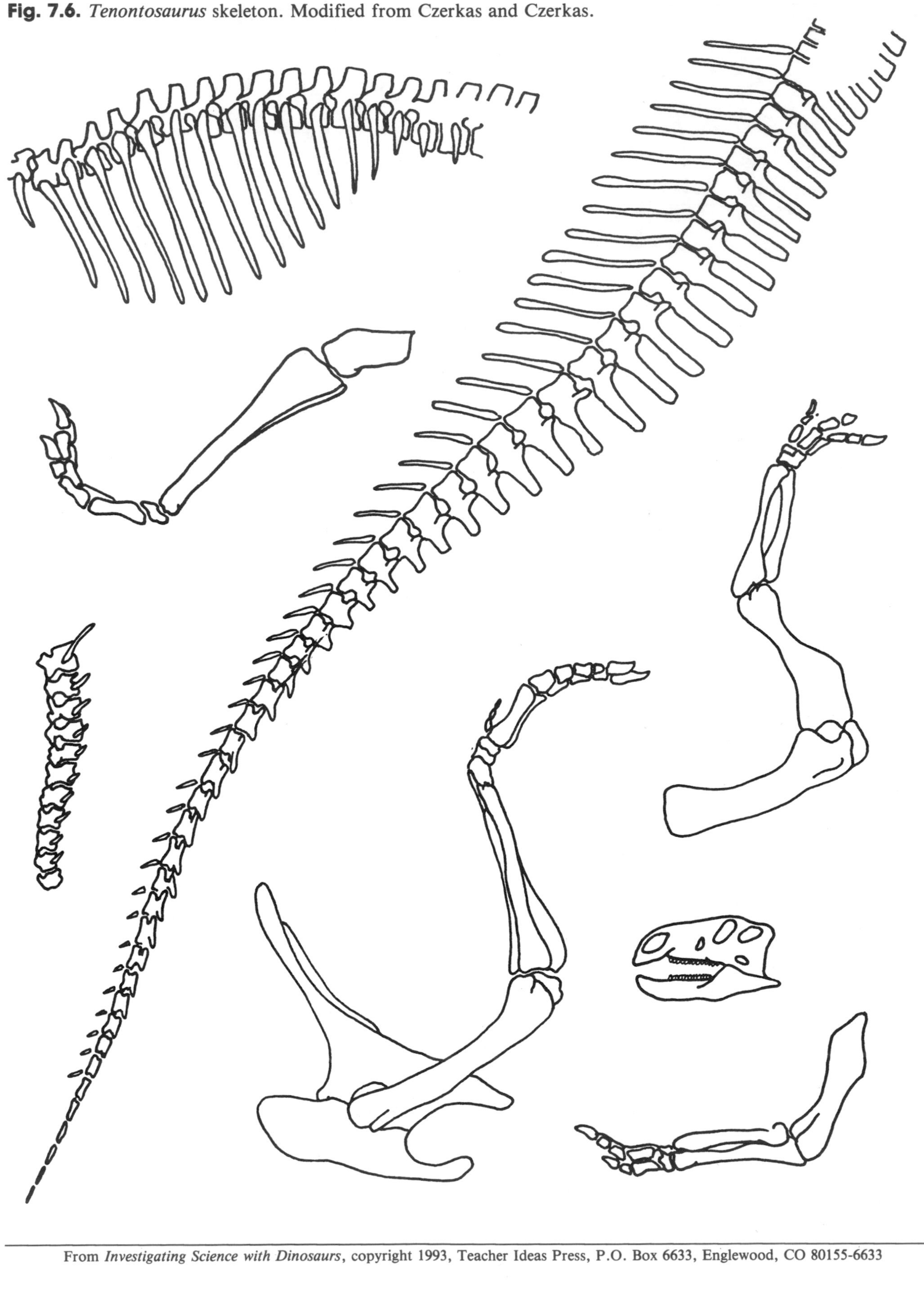

Fig. 7.7. *Stegoceras* skeleton. Modified from Norman.

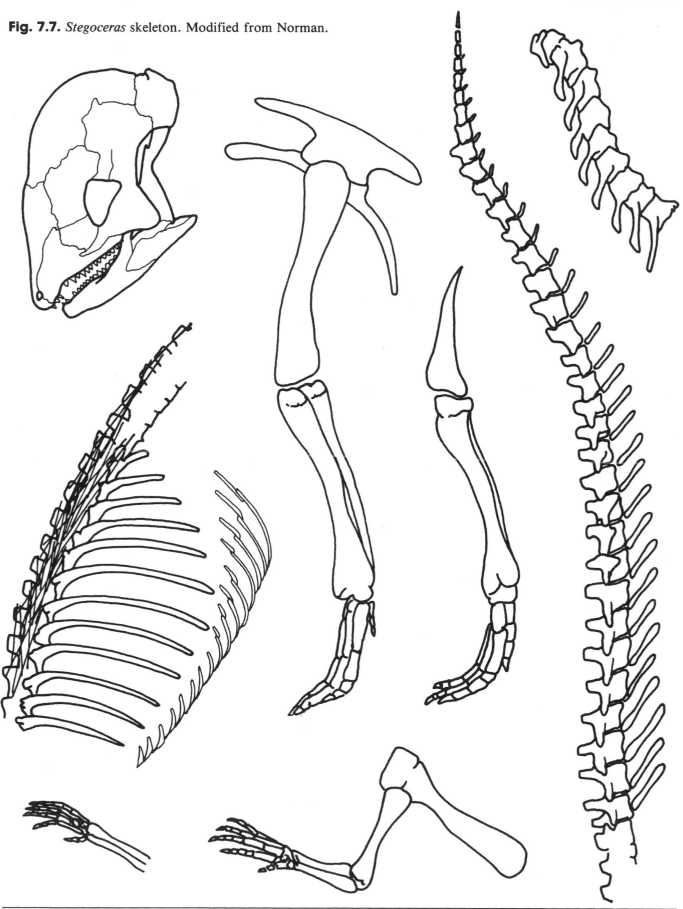

Fig. 7.8. *Sauropelta* skeleton. Modified from Czerkas and Czerkas.

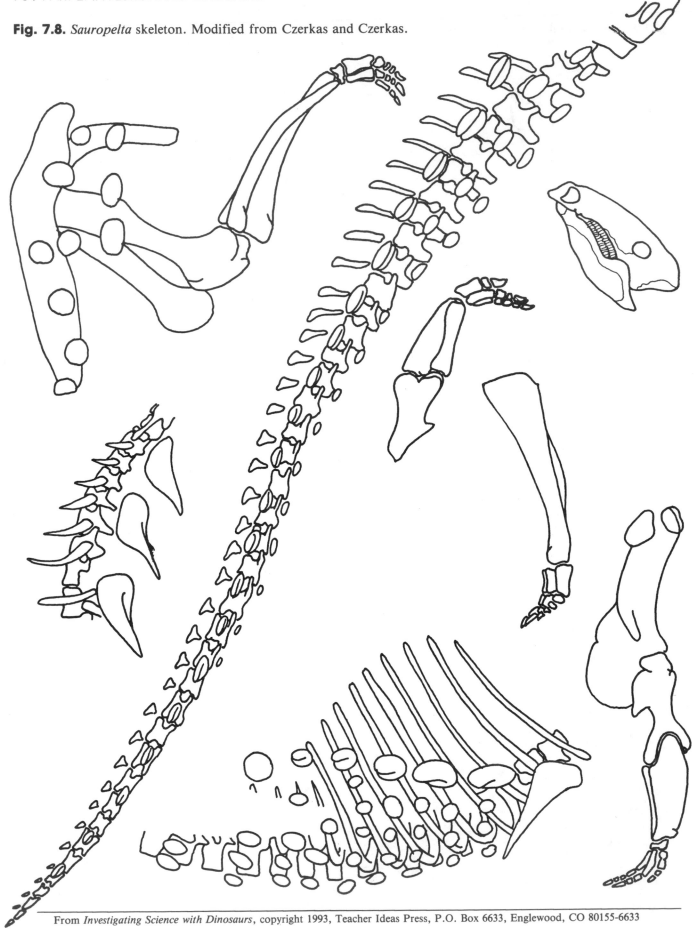

Fig. 7.9. *Protoceratops* skeleton. Modified from Norman.

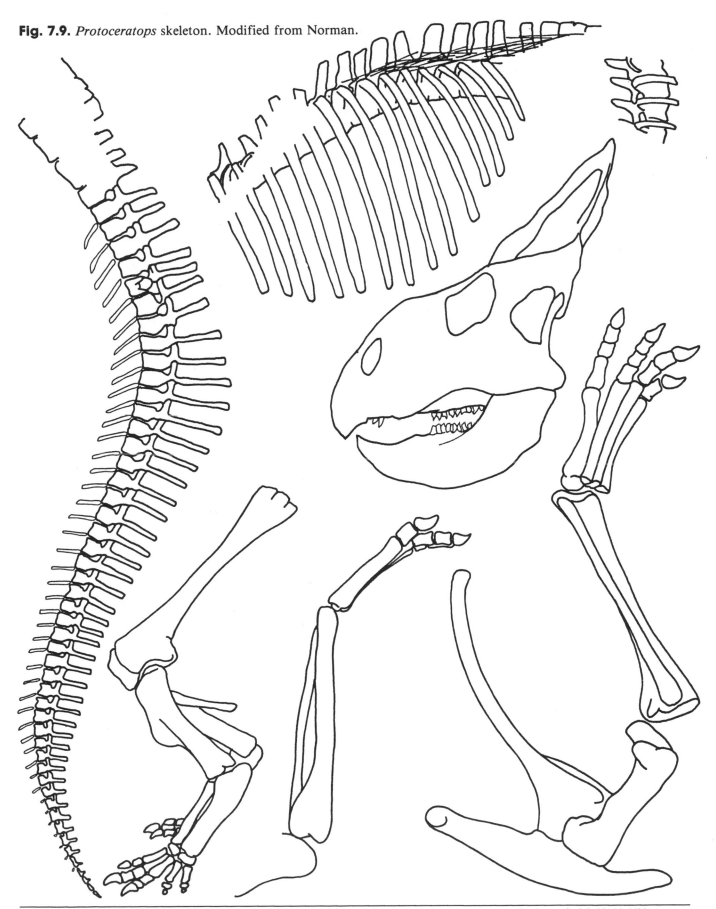

Fig. 7.10. *Parasaurolophus* skeleton. Modified from Norman.

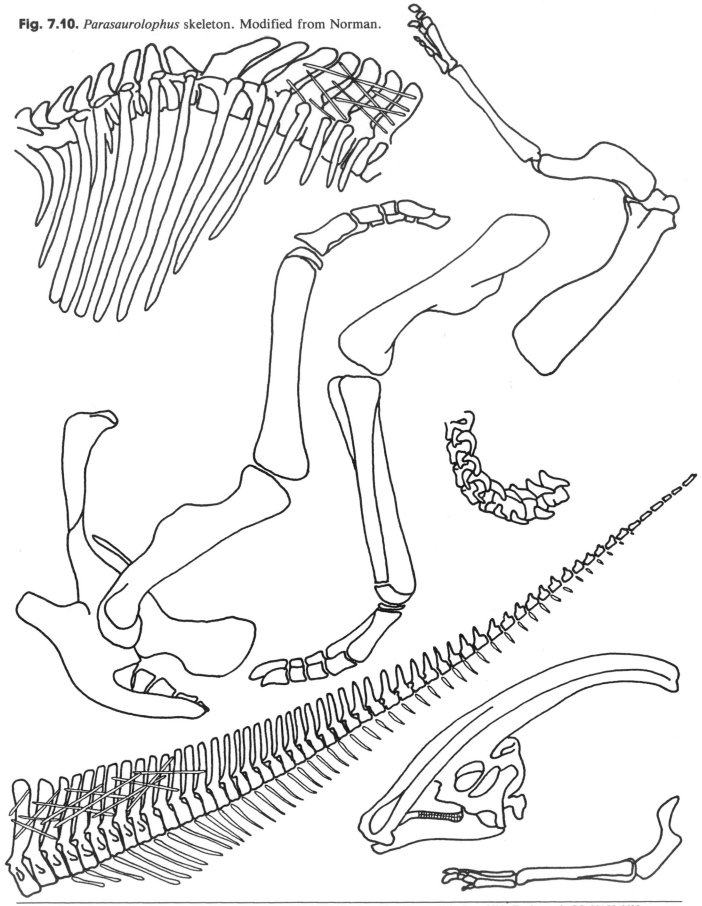

Fig. 7.11. *Hypsilophodon* skeleton. Modified from Norman.

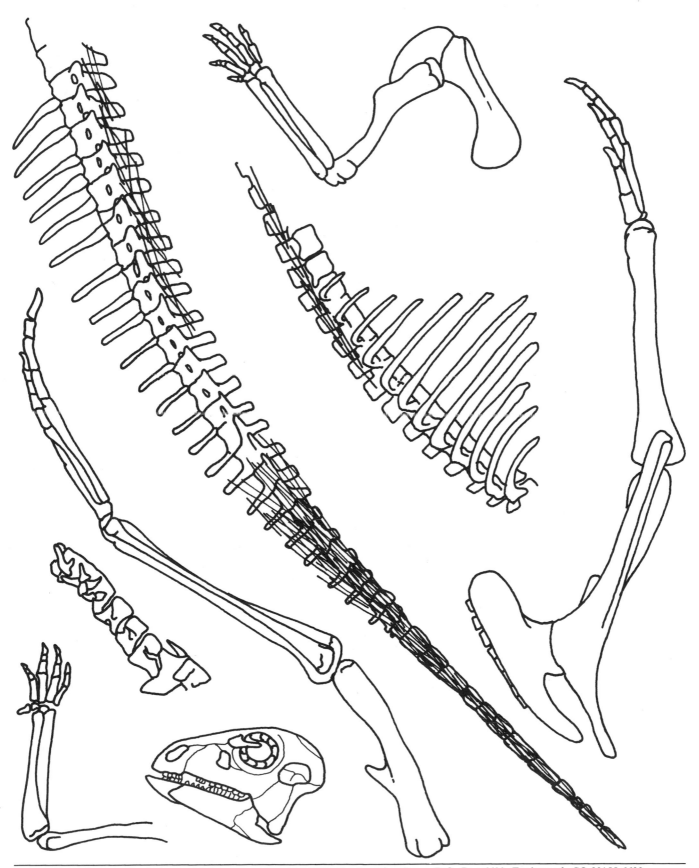

Fig. 7.12. *Centrosaurus* skeleton. Modified from Norman.

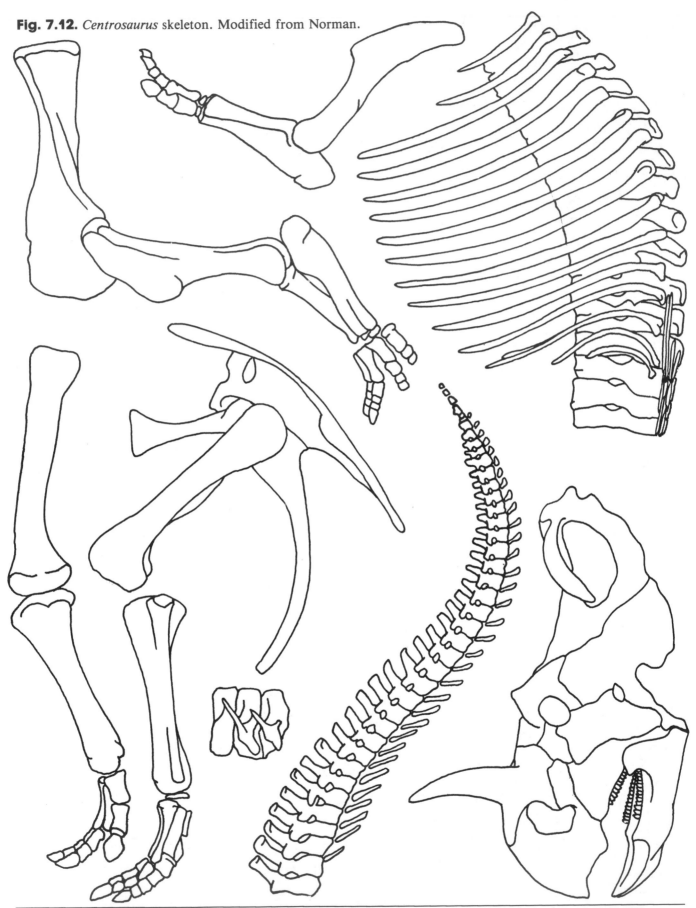

Part 2

1. Seat student pairs at tables or on the floor.

2. Give the students the following instructions: Each group is a museum expedition to a foreign country that has discovered a new bone site. Not much is known about the bones. No one knows what the animals looked like, how big they were, how many animals are in the bone site, or whether they are all the same or all different. The skeletons may be complete or parts may be missing. There may be extra bones. Your museum has asked you to solve the mysteries of the bone site. How many animals are there? What did they look like? Based upon the evidence you have, what can you discover about the animals? Were they carnivores or herbivores? Did they walk on two legs or four? At the conclusion of the dig, you will be required to prepare a detailed written report and present your findings to the board of directors of the museum (the class).

3. Students should be advised that there is no correct way to assemble the skeletons. Because they are the first people to find these bones, any reasonable assembly is acceptable as long as they can defend their choices.

4. Distribute one envelope to each pair, making certain that students do not receive the envelope with their names on it. Have the students dump the contents of the envelope into a small pile. This is their "bone site."

5. Distribute the tape or glue and large sheets of paper to the pairs. Pairs should be reminded to try different arrangements of the skeleton pieces until they are satisfied they all fit. Only then should they assemble them by taping or gluing them to the large piece of paper.

6. Have students put their names and periods on the back of the paper.

7. Provide a place where the materials of a single group can be stored undisturbed between periods.

Part 3

1. Have students prepare the written report. This report should involve both members of the pair and should include discussions of the results of the expedition and how the pair arrived at their conclusions about the animals. Encourage students to use outside references. Add a library research period to the project and have students bring in their own dinosaur books. Any references used should be cited in the final report. Drawings should be encouraged. Give students a standard format to be followed: cover page, table of contents, two pages of text, drawings, comparisons to skeletons of modern animals, references, or any other details you may select. Each group member should specify what he or she contributed to the report.

2. Class presentations should communicate the methods and conclusions given in the written report, using the assembled dinosaur skeletons as visual aids. Permitting students to make an overhead transparency of a significant drawing will improve the presentation. Presentations should be three to five minutes long, and both members of the group should participate. The class, serving as the museum board of directors, should be encouraged to ask questions of the presenters.

EXTENSIONS

1. The activity may also be done by scattering the cut skeleton sections in various places around the room and asking the students to find them. Groups will then be required to prepare a report listing their finds and the conclusions they have drawn.

2. In a smaller class situation have students sit in a circle on the floor. All bones from all the envelopes can be dumped into the middle of the circle to create a bone site. The class can be divided into small, competing discovery groups. Taking turns, each group can select three or four bones until all bones have been distributed. The groups will then have to assemble their dinosaurs based only upon the bones they have. Many skeletons will then be incomplete, but it is a more realistic simulation of a dig.

3. Students may be asked to create a "scene" (perhaps a description, drawing, or model) in their reconstruction or interpretation, showing how the various animals they found might have interacted with each other and their environments.

4. In lieu of a formal report each student pair may be asked to prepare a newspaper announcement of their discoveries, distribute it to the class, and then hold a press conference to answer questions from the class.

★ ★ ★

ACTIVITY: LIFE-SIZE SKELETONS

Although the smallest dinosaurs were approximately the size of small birds, the majority of them were considerably larger. The study of dinosaurs usually involves discussion of these extinct giants, supported by small drawings, models, or photographs. Full-size dinosaurs can be seen in museums but are not easily accessible on a daily basis. In this activity students will be able to assemble a full-size drawing of a dinosaur skeleton, which can be displayed on a classroom or hallway wall (see chapter 4, "Bigger Than You Think" [page 31], fleshed out). While studying dinosaurs in class, the presence of a life-size example will provide the perspective on size that is often lacking in school studies. This activity is constrained to "wall-size" dinosaur skeletons and limits drawings to those that will fit onto a wall 8 feet high and no more than 20 feet long. A full-size drawing of just the front half of a *Stegosaurus* (see fig. 7.18, page 80) in the room, peering over a student's shoulder, will be a constant reminder of the greatness dinosaurs represent.

REQUIREMENTS

Time

45-90 minutes; part of the activity may also be given as homework

Materials

• Rulers (metric or English)

• 1 large sheet of blank paper for each student (newsprint pads come in large sizes and are relatively inexpensive)

• 1 copy of a dinosaur-skeleton-in-a-grid selected from figures 7.13-7.21

• Pencils

• Large wall

• Wide black markers, one per student

• Scissors, one per student

• Blank grid for the dinosaur selected, showing only the numbered spaces (not the skeletal outlines) and prepared as an overhead transparency or blackboard drawing.

Grouping

Individuals and group

DIRECTIONS

1. Select and clear a wall area that will accommodate the skeleton assembly you have selected.

2. Select a drawing from figures 7.13-7.21, pages 77-81, that has *at least* enough grid spaces for the class size. If there are more grid spaces than students, students may be given more than one grid to complete.

3. Enlarge the drawing slightly so the lines within each grid are easier to see and cut the grid apart into individual squares.

4. Assign each student a number in sequence, starting with one (leftover or extra numbers can be given as a reward to students with good behavior). This number will be the grid space for which the student is responsible.

5. The caption for each drawing in this book indicates the size the students' grid boxes should be. Each student must cut a piece of paper to match this size (6" × 6", 1' × 1', or 2' × 2').

Fig. 7.13. *Tyrannosaurus rex* legs. 1' × 1' grid. Modified from Norman.

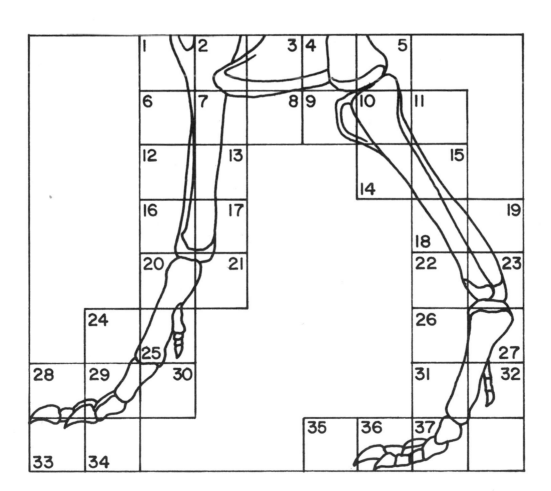

(Text continues on page 82.)

Fig. 7.14. *Heterodontosaurus*. 6" × 6" grid. Modified from Norman.

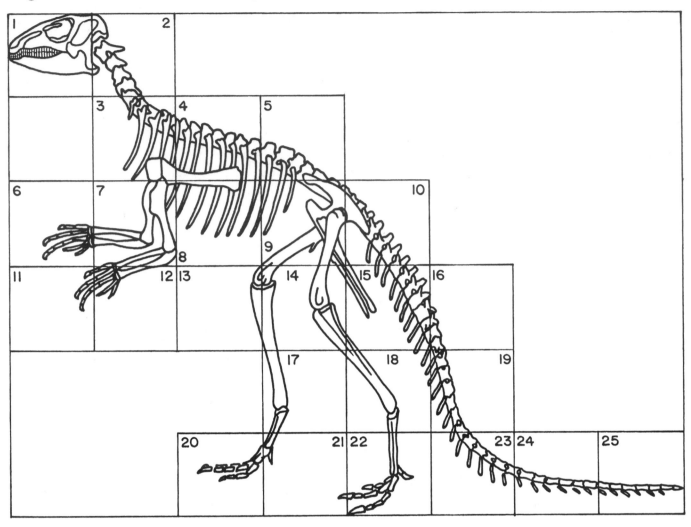

Fig. 7.15. *Protoceratops*. 1' × 1' grid. Modified from Norman.

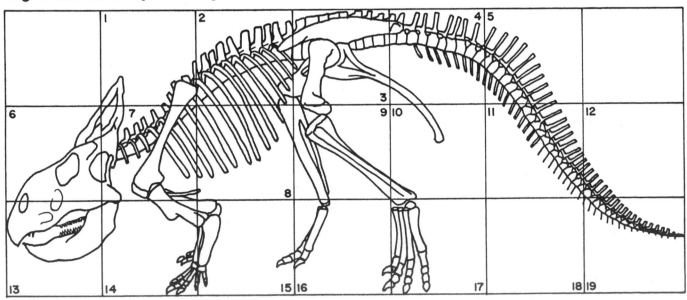

Fig. 7.16. *Diplodocus* neck. 2' × 2' grid. Modified from Norman.

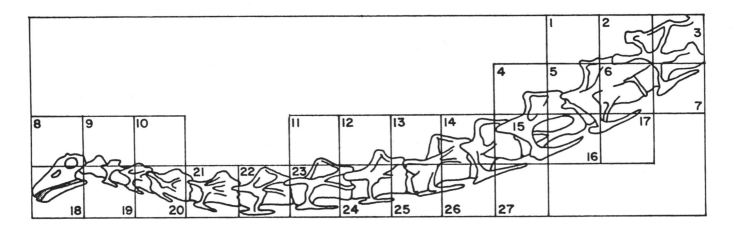

Fig. 7.17. *Hypsilophodon*. 1' × 1' grid. Modified from Norman.

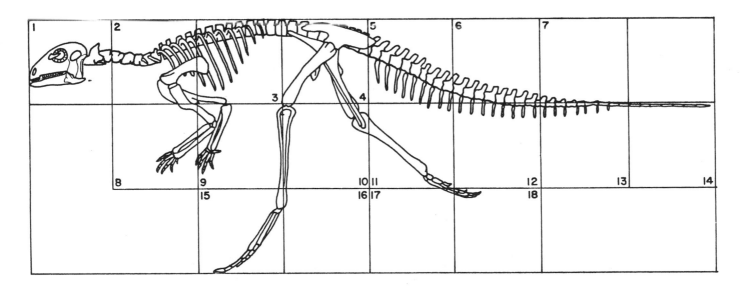

Fig. 7.18. Front of *Stegosaurus*. 1' × 1' grid. Modified from Norman.

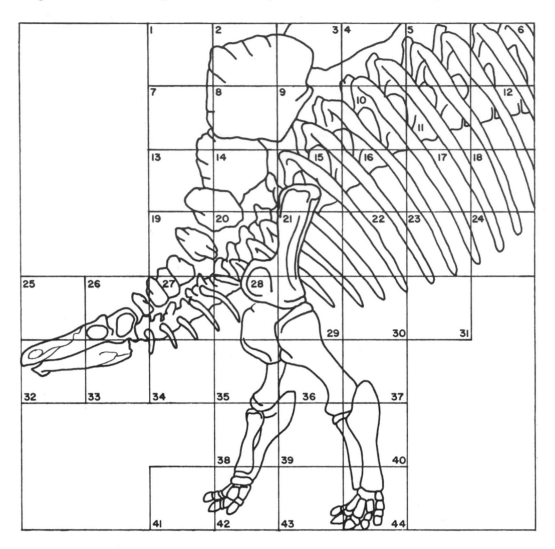

Fig. 7.19. *Compsognathus*. 6" × 6" grid. Modified from Norman.

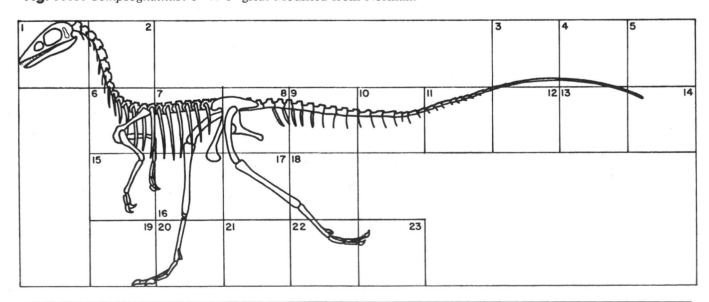

Fig. 7.20. *Velociraptor*. 9" × 9" grid. Modified from Norman.

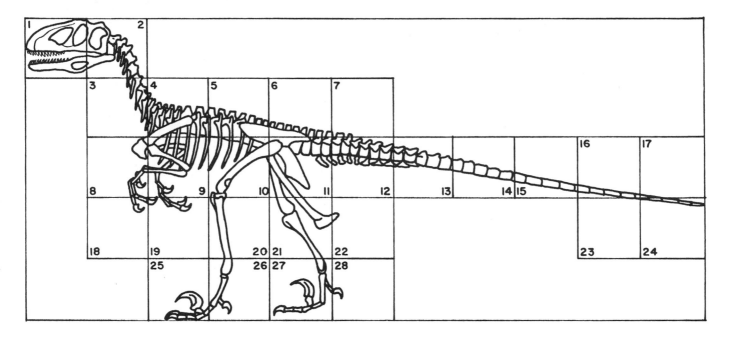

Fig. 7.21. *Struthiomimus*. 1' × 1' grid. Modified from Norman.

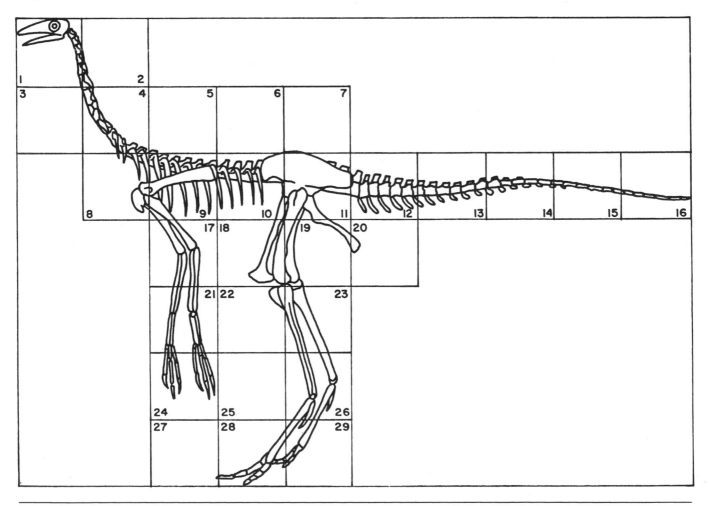

6. *Using pencil* students should reproduce the drawing of the skeleton grid box on their piece of news-print, completely filling the page. Tell students that lines of the drawings must continue to the edge of the paper; they must not create a border.

7. Students should compare their expanded drawing with the adjoining grid spaces to be certain of continuity of lines (bones). Any adjustments should be made in pencil. It is helpful to prepare several small drawings of the original numbered grid for student reference; draw the grid only, not the skeleton lines.

8. Ask students whether they have any ideas about what the animal might be like. Is it big, small, herbivorous, carnivorous, bipedal, quadrupedal?

9. Once students have completed the drawings in pencil and checked them for continuity with the adjoining drawings, the assembly can proceed. If nontransparent tape is used, the tape can be applied to the reverse side. If the markers will write on the clear tape, then it can be applied to the front.

10. When the taped assembly is complete, all pencil lines should be gone over with the wide markers to improve visibility.

EXTENSIONS

1. As a class project for secondary students, a mural depicting the animals of *Jurassic Park* by Michael Crichton (Ballantine Books, 1991) might be built. Reading the book with the life-size skeletons in the room would bring the novel to life. Intermediate students can complete a similar project using any of the books by Angela Sheehan listed in the bibliography at the end of this book.

2. This activity can be tied to units on human anatomy, bones, or structure. Figure 7.22 is a human skeleton on a 1' × 1' grid. After a library period have students compare the human skeleton to those of the dinosaurs for adaptations (length or thickness of limbs). Students can label bones on a drawing of a life-size human skeleton, then locate comparable bones on the dinosaur skeleton. How are the bones different? Why? How has the human skeleton adapted to functions that are different than those of the dinosaurs?

3. Different classes can compete, making different animals. The constructed animal can be used to introduce a dinosaur unit or a multiple-day lesson studying the lifestyle and habits of the animal, using videos and library research.

4. If space is available (perhaps the gymnasium or side of the building), to-scale drawings of many of the taller and longer dinosaurs can be created in this same way (you may assign grid squares for a single large dinosaur to several classes on the same grade level).

★ ★ ★

Fig. 7.22. Adult human skeleton. 1' × 1' grid. Modified from Oram, Hummer, and Smoot.

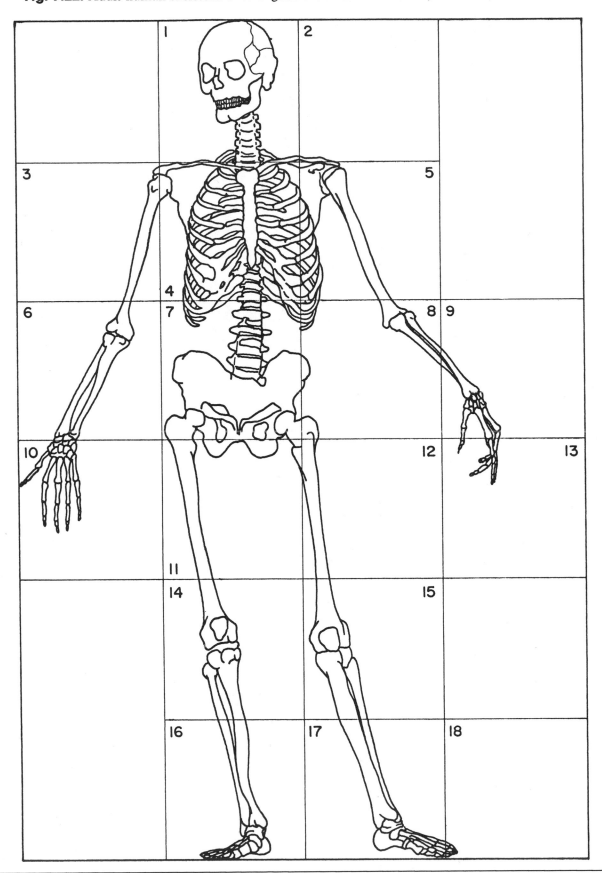

FURTHER READING FOR STUDENTS

Many excellent books have been written about digs and the resurrection of dinosaur fossil skeletons.

For primary students:

Aliki. *Digging Up Dinosaurs*. New York: Thomas Y. Crowell, 1981. Grades 1-4.

For intermediate students:

Arnold, Caroline. *Dinosaur Mountain: Graveyard of the Past*. New York: Houghton Mifflin, 1988. Grades 4-6.

Colbert, Edwin H., and William A. Burns. *Digging for Dinosaurs*. Chicago: Children's Press, 1967. Grades 4-6.

Daeschler, Ted. *The Dinosaur Hunter's Handbook*. Philadelphia: Running Press, 1990. Grades 4-6.

Ipsen, D. C. *The Riddle of the Stegosaurus*. Reading, Mass.: Addison-Wesley, 1969. Grades 4-6.

Selsam, Millicent. *Tyrannosaurus rex*. New York: Harper & Row, 1978. Grades 4-6.

Shuttlesworth, Dorothy E. *Dodos and Dinosaurs*. New York: Hastings House, 1968. Grades 4-6.

Whitaker, George O., and Joan Meyers. *Dinosaur Hunt*. New York: Harcourt, Brace & World, 1965. Grades 4-6.

For secondary students:

Andrews, Roy Chapman. *All About Dinosaurs*. New York: Random House, 1953. Grades 6 and up.

Bird, Roland T. *Bones for Barnum Brown*. Forth Worth, Tex.: Texas Christian University Press, 1985. Grades 8 and up.

Casier, Edgar. *Les Iguanodons de Bernissart*. Brussels: Institut Royal des Sciences Naturelles de Belgique (in French), 1960. Grades 8 and up; knowledge of French required.

Horner, John R., and James Gorman. *Digging Dinosaurs*. New York: Workman, 1988. Grades 8 and up.

Ostrom, John H., and John S. McIntosh. *Marsh's Dinosaurs: The Collections from Como Bluff*. New Haven, Conn.: Yale University Press, 1966. Grades 8 and up.

West, Linda. *Dinosaurs and Dinosaur National Monument*. Jensen, Utah: Dinosaur Nature Association, 1985. Grades 6 and up.

REFERENCES

Williston, Samuel W. 1878. "American Jurassic Dinosaurs." *Transactions of the Kansas Academy of Science* 6: 42-46.

SUGGESTED READING

Czerkas, Sylvia J., and Stephen A. Czerkas. *Dinosaurs: A Global View*. New York: Mallard Press, 1991.

Lanham, Url. *The Bone Hunters*. New York: Columbia University Press, 1973.

Norman, David. *The Illustrated Encyclopedia of Dinosaurs*. New York: Crown, 1985.

Oram, Raymond F., Paul J. Hummer, and Robert C. Smoot. *Biology: Living Systems*. Columbus, Ohio: Charles E. Merrill, 1983.

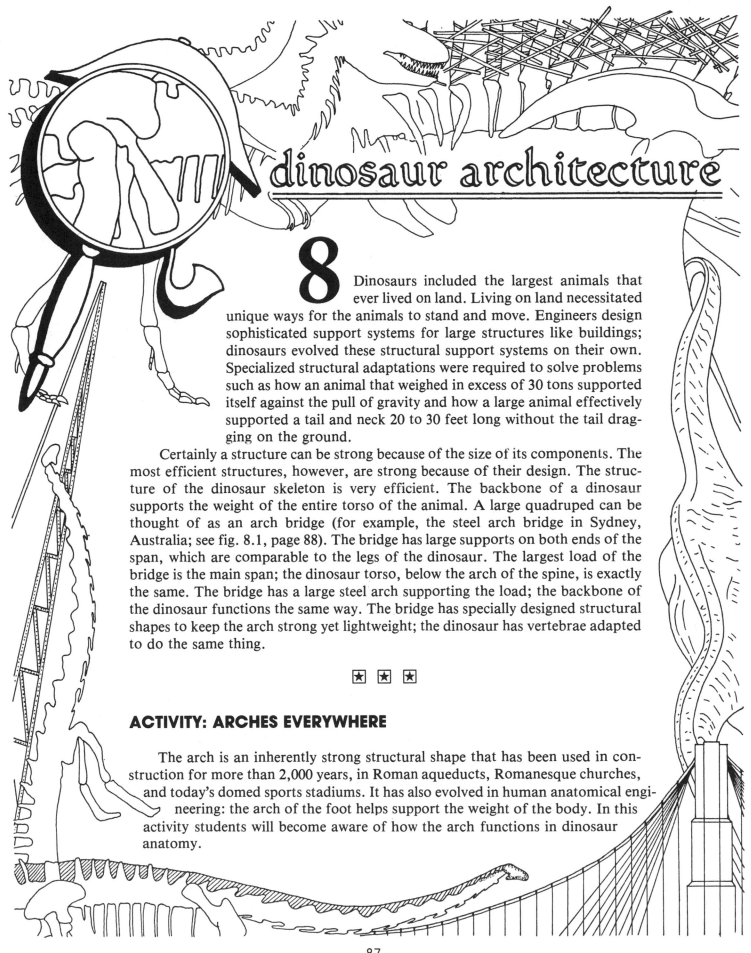

dinosaur architecture

8 Dinosaurs included the largest animals that ever lived on land. Living on land necessitated unique ways for the animals to stand and move. Engineers design sophisticated support systems for large structures like buildings; dinosaurs evolved these structural support systems on their own. Specialized structural adaptations were required to solve problems such as how an animal that weighed in excess of 30 tons supported itself against the pull of gravity and how a large animal effectively supported a tail and neck 20 to 30 feet long without the tail dragging on the ground.

Certainly a structure can be strong because of the size of its components. The most efficient structures, however, are strong because of their design. The structure of the dinosaur skeleton is very efficient. The backbone of a dinosaur supports the weight of the entire torso of the animal. A large quadruped can be thought of as an arch bridge (for example, the steel arch bridge in Sydney, Australia; see fig. 8.1, page 88). The bridge has large supports on both ends of the span, which are comparable to the legs of the dinosaur. The largest load of the bridge is the main span; the dinosaur torso, below the arch of the spine, is exactly the same. The bridge has a large steel arch supporting the load; the backbone of the dinosaur functions the same way. The bridge has specially designed structural shapes to keep the arch strong yet lightweight; the dinosaur has vertebrae adapted to do the same thing.

★ ★ ★

ACTIVITY: ARCHES EVERYWHERE

The arch is an inherently strong structural shape that has been used in construction for more than 2,000 years, in Roman aqueducts, Romanesque churches, and today's domed sports stadiums. It has also evolved in human anatomical engineering: the arch of the foot helps support the weight of the body. In this activity students will become aware of how the arch functions in dinosaur anatomy.

Fig. 8.1. The Sydney Harbor arch bridge compared to the skeleton of a *Diplodocus*. Scales are not the same. *Diplodocus* modified from Norman.

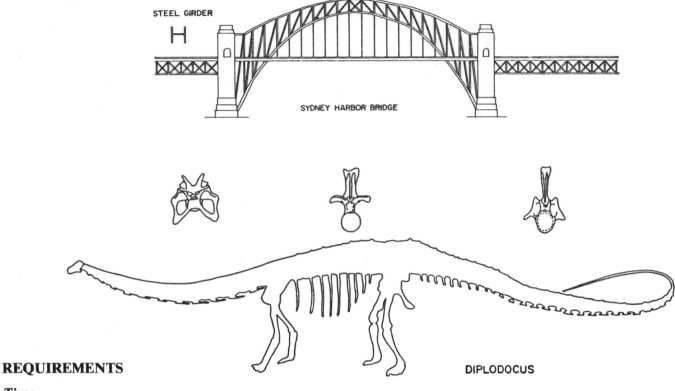

REQUIREMENTS

Time

Weekends or two to three evenings to complete homework

Materials

Student provided

Grouping

Individuals

DIRECTIONS

1. Introduce students to the arch as an important shape in dinosaur architecture and engineering.

2. Have students create a poster about the arch from library sources, using drawings rather than magazine cutouts. They should use a motif—the arch in architecture, the arch in animals, the arch in designs and symbols.

EXTENSION

Students can build arch models using sugar cubes or small blocks of wood either as a class project or homework. This will give students a better idea of how an arch works. Arches can be constructed on a horizontal surface then raised into a vertical position for testing.

Some modern animals have tails, which they use for all kinds of things: Monkeys use their tails to swing from branches, cattle to swat at insects, certain squirrels to shade their bodies from the sun, fishes and crocodiles to propel their bodies through the water, beaver to warn of danger, and birds as control surfaces during flight. All dinosaurs had tails. They were probably used for defense by some dinosaurs. Herbivores like *Stegosaurus* and *Ankylosaurus* could swing their tails like a medieval mace at an approaching enemy. The defensive end of a *Triceratops*, on the other hand, is the front; the tail serves no combative purpose. Other herbivores may have used their tails and their hind legs to support their bodies (see fig. 8.2) while "standing" to browse on trees, much like a kangaroo "sits" back on its tail and two hind legs. For many dinosaurs, especially the bipedal ones, the tail helped balance the body while the animal was feeding and moving (see fig. 8.3., p. 90).

Fig. 8.2. *Diplodocus*, showing the location of the ligament along the neck, body, and tail that provided the control for many of the animal's postures. Modified from Norman.

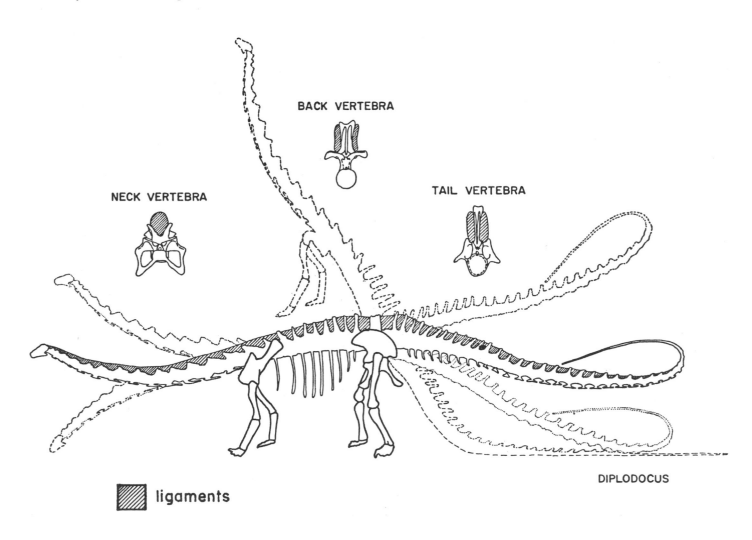

NECK VERTEBRA

BACK VERTEBRA

TAIL VERTEBRA

DIPLODOCUS

ligaments

Fig. 8.3. *Tyrannosaurus rex*, showing movement of neck and compensating movement of tail. Modified from Norman.

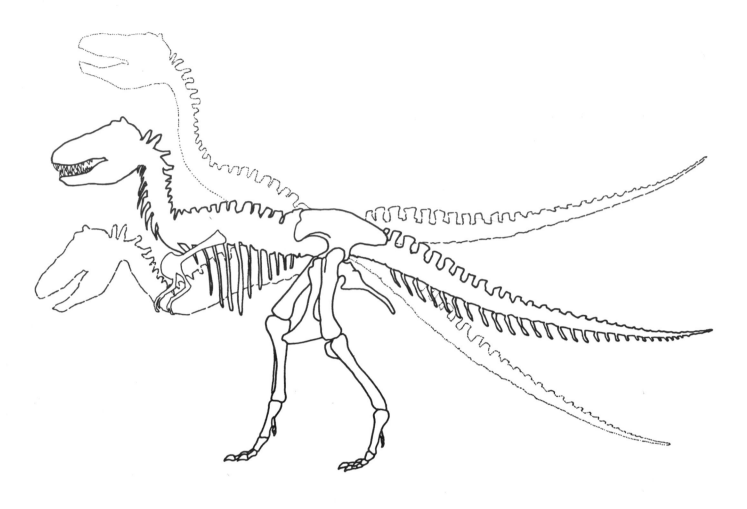

Although many dinosaur trackways have been found, none have tail impressions preserved from while the animal was walking, suggesting, at least, that no matter how long the tail might have been, the animal was able to support it above the ground. It takes a lot of energy and muscle control for a person merely to hold an arm out horizontally, away from the body. Imagine the energy consumed by *Diplodocus* to hold up a 30-foot neck and 30-foot tail at either end of its body, all the time! The shape of the neck, back, and tail vertebrae indicate there are places where large ligaments may have been located along the spine of the animal, from head to tail (see fig. 8.2). This ligament may have acted as a long rubber band, linking the motions of the front and rear ends of the animal so that when the head went down, the tail went up (see figs. 8.2, 8.3, and 8.4).

Fig. 8.4. *Diplodocus* drinking. Note that head and neck are down, the compensating tail, up. Modified from Paul.

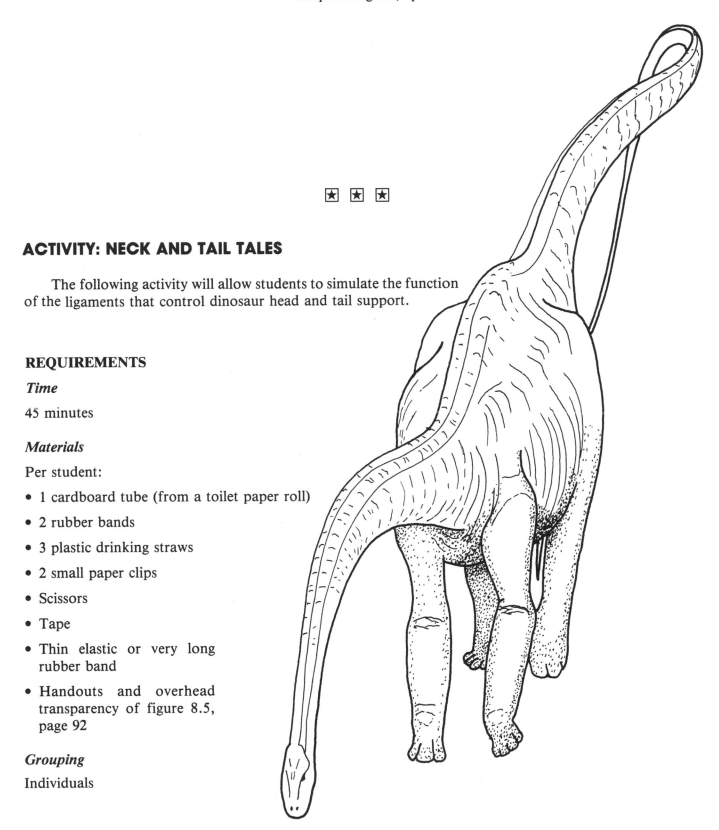

★ ★ ★

ACTIVITY: NECK AND TAIL TALES

The following activity will allow students to simulate the function of the ligaments that control dinosaur head and tail support.

REQUIREMENTS

Time

45 minutes

Materials

Per student:

- 1 cardboard tube (from a toilet paper roll)
- 2 rubber bands
- 3 plastic drinking straws
- 2 small paper clips
- Scissors
- Tape
- Thin elastic or very long rubber band
- Handouts and overhead transparency of figure 8.5, page 92

Grouping

Individuals

Fig. 8.5. Diagrams for assembling *Diplodocus* neck and tail support model.

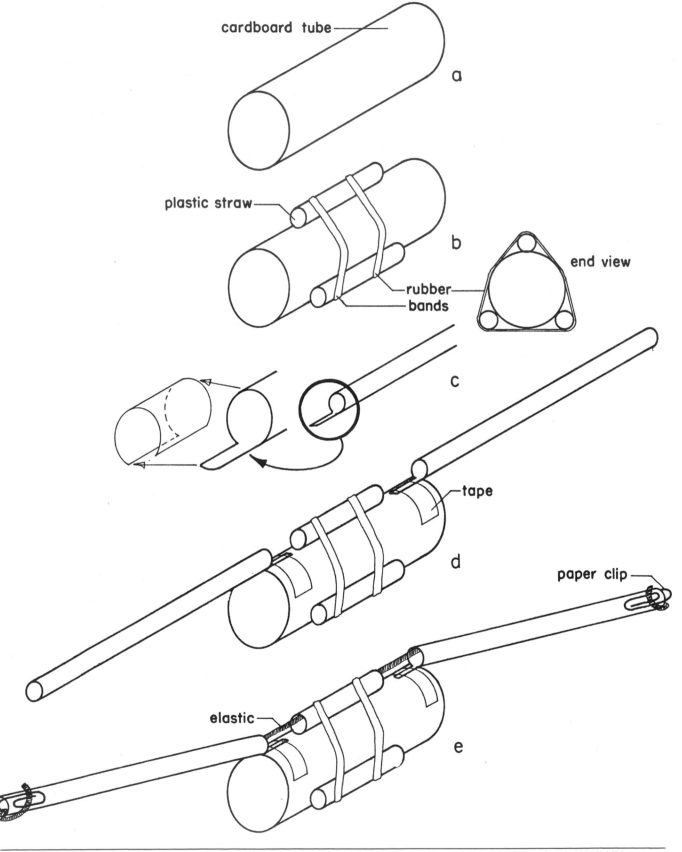

DIRECTIONS

1. Introduce the concept of long tails and necks of dinosaurs. Open a discussion of how an animal might be able to hold up such a long appendage. To help students understand how much work it takes to hold up an appendage of the body, ask them to stand, extend both arms forward, and hold them straight out for three minutes.

2. Tell them they will be building a model of a way *Diplodocus* might have been able to hold up its neck and tail with only a minimum of work by its muscles.

3. Provide each student with all required materials.

4. Distribute figure 8.5 and show the transparency.

5. The following instructions for figure 8.5 are straightforward (depending upon the class you might want to spend some time briefly reviewing the procedures):

    Step 1. Cut one straw in thirds, place the three pieces around the cardboard tube, and hold in place using the two rubber bands as shown in figure 8.5b.

    Step 2. Cut one end of each of the remaining straws as shown in figure 8.5c. Total cut length should be approximately 1/2".

    Step 3. Tape the two straws prepared in step 2 on the top of the tube so they are aligned with the short straw section already there, with the two cut sections resting on the tube. Tape the two straws in place as shown in figure 8.5d.

    Step 4. Attach a paper clip at the end of each projecting straw.

    Step 5. Run the elastic or long rubber band (cut so that it is one long piece) completely through all three straw sections on the top of the tube and securely hold it with the paper clips at each end as shown in figure 8.5e.

    Step 6. Adjust the tension of the elastic so that as one straw is pressed down, the other straw rises; this is a little tricky.

6. The *Diplodocus* model is now complete. The two straws represent the neck and tail and the elastic represents the ligament. Figure 8.2 shows how the ligaments might have worked on *Diplodocus*. Some scientists believe many of the large dinosaurs might have been able to support themselves on rear legs and tails to reach high into trees for food. In the case of *Diplodocus*, it might have been able to reach 40 or 50 feet above the ground, giving it a significant edge over other animals when food was scarce.

★ ★ ★

With the *Diplodocus* model, students may have noticed that it is most difficult to move the neck or tail when both are horizontal. The only way the ligament can raise the tail is if it pulls at an angle to the tail; the greater the angle, the easier it is to pull. A construction crane is designed so there is a large angle between the cable and the boom. This is accomplished by a brace that works exactly like the vertebrae of the *Diplodocus* to increase the angle of pull (see fig. 8.6, p. 94).

Fig. 8.6. Comparison of *Diplodocus* tail vertebrae and ligament with construction crane. *Diplodocus* modified from Norman.

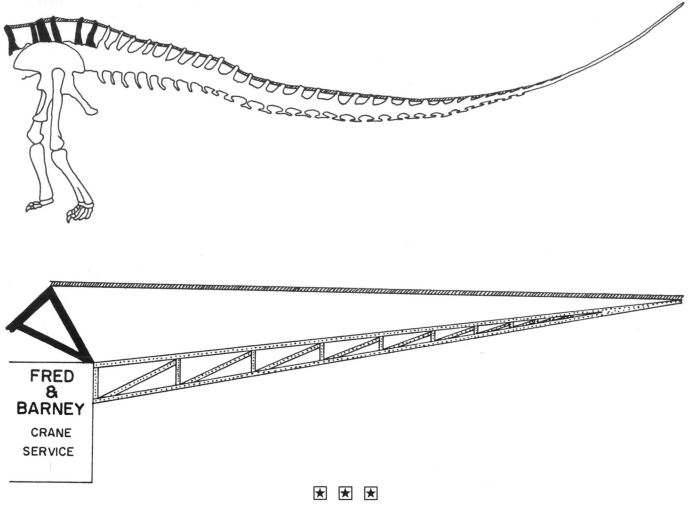

⊠ ⊠ ⊠

ACTIVITY: THE ANGLE MAKES IT EASY

It is possible to simulate the effect of the tail vertebrae on the ease of pulling up the tail by building and testing a small model of the system.

REQUIREMENTS

Time

90 minutes

Materials

Per team:

- Cardboard (8½" × 11" or larger)
- Scissors
- 15 paper clips

- Stapler

- Thumbtacks or pushpins

- Sewing thread (approximately 12")

- Nylon fishing line (approximately 15", 20#-30# test)

- Sharpened new pencil with eraser

- Hole punch

- Graph paper (2 sheets)

- Protractor

- Handouts and overhead transparency of figure 8.7, page 96

- Wood (1" × 4" × 12" dimension lumber, or similar)

Grouping

Pairs

DIRECTIONS

1. Using figure 8.6 discuss how the angle between the ligament and the tail makes it easier to control the tail. Show the analogy to the construction crane. Tell the students they will be building a model of the same system.

2. Provide all materials to students.

3. Distribute figure 8.7, page 96, and show the transparency.

4. The following are instructions for assembly of the apparatus shown in figure 8.7 (you may want to review these before you begin:

   Step 1. Cut the cardboard as shown in figure 8.7a, including the tabs at the bottom of part A.

   Step 2. Using the hole punch, make a vertical column of holes 1" apart starting at the top of A and running down the middle. The bottom point (X) should not be punched. Point X should be started with the thumbtack or pushpin and enlarged slightly with the pencil point.

   Step 3. Staple A to the middle of B as shown in figure 8.7b.

   Step 4. Pin the A/B assembly to the wooden base.

   Step 5. Make a brace using sewing thread, attaching it to a pin on the base and stapling it to the top of A; part A should now be vertical.

   Step 6. Push the remaining pin into the eraser of the pencil and push the sharpened end of the pencil through the bottom hole (X) in A so the pencil rests as shown in figure 8.7c.

   Step 7. Attach the fishing line to the pin at the eraser end of the pencil and run the other end of the line through the top hole in A as shown in figure 8.7c.

   Step 8. Bend a paper clip as shown in figure 8.7c to make a hook and attach it to the fishing line with an overhand knot.

Fig. 8.7. Diagrams for assembling the angle-of-pull activity.

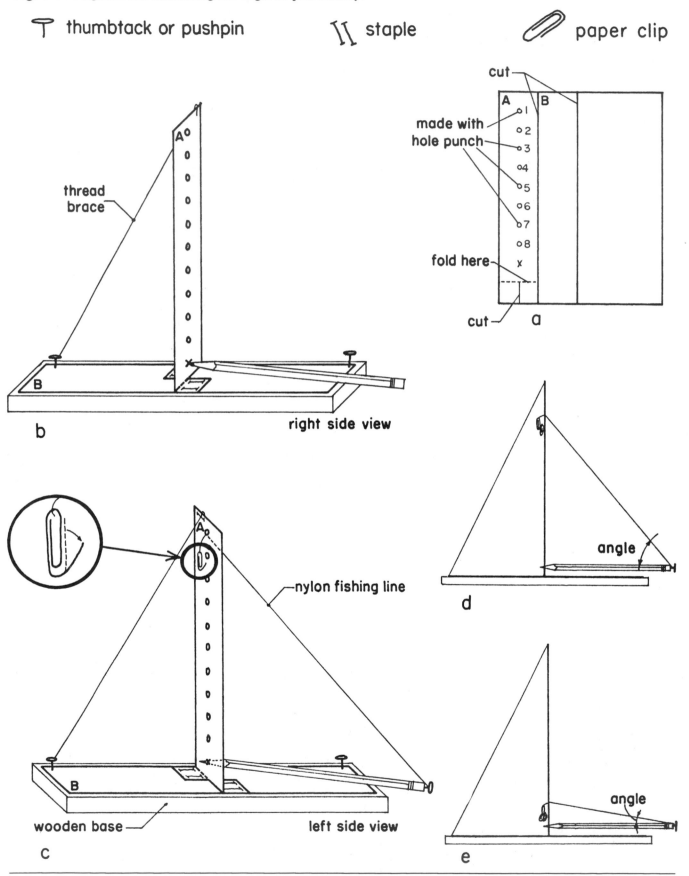

Step 9. The pencil will now be resting on the base. Add paper clips to the hook, one at a time, until the pencil is just held in a horizontal position by the weight of the paper clips as shown in figure 8.7d. It might be necessary to jiggle the pencil a little to be certain it is being supported.

Step 10. Take a piece of paper and make three columns. Label one "Hole Number"; the second, "Number of Clips"; and the third, "Angle." Record the hole number, the number of clips used to balance the pencil, and, after measuring it with a protractor, the angle the fishing line makes with the pencil (see fig. 8.7d and 8.7e).

Step 11. Repeat the procedure for the remaining holes, adding paper clips as necessary and completing the table as you go.

5. At the completion of the exercise, each student will prepare a graph from the completed table, plotting angle on the vertical axis and number of clips on the horizontal axis.

6. Ask each student to analyze the graph by writing a paragraph explaining how the degree of the angle makes it harder or easier for the dinosaur to move its tail.

EXTENSION

This activity can be made more real by using a model made of wood, replacing the pencil with a 1" × 2" strip, using a hinge where A attaches to the base, adding weights to the end of the 1" × 2", and using a spring balance to measure the force needed to pull up a known weight.

★ ★ ★

For many dinosaurs, such as *Diplodocus* or *Stegosaurus*, tail flexibility was critical. Both probably used their tails as weapons, and it was important that the tails were capable of rapid swings from side to side. For other bipedal dinosaurs, such as *Iguanodon*, *Pachycephalosaurus*, and *Parasaurolophus*, who used their tails as a counterbalance, tail stability was more important than flexibility. Along the spine from in front of the hips to back along the tail, thin bones or tendons were arranged diagonally along the sides of the vertebrae. These diagonal "stays" helped reinforce the spine for added strength, but at the same time reduced lateral, or sideways, flexibility of the tail. This structural system did not disappear with the dinosaurs. In 1883 the Brooklyn Bridge opened to traffic, spanning the East River between Brooklyn and New York. John Roebling, the engineer in charge, recognized early in the design process that a suspension bridge was inherently flexible. To reduce that flexibility, he added a series of diagonal cables (stays) radiating from the towers and interlocking with the suspenders. See figure 8.8, page 98, which shows the structural similarity between the bony tendons along the spine of a hadrosaur and the diagonal cables of the Brooklyn Bridge. The bridge still stands. By contrast, the Tacoma-Narrows Bridge in Washington State, built in 1950, literally shook itself to pieces because of wind-induced forces that caused the bridge to twist violently, earning it the nickname "Galloping Gertie." It had no stays. It had great flexibility, but as Roebling recognized, flexibility is not an asset for a suspension bridge.

Flexibility without stability is meaningless (rubber bands twist, but if they snap when they are stretched, they are worthless). For the human body, flexibility is important for all athletics; however, if our body structure is unstable and allows us to fall over, flexibility is unnecessary because, unable to stand, we will not have the opportunity to use it. Dinosaurs had similar problems. Defense, aggression, and movement certainly required flexibility; however, without the stability (balance) provided by its tail, the fearsome bipedal *Tyrannosaurus* would have fallen flat on its face.

Fig. 8.8. Comparison of stiffening structures of a hadrosaur spine and diagonal stays of the Brooklyn Bridge. Hadrosaur modified from Norman.

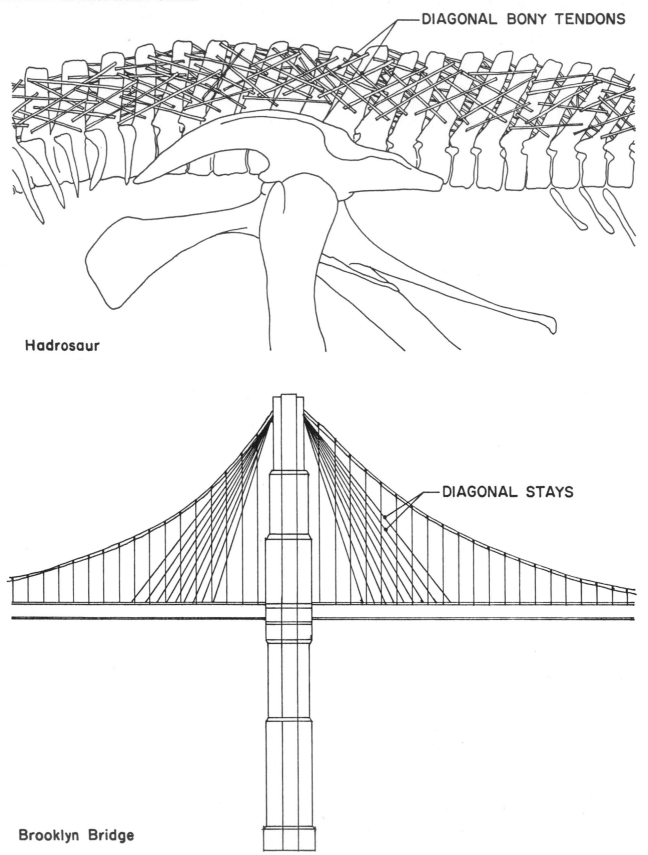

DIAGONAL BONY TENDONS

Hadrosaur

DIAGONAL STAYS

Brooklyn Bridge

Bipedal dinosaurs were able to keep both feet on the ground and used their tails to help provide balance when they leaned over. Demonstrate the importance of the tail in dinosaur balance by projecting an overhead transparency of figure 8.9a, which shows a *Ceratosaurus* without its tail. It not only looks weird, it also looks as though any second its head will come crashing to the ground. Most of its body weight is positioned far ahead of the support at its hips. Ask students how the situation could be changed: What would make the animal balance? One of their answers should be a tail. Place a transparency of figure 8.9b, the *Ceratosaurus* tail, on top of the transparency of figure 8.9a so that the dinosaur's tail attaches to its body in the appropriate place. The animal should now look balanced. The tail likely served as a counterweight, or force to balance the weight of the front end and the massive head. As a bipedal dinosaur moved its head up or down, the tail moved in the opposite direction as a counterweight or balance (see fig. 8.1).

Fig. 8.9. *Ceratosaurus* torso and tail, designed to be used as two overhead transparencies.

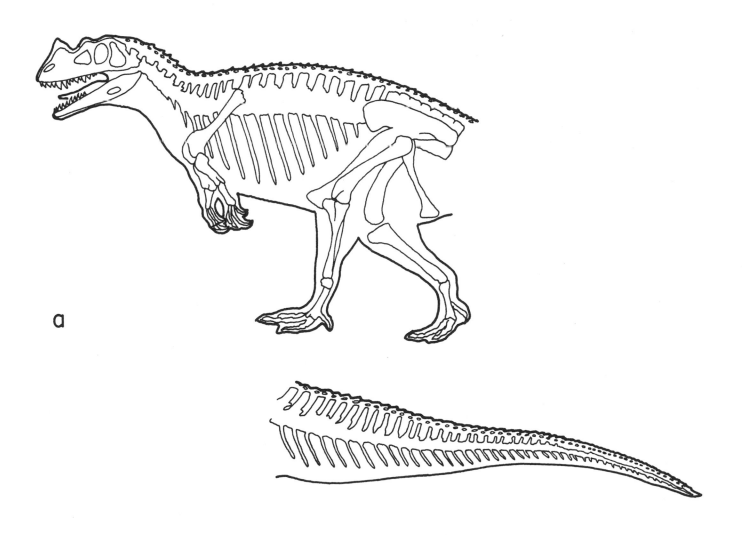

a

b

✵ ✵ ✵

ACTIVITY: COUNTERBALANCE

Students can easily demonstrate the concept of a counterweight to each other.

REQUIREMENTS

Time

5 minutes

Materials

Pencil

Grouping

Pairs

DIRECTIONS

1. Have one student place a pencil on the floor.

2. Have the second student stand on one leg, and without bending the knee (just bending over from the waist), reach the pencil on the floor. The observing student should notice that the student bending over extends the second leg backward as a counterweight. Dinosaurs do the same thing but use their tails instead.

3. Reverse student roles and repeat the activity.

✵ ✵ ✵

A simple examination of a teeter-totter, or see-saw, provides an example of how the balancing system works. Two people of the same weight sitting at equal distances from the center pivot, or fulcrum, results in a balanced system and a horizontal plank (see fig. 8.10a). If a heavy person and a light person are equidistant from the fulcrum, the heavy end will always go down (see fig. 8.10b). What happens, however, if that heavy person moves closer to the fulcrum? Now the end of the board with the light person on it will go down, and the end with the heavy person will go up (see fig. 8.10c). The weight on either side of the board did not change, so what made the board tilt the other way?

Balancing of the board is caused by two things: the weight on either side of the fulcrum and the distance of that weight from the fulcrum. The tilt of the board is determined not by the weight (known as the *force*) on either side alone, but by the product of the force times the distance from the fulcrum. This is called the *moment*. A small force a large distance from the fulcrum is equivalent to a large force close to the fulcrum. We use moments to our advantage every day. A door opens easily when the doorknob or handle is pulled, because the handle is located the maximum distance from the hinge, or fulcrum. The force (how hard we pull) is multiplied by the distance from the fulcrum (hinge) to create a large moment. To enhance the aesthetics of door design, occasionally the doorknob is moved to the center of the door, closer to the hinge. If you have ever opened such a door, you can feel the effect of a smaller moment. Because the doorknob is closer to the hinge, the distance to the fulcrum is smaller; because the distance is smaller, the force (or pull) must be greater. The door may look prettier, but it takes more effort to open it. Use of levers and crowbars is also an example of a moment. The longer the crowbar or lever, the less force is necessary to accomplish the task.

Fig. 8.10. Teeter-totter, or see-saw, introduction to moments. The relative weights are indicated by "W," distances from the fulcrum are shown by "d."

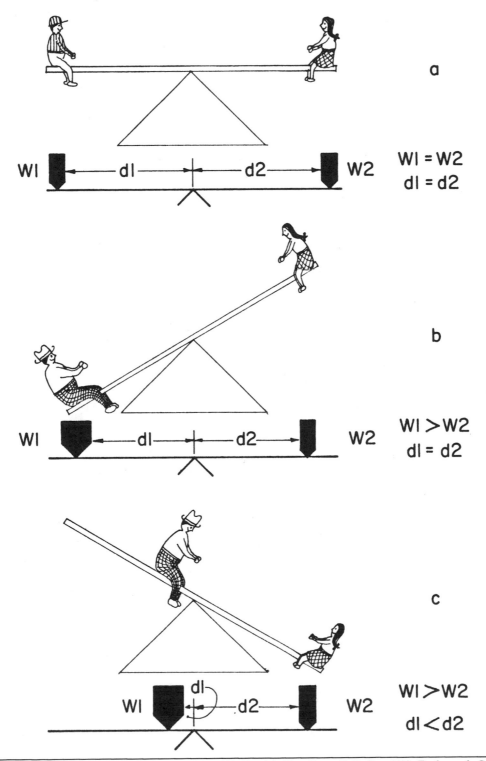

⭐ ⭐ ⭐

ACTIVITY: MOMENT TO MOMENT

Moments are easy to study by building a model of a see-saw or balance and having students manipulate some small weights and perform simple arithmetic.

REQUIREMENTS

Time

45-90 minutes

Materials

Per team:

- Cardboard (8½" × 11", or larger)
- 10 paper clips
- Hole punch
- Stapler
- Paper or plastic cup with flat bottom
- Sewing thread (12")
- Handouts and overhead transparency of figure 8.11.

DIRECTIONS

1. Distribute figure 8.11 to students and show the transparency.

2. Following are instructions for building the apparatus shown in figure 8.11:

    Step 1. Cut strips A and B from cardboard as shown in figure 8.11a.

    Step 2. Punch holes as shown in A, 1" apart along a straight line as shown in figure 8.11b. Number the holes outward from the center as shown.

    Step 3. The "X" is exactly in the middle of A. At the X make a small hole with a sharp pencil point; attach the thread as shown in figure 8.11c.

    Step 4. Fold and staple support B as shown in figure 8.11c. Put a hole in the top of B to attach the other end of the thread so that A hangs horizontally from B (see fig. 8.11c).

    Step 5. Bend two paper clips as shown in figure 8.11d to make hangers.

    Step 6. Place the completed balance on the inverted cup as shown in figure 8.11e.

    Step 7. Hangers can be placed in any hole and additional paper clips placed on the hangers to add weights.

Fig. 8.11. Diagrams for assembling and table for completing the moments activity.

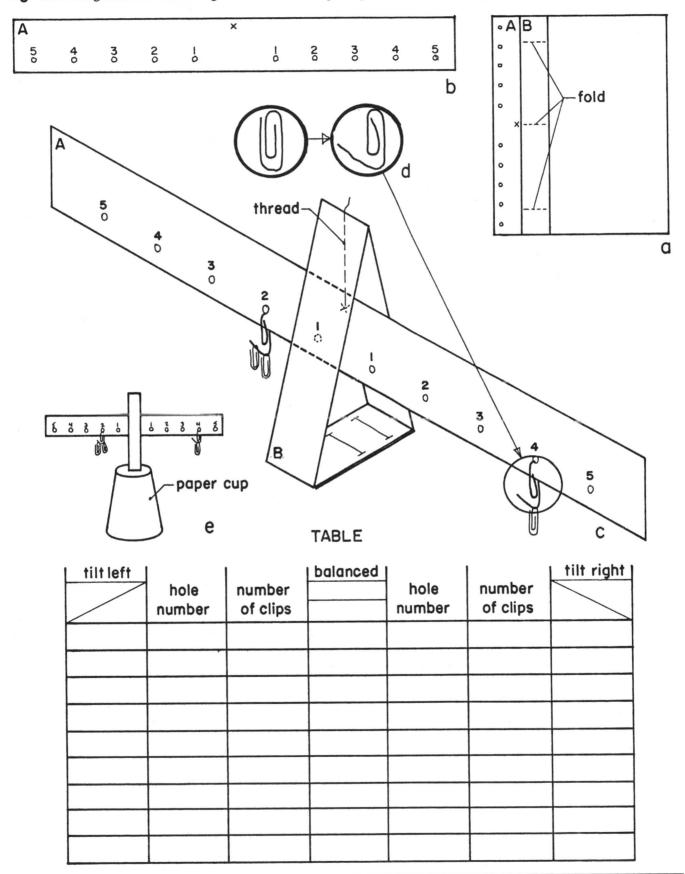

tilt left	hole number	number of clips	balanced	hole number	number of clips	tilt right

3. By playing with the combinations of distance from the fulcrum (X) and number of clips suspended from pairs of holes, one on either side of the fulcrum, students should be able to obtain left tilt, right tilt, and balance. As they proceed, have them complete the table shown in figure 8.11.

4. Ask students to draw their own conclusions about the conditions under which balance is achieved by looking at the data in their completed tables.

EXTENSIONS

1. If a see-saw is available, actual measurements and student weights can be determined and moments can be calculated.

2. Ask students to find other situations in which a force acts at a distance from a fulcrum. Examples include doors (force acts on the doorknob a certain distance from the hinge) and raising something with a lever. The longer the lever, the easier it is to raise something; using a longer lever, the smallest student in the class can lift a heavy object (such as another student) easier than the largest student can.

OTHER ACTIVITIES

R. McNeill Alexander (1989, 16-26) describes a simple method by which the center of gravity of an animal can be determined. The reason this determination is useful is that it is then a relatively simple matter to answer questions such as how much of the weight of an animal was supported on its front or rear legs, whether the animal's legs were strong enough to support its body weight on land or did it necessarily live in water, and whether the bone structure was strong enough to allow the animal to be agile or "athletic."

★ ★ ★

REFERENCES

Alexander, R. McNeill. 1989. *Dynamics of Dinosaurs and Other Extinct Giants*. New York: Columbia University Press.

SUGGESTED READING

Alexander, R. McNeill. "How Dinosaurs Ran." *Scientific American* 264, no. 4 (1991): 130-136.

Bakker, Robert T. *The Dinosaur Heresies*. New York: Zebra Books, 1986.

Norman, David. *The Illustrated Encyclopedia of Dinosaurs*. New York: Crown, 1985.

Paul, Gregory S. *Predatory Dinosaurs of the World*. New York: Simon & Schuster, 1988.

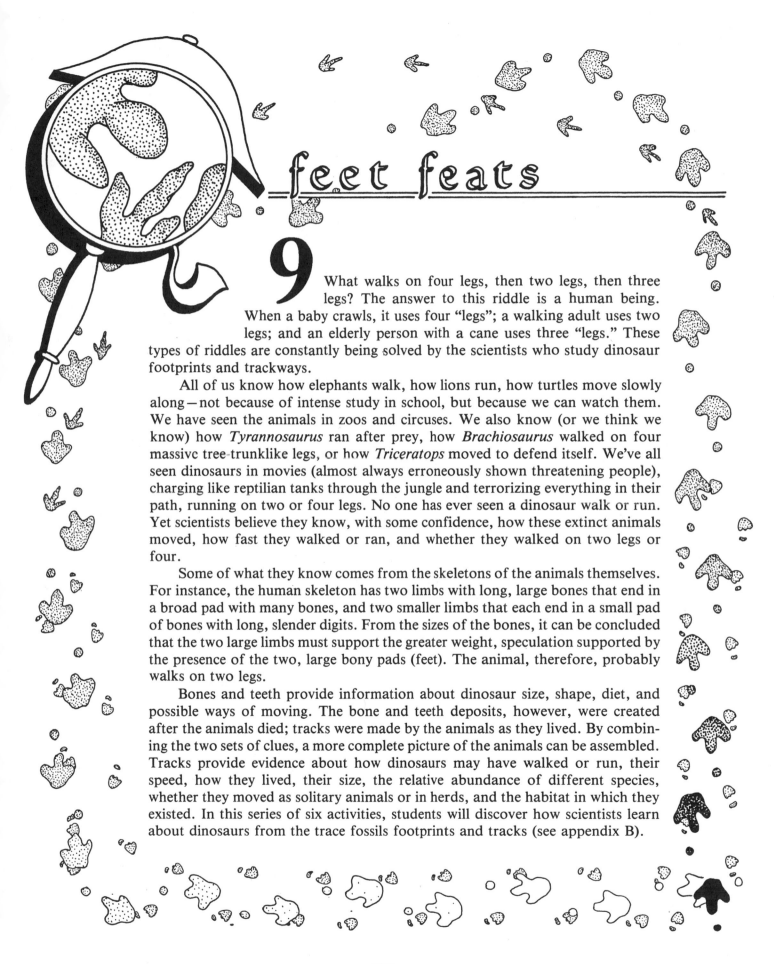

feet feats

9

What walks on four legs, then two legs, then three legs? The answer to this riddle is a human being. When a baby crawls, it uses four "legs"; a walking adult uses two legs; and an elderly person with a cane uses three "legs." These types of riddles are constantly being solved by the scientists who study dinosaur footprints and trackways.

All of us know how elephants walk, how lions run, how turtles move slowly along—not because of intense study in school, but because we can watch them. We have seen the animals in zoos and circuses. We also know (or we think we know) how *Tyrannosaurus* ran after prey, how *Brachiosaurus* walked on four massive tree-trunklike legs, or how *Triceratops* moved to defend itself. We've all seen dinosaurs in movies (almost always erroneously shown threatening people), charging like reptilian tanks through the jungle and terrorizing everything in their path, running on two or four legs. No one has ever seen a dinosaur walk or run. Yet scientists believe they know, with some confidence, how these extinct animals moved, how fast they walked or ran, and whether they walked on two legs or four.

Some of what they know comes from the skeletons of the animals themselves. For instance, the human skeleton has two limbs with long, large bones that end in a broad pad with many bones, and two smaller limbs that each end in a small pad of bones with long, slender digits. From the sizes of the bones, it can be concluded that the two large limbs must support the greater weight, speculation supported by the presence of the two, large bony pads (feet). The animal, therefore, probably walks on two legs.

Bones and teeth provide information about dinosaur size, shape, diet, and possible ways of moving. The bone and teeth deposits, however, were created after the animals died; tracks were made by the animals as they lived. By combining the two sets of clues, a more complete picture of the animals can be assembled. Tracks provide evidence about how dinosaurs may have walked or run, their speed, how they lived, their size, the relative abundance of different species, whether they moved as solitary animals or in herds, and the habitat in which they existed. In this series of six activities, students will discover how scientists learn about dinosaurs from the trace fossils footprints and tracks (see appendix B).

Fig. 9.1. Series of trackways made by various human movements.

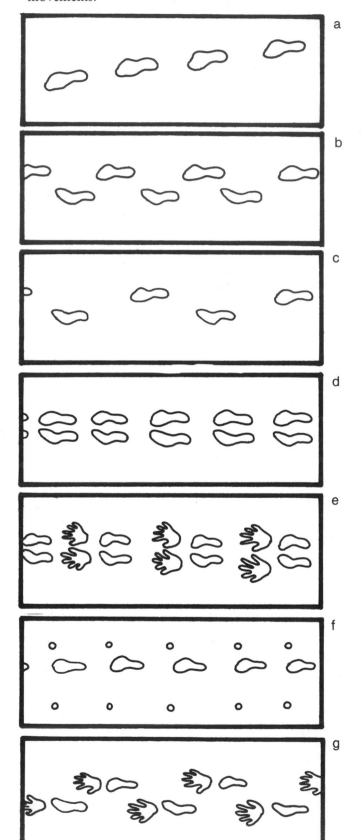

ACTIVITY: HOW DID THEY DO THAT?

This activity will introduce students to the various ways tracks can be made and how those tracks can be interpreted.

REQUIREMENTS

Time

Approximately 45 minutes

Materials

Teacher materials:

- Overhead projector

- Overhead transparency prepared from figure 9.1

- 1 pair of crutches (often can be borrowed; students may have some)

Class materials (for each student):

- 2 colored pencils

- 4 sheets of paper, each 5½" × 8½" (8½" × 11" cut in half)

Grouping

Entire class; some steps in pairs

DIRECTIONS

1. Arrange the class desks in a horseshoe that allows students to face the overhead projector and surrounds a large open space in the center of the room.

2. Have students pair off. Ask students to look at the soles of their partner's shoes. Discuss how the left and right shoes are different. How are the left and right feet different? Will they make the same footprints? How could you tell the difference?

3. Distribute materials to students.

4. Explain that you will be naming six activities that animals perform and students will need to draw what the tracks will look like.

---

5. Before you begin this list, explain that you will use hopping on one foot as an example. Note that humans are the only animals who can do this. Select a student to demonstrate hopping on one foot in a straight line. Ask students to watch carefully, then draw the footprints the student would leave if he or she were hopping on snow.

6. Show students the overhead transparency of figure 9.1a. Have them compare their drawings to the transparency. Discuss any differences to be certain they understand the concept.

7. Instruct students to use one color for the left hands or feet and a different color for the right.

8. Name each of the six activities below and select one student to demonstrate each. After the demonstration allow sufficient time for students to complete their drawings before continuing to the next step.

   1. Walking (shown in fig. 9.1b)

   2. Running (shown in fig. 9.1c)

   3. Jumping, using two feet together like a bird or kangaroo (shown in fig. 9.1d)

   4. Jumping, crouching on the floor with two feet and two hands together like a frog (shown in fig. 9.1e)

   5. Walking on one foot with two crutches (shown in fig. 9.1f)

   6. Crawling (shown in fig. 9.1g)

9. At the completion of all activities, show the series of overhead transparencies (figs. 9.1b to 9.1g) and have students compare their drawings to these transparencies. Demonstrate the footprints again if the student drawings are in error.

EXTENSION

This activity may be done outdoors on snow or sand. Doing it on mud will work as well but is not recommended for obvious reasons.

★ ★ ★

ACTIVITY: TRACKWAY INTERPRETATION

In small groups students will create and interpret trackways. Students will learn that the activity of an animal can be interpreted from its footprints and tracks. This activity will require two to three 45-minute periods. During the first and second periods, students will gather data to be graphed and interpreted during the second and third periods.

REQUIREMENTS

Time

Three 45-minute periods

Materials

• 1 large (3' × 6') piece of butcher paper (brown paper that comes on large rolls) per group

• 2 wide black markers per group

- 3 soft pencils per group

- 4 colored pencils per group

- Overhead transparency of figure 9.2

- A large open area in which to lay out the paper and create the trackways

Grouping

Groups of four

Period 1

Divide the class into groups of four students (using smaller groups is possible, but four seems to work best; larger groups become too confusing). Give each group one piece of the butcher paper. Each student in the group will be creating a trackway (show the transparency of fig. 9.2a) by moving across the sheet of paper while others in the group trace (using the pencil) the outline of the footprint or any part of the student's body that contacts the paper (knee, elbow, hand, and so forth). *Make certain students do not use the markers in this stage because they will discolor feet and damage stockings*. Ideally, all groups of students will be able to create their footprints at the same time. If available, the gymnasium, cafeteria, or hallway might provide more room than the classroom. Distribute the pencils and markers to each group. Have students remove their shoes so the paper will not be torn as they walk upon it. Each member of the group will take a turn, so that ultimately there are four different trackways on each sheet of paper. Urge students to be as imaginative as possible: walk, hop, crawl, stretch their legs as far apart as possible, walk in circles, hold their feet in funny positions. The only rule is that each trackway must include some foot impressions. After all trackways have been marked in pencil, have students trace over them using the wide black markers. A demonstration for the students is very helpful. Ideally, students should be allowed to complete making their trackways in the first period. If necessary, however, the activity can be extended into period 2.

Period 2

Complete trackways as needed.

When the trackway is completed, each group should select the name of a dinosaur and write that name on the back of the sheet (show transparency of fig. 9.2b). That name should be kept secret so the group identity remains unknown to other groups. All sheets will then be given to the teacher for redistribution, so that each group gets another group's trackway.

Each group will then need to take the new sheet and interpret that trackway. Using the four colored pencils provided (one for each of the tracks on the sheet of paper), the group should color each track with a different pencil (show the transparency of figure 9.2c). Once distinguished by color, each track should be interpreted: How was it made—by walking, hopping? Once this phase is completed, the teacher should divulge which group made which trackway and who the group members are. Students in each group should record the appropriate names and then attempt to determine which person made which track, using foot size, for example, as a criterion.

Period 3

This last period will involve group presentations of their interpretations as well as conclusions that could be drawn from the exercise. Each sheet should be put on the wall, or on the floor with the class gathered around it. In turn, each of the groups will explain to the class their interpretation of the trackways they deciphered, including which student made which tracks. The group that made the trackway should respond, explaining how accurate the interpretation is. Keep score on the board for which group made the most correct interpretations.

☒ ☒ ☒

Fig. 9.2. Progressive illustrations of classroom trackways.

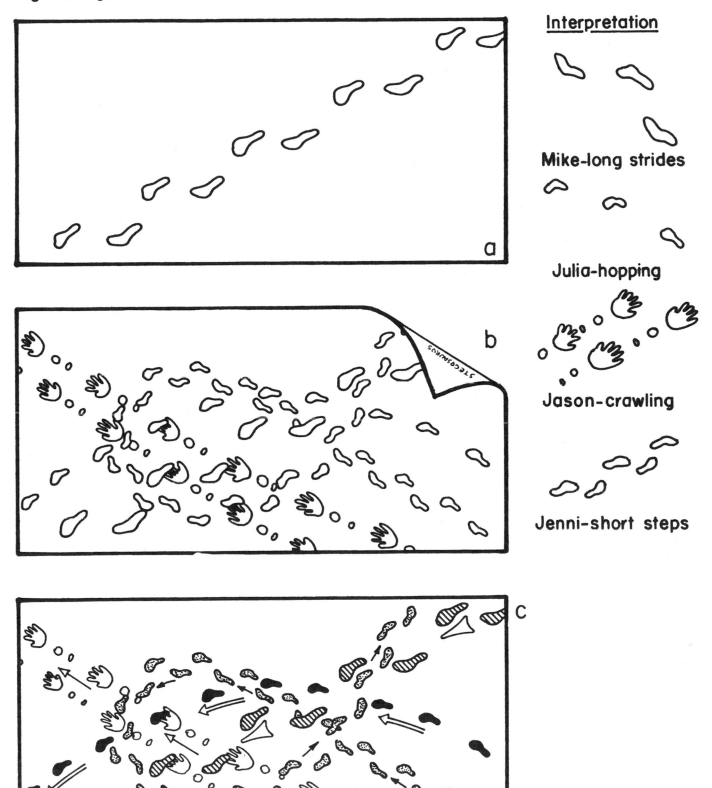

Interpretation

Mike-long strides

Julia-hopping

Jason-crawling

Jenni-short steps

A dinosaur restoration standing mute in a museum is impressive. A seven-ton, 40-foot-long eating machine like the *Tyrannosaurus rex* moving faster than a human can run is awesome (in the truest sense of the word). The bones provide clues to the size of the animal; the footprints and tracks supply the evidence for how quickly it moved. Because no one has ever seen a dinosaur making tracks, scientists use today's animals as an analog, or model. In the absence of dinosaurs, emus (a large ostrichlike bird from Australia) and many large herding animals (for example, elephants) have been studied as they move. Although they are not considered dinosaur descendants, large bipedal mammals are used because they are more commonly available than emus. Relationships among the footprint length, stride, speed, and height of students will be related to similar measurements for dinosaurs.

☒ ★ ☒

ACTIVITY: HOW FAST DID THEY DO THAT?

The class will measure their own strides and footprints and determine their speed. Data will be graphed for comparisons.

REQUIREMENTS

Time

Three 45-minute periods

Materials

- Optional: measuring tape and calculators for each group
- 2 metersticks
- Pad or notebook and pencil
- Stopwatch (or watch that will indicate seconds)
- Masking tape
- Piece of chalk or two small markers
- Handouts of table 9.1 for each student
- Handouts of figure 9.3 for each student

Grouping

Groups of four

Part 1

One student will run and walk the length of a measured course while other students in the group will time, measure, and record his progress. Note that this exercise is written in the metric system, first, because the numbers from the metric system are much easier to manipulate and, second, because the metric system is the "language of science" and students need to become familiar with it.

A large area will be needed for this activity (gymnasium, cafeteria, hallway, or outside). Divide the class into groups of four. In each group, one student will complete the course, and the other three will be the timer, the measurer, and the recorder. Each group member will have the opportunity to perform each activity. Each group will need a measured "track" or "course" 20 meters long. Indoors, both ends can be marked with masking tape, outdoors by a stake, book, or jacket. Designate one end "Start" and the other end "Finish." Group members will do the following:

The recorder should have a copy of table 9.1 and complete it with information as it becomes available for each member of the group. The recorder will also assist the measurer to determine stride length.

The timer will stand at the finish line with the stopwatch, say "Go!" when the student is at the starting line, and time how long it takes for the student to first walk, then run the length of the course.

The measurer (with the help of the recorder) will determine the stride length for the walking and running trials by counting strides and dividing the length of the course by number of strides.

All students in the group should rotate through all positions until all data for table 9.1 are recorded.

To complete table 9.1 it will be necessary to determine the students' speed. Divide the length of the course (20 meters) by the time (in seconds). This will give a speed in meters per second to be entered in the appropriate column. Other data for table 9.1 are straightforward.

Certain anatomical relationships have been determined for dinosaurs. For students to better understand the relationships as applied to dinosaurs, they can first determine those relationships for themselves. Figure 9.3, page 112, provides a place for recording and graphing the hip height, foot length, and total height.

Hip height is measured from the ground to where the top of the femur (thighbone) joins the pelvis (to find this spot, have students lift a leg so the femur is parallel to the ground; it is now easy to see where the top of the femur joins the pelvis). Foot length and total height are self-explanatory.

Table 9.1
Student Data

NAME_____ PERIOD_____ DATE_____

STUDENT	WALKING				RUNNING				footprint length (m)	leg length (m)	student height (m)
	stride length (m)	time (sec)	distance (m)	speed (m/sec)	stride length (m)	time (sec)	distance (m)	speed (m/sec)			

Fig. 9.3. Table and graph to be prepared comparing hip height and total height to foot length.

student name	A foot length (cm)	B hip height (cm)	C total height (cm)	ratio B/A	ratio C/A
_____	_____	_____	_____	_____	_____
_____	_____	_____	_____	_____	_____
_____	_____	_____	_____	_____	_____
_____	_____	_____	_____	_____	_____

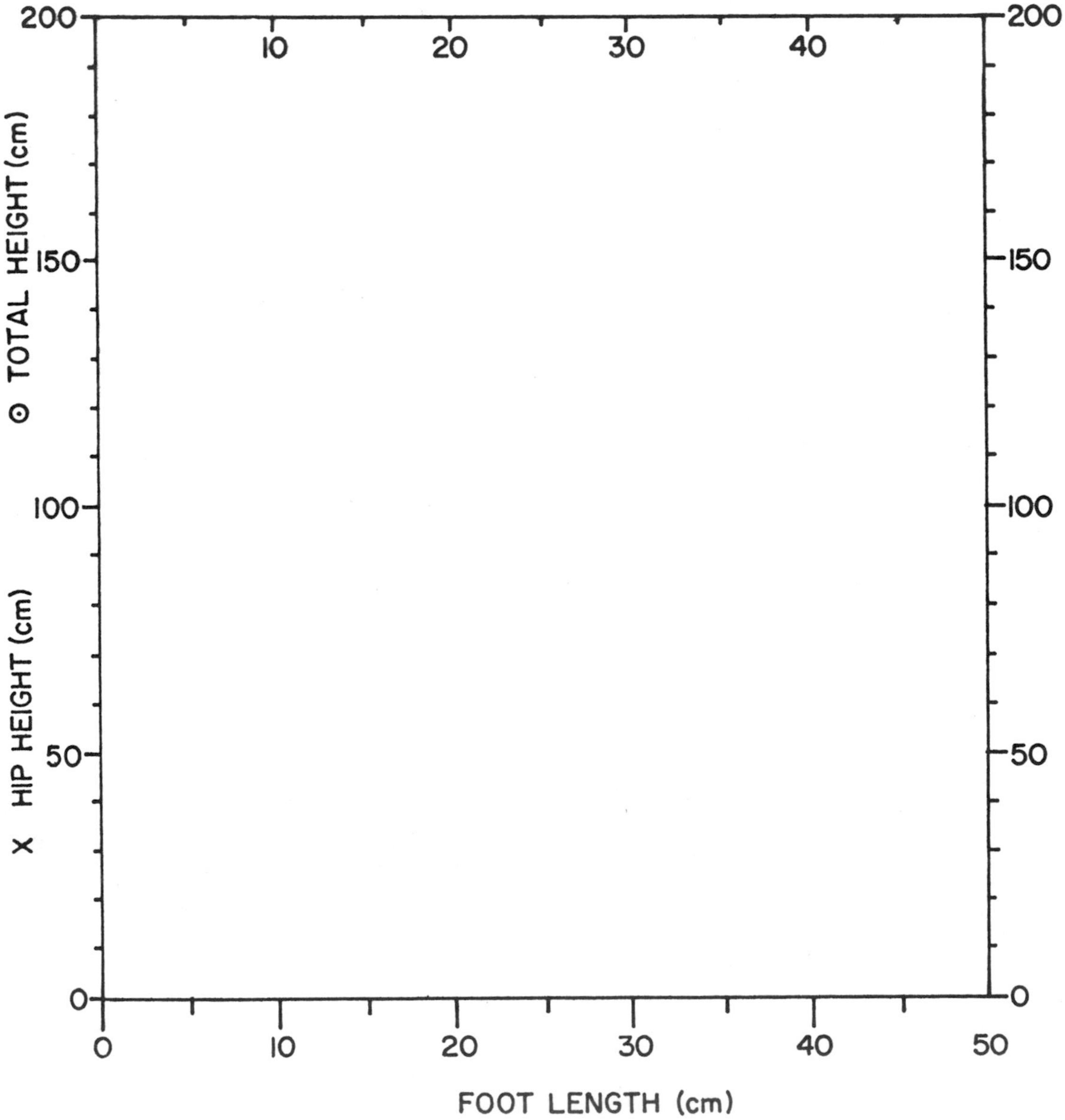

FOOT LENGTH (cm)

Part 2

Graphs of various measured quantities provide good opportunities for data manipulation and interpretation. Examples of graphs the teacher can make based on information recorded in table 9.1 are stride length versus speed (separately or together), stride length versus height, and height versus speed. Once graphs have been plotted, students can be asked to interpret them. Do taller people always have longer strides? Do the fastest runners always have the longest strides? Are the tallest people the fastest? These graphs can be prepared for the entire class on very large sheets of graph paper (available from drafting or engineering supply dealers). Data for individual students can be determined by symbols or initials.

EXTENSIONS

1. Students can research trackways made by different types of native wildlife. The U.S. Fish and Wildlife Service, Project Wild, or state agencies are excellent resources.

2. Through library study, students can determine the same data for various animals that they determined for themselves. Do the same relationships hold for stride, height, and speed? More ambitious extensions can involve student pets. Rabbits, cats, dogs, turtles, and horses make good subjects for obtaining the necessary data.

★ ★ ★

ACTIVITY: DID THEY WALK, TROT, OR RUN?

Animals move at different rates of speed. It is possible to watch a horse first walk, then trot, and finally run as its rate of speed increases. It is not possible to watch a dinosaur. Yet it is possible to know how the dinosaur moved by examining its tracks.

As the speed of an animal (two- or four-legged) increases, its stride length also increases, so that for an animal of a certain size, the longer the stride length, the faster the animal is moving. The size of the animal is very important: An adult giraffe walking slowly will have a much longer stride length than a mouse running at top speed. Therefore, to determine whether an animal is walking, trotting, or running, both the stride length and the size of the animal must be known.

During walking, each foot (for both bipedal and quadrupedal animals) is in contact with the ground more than half the time. For people and other bipedal animals this means that sometimes one foot, and sometimes both feet, are in contact with the ground. During running, however, each foot comes in contact with the ground less than half the time, and there are times when no feet are touching the ground and the animal's body is completely in the air. Trotting, which is faster than walking and slower than running, is less well defined.

Using the following information, students will reconstruct dinosaur trackways in the classroom. Figures 9.4 and 9.5, pages 114 and 115, are tracings of dinosaur footprints from Upper Cretaceous rocks just west of Denver, Colorado. Sizes of the footprints are reduced here, but actual measurements are given so the two figures may be enlarged to life size. Figure 9.6, page 116, is a scale drawing of the track of the quadruped that made the footprint shown in figure 9.4. Figure 9.7, page 116, is a similar drawing of the track of the bipedal dinosaur that made the footprint in figure 9.5. Using the information contained in these four figures, it is possible to duplicate for student use in the classroom the life-size tracks made by these two animals. Students will determine how fast the animals were traveling.

(Text continues on page 117.)

Fig. 9.4. Tracing of quadrupedal footprint of a Cretaceous dinosaur.

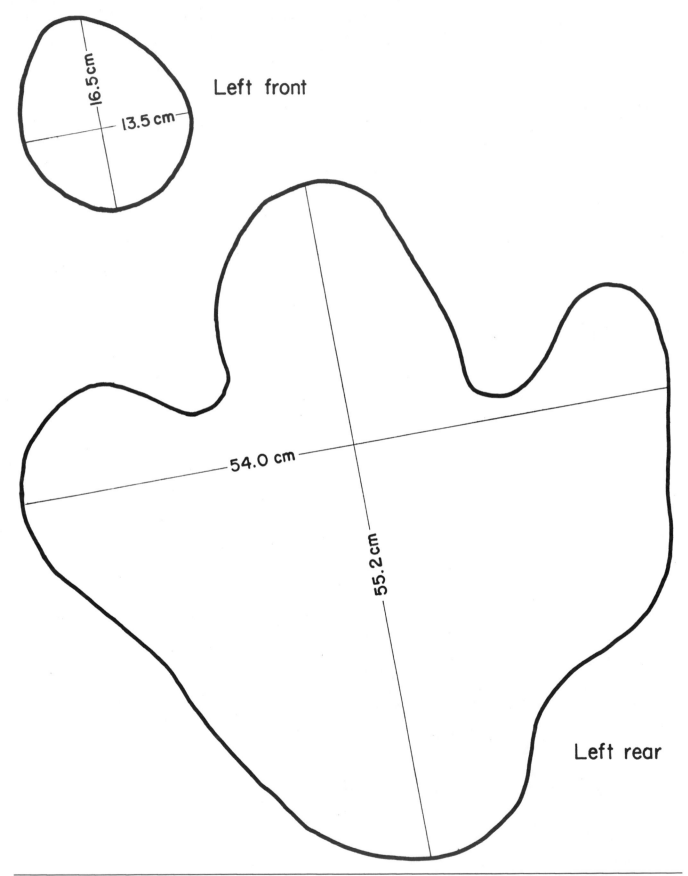

Left front

16.5 cm

13.5 cm

54.0 cm

55.2 cm

Left rear

Fig. 9.5. Tracing of bipedal dinosaur footprint of a Cretaceous dinosaur.

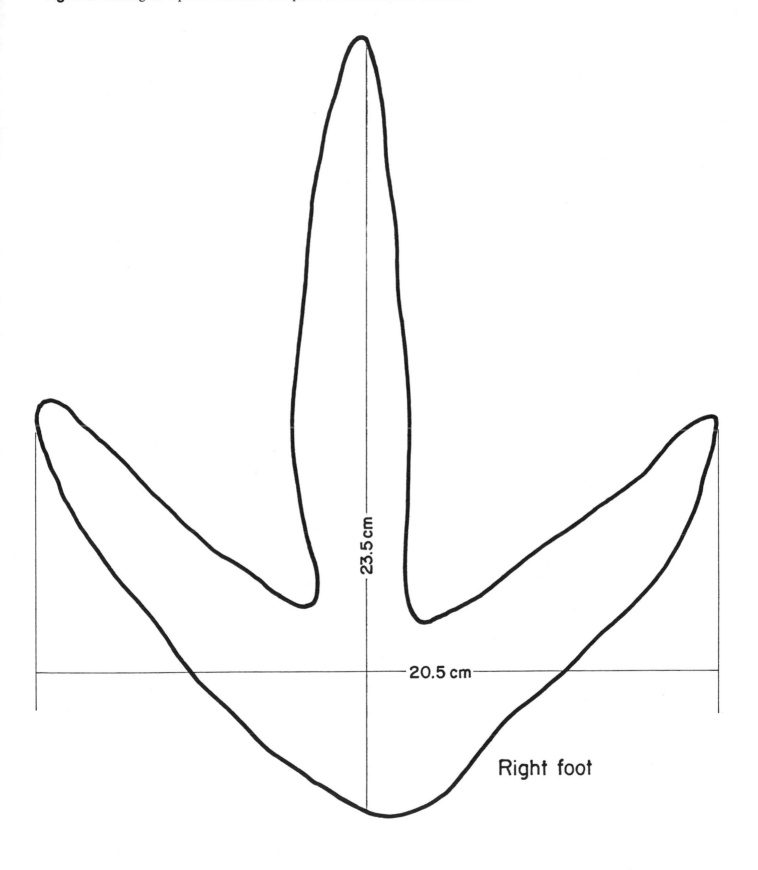

23.5 cm

20.5 cm

Right foot

Fig. 9.6. Scale drawing of the track of the quadrupedal dinosaur from figure 9.4.

Fig. 9.7. Scale drawing of the track of the bipedal dinosaur from figure 9.5.

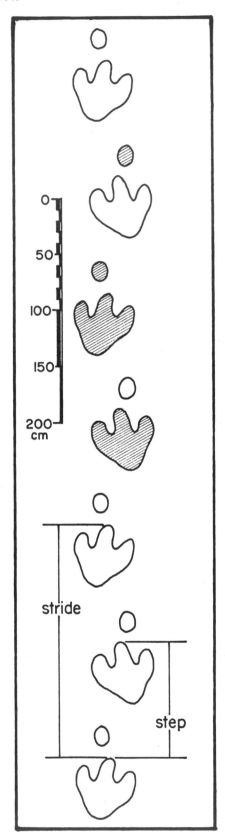

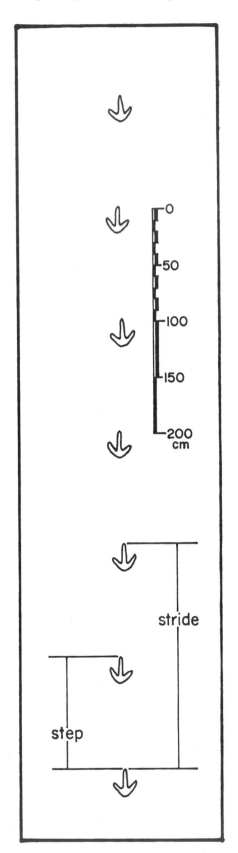

REQUIREMENTS

Time

One or two 45-minute periods

Materials

- Sets of animal tracks made from figures 9.4 through 9.7
- 1 meterstick per student
- Handouts of table 9.2 for students
- Calculators (optional)

Grouping

Individuals or pairs

Table 9.2

Walk, Trot, or Run

NAME _____ PERIOD ____ DATE _____

TRACK	FL footprint length (cm)	h hip height FL x 5 (cm)	SL stride length (cm)	SL/h ratio	WALK (W) TROT (T) RUN (R)	NOTES

DIRECTIONS

1. Create several tracks on the floor, using figures 9.4 to 9.7. Enlarge the footprints as indicated in figures 9.4 and 9.5. Make as many footprints as needed to fill the available space—at least three of each—and cut them out (to make left and right footprints, merely flip them over). Figures 9.6 and 9.7 show the full track of each animal to scale. By referring to these figures and measuring carefully, the trackways can be duplicated in the classroom. Reduce or enlarge footprints to different sizes to create tracks of animals of different sizes (adults, juveniles, perhaps family units or herds of many animals).

2. Building on the previous activities in this chapter, discuss with students what happens to footprints as animals move faster (they get further apart; on softer ground a running animal will also leave deeper footprints). Also discuss the relationship of height to stride length and to rate of movement (a good example would be a comparison of a giraffe and a mouse).

3. Tell students that they have come upon a large track site made by many different animals. Allow the students to determine how many different ones there are.

4. Their task is to determine whether the animals were walking, trotting, or running. Allow the class to discuss (in general terms) how they might solve the problem.

5. Distribute copies of table 9.2, page 117.

6. By measuring the stride length (SL) and footprint length (FL) and calculating the hip height (h), students will be able to determine whether the animals were walking, trotting, or running using the following relationships:

   Walking

   SL/h = less than 2.0

   Trotting

   SL/h = 2.0 through 2.9

   Running

   SL/h = greater than 2.9

7. Write the relationships on the board or an overhead transparency, review them with the students so they understand what they are expected to do, and have them write these relationships on their copies of table 9.2 for reference.

8. Have students complete table 9.2. Once they determine whether the gait was a walk, trot, or run, have them enter the ratio determined and "W," "T," or "R" in the appropriate columns.

9. Under the "Notes" column in table 9.2, students are asked to comment on the tracks: for example, "Track 1 is the same as Track 4 but from a smaller animal."

★ ★ ★

ACTIVITY: CAN WE TELL HOW BIG THEY WERE?

The easiest way to determine the size of a dinosaur is to measure its assembled skeleton. Unfortunately, relatively few dinosaurs are represented by complete skeletons. Each animal was equipped with only one skeleton during its lifetime; footprints are far more abundant.

REQUIREMENTS

Time

45 minutes

Materials

- Tracks placed on classroom floor from previous activity

- Meterstick for each student

- Figures 9.8 and 9.9 prepared for distribution or as overhead transparencies

- Copies of table 9.3 for each student

Grouping

Individuals

Scientists have established certain relationships by comparing various parts of the skeleton and by determining the foot size so that it is possible to estimate the size of an animal from the footprints and tracks alone. These estimates will obviously not be as accurate as measurements taken from a complete skeleton, but they can provide a fair idea of the size of an animal when only a track is available, and they may be just as accurate as measurements extrapolated from only a partial skeleton.

> For quadrupedal animals:
>
> overall length = 4 × shoulder-hip dimension (see fig. 9.8, p. 120)

> For bipedal animals:
>
> hip height = 5 × footprint length
>
> head-to-tail length = 10 × footprint length (minimum) (see fig. 9.9, p. 120)

Measuring the trackways placed on the classroom floor in the previous activity, students can determine the animals' size using the above relationships.

DIRECTIONS

1. Figures 9.8 and 9.9 should either be distributed to students or shown on an overhead projector as a reference during the exercise.

2. Provide students with the above relationships, either as a handout or written on an overhead transparency or the chalkboard.

3. Review the relationships and the figures to be certain students understand what they need to do.

4. Have students complete table 9.3, page 121, to determine the size of the animal that made each prepared track.

Fig. 9.8. Skeleton and track of iguanodontoid dinosaur associated with figures 9.4 and 9.6. Shaded footprints indicate a single sequence of footprints. This figure demonstrates how to determine shoulder-hip length, the distance from the shoulder socket to the hip socket, for a quadruped. To find the shoulder socket, determine the midpoint of the distance between the two front footprints (A); to find the hip socket, determine the midpoint of the distance between the two hind footprints (B). The distance between the two midpoints is the shoulder-hip length.

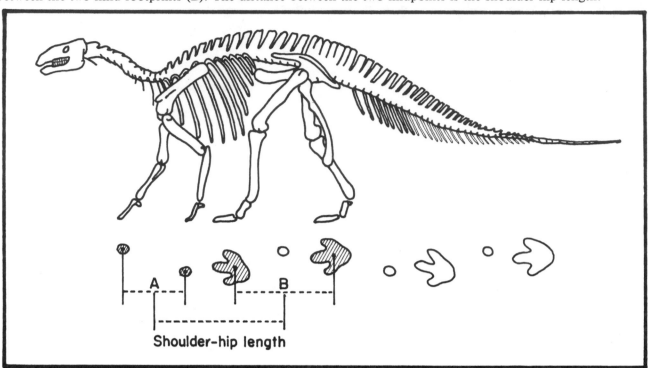

Fig. 9.9. Skeleton and track of ostrichlike dinosaur associated with figures 9.5 and 9.7.

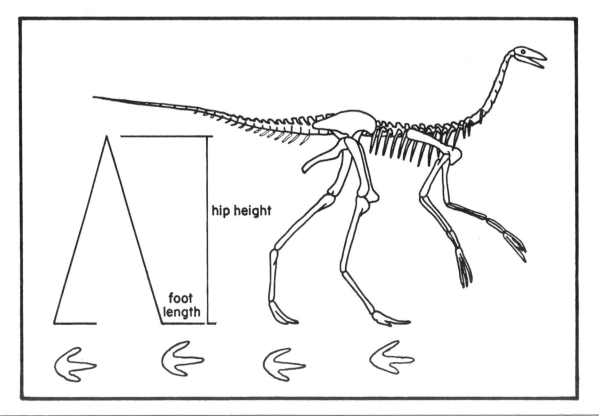

EXTENSIONS

1. As with other track activities, examples of the tracks of modern animals can be obtained from various sources, and similar calculations can be done for these animals, especially pets. If skeletons of cats or dogs (perhaps these can be borrowed from a museum or university) are available for classroom use, students can determine relationships using observed footprints and skeletal measurements.

2. The activities here can provide a measure of the dimensions of the animal but not its mass. R. McNeill Alexander (1989, 16-26; 1991, 130) explains a method by which the mass of the dinosaur (and therefore its weight) can be approximated using museum models. Accurate museum models are scaled-down versions of what scientists think the animals actually looked like. By submerging the models in water, the volumes of the models can be determined. If the scale of the model is known, the volume of the original animal can be determined. Because the density of the bodies of both mammals and crocodiles is approximately the same as that of water, the mass of the original animal can be determined as well.

Table 9.3

Size

NAME_____PERIOD_____DATE _____

TRACK	BIPEDAL		QUADRUPEDAL	
	FL footprint length (m)	head-to-tail length FL x 10 (m)	SHD shoulder-hip dimension (m)	overall length SHD x 4 (m)

★ ★ ★

Skeletons can provide some clues about how an animal might have moved. Do the leg bones show signs of the attachment of large muscles? Were the bones strong enough to support the weight of the animal on only two legs? Were the leg bones long enough to allow the animal to run rather than walk? Did the joints have the flexibility to allow the animal to move rapidly or only stiffly? Did the joints have the strength to support high speeds? Calculations based upon skeletal proportions can also be used to estimate the speeds of the animals. Speeds determined from skeletal evidence are largely speculative. Trackways, too, can provide clues about dinosaur speeds; tracks are made while the animal is in motion and are a direct function of the speed of the animal. Neither source of evidence, however, provides the precise information scientists would like, and, unfortunately, the results of calculations based on tracks and skeletal evidence do not agree very well.

★ ★ ★

ACTIVITY: HOW FAST DID THEY MOVE?

There is not much agreement among paleontologists who estimate dinosaur speed from dinosaur tracks. Some have examined the relationship of tracks to speed for modern animals and used their conclusions as a basis for comparison. Others have determined mathematical relationships of varying complexity integrating leg length, stride length, strides per second, or footprint length. The suggested reading at the end of this chapter will provide details of those methods. This activity is empirical and will allow students to compare the measurements they have taken of the prepared tracks in the classroom with those taken by various investigators in the field and determine the speeds of their animals through reference to a prepared graph.

Figure 9.10 is a graph of the relationship of stride length to speed of dinosaur as determined from trackway and skeletal information found in Alexander (1976, 129-130; 1989, 40), James O. Farlow (1981, 747-748), and Richard A. Thulborn (1982, 238, 241). One thing loco-paleontologists ("loco-" referring to locomotion — not the Spanish word for "crazy") all agree upon is that animals spend only a small fraction of their lives moving at maximum speed. Think about how infrequently you sprint each day! More data is therefore available from trackways of walking dinosaurs than running dinosaurs.

Based upon their tracks, dinosaurs seem to have walked slowly most of the time. After all, if they were herbivores, their food was not going anywhere, and if they were carnivores, they needed to conserve their energy to pursue their food. In this dinosaurs were not unique. Modern animals behave in the same manner. Speeds determined from trackways of walking dinosaurs are on the order of one to three meters per second, approximately the same as a human walk.

(Activity continues on page 124.)

Fig. 9.10. Graph of relationships of stride length and speed as determined from trackway and skeletal data. Circles are trackway data points, triangles are skeleton data. Graph represents data from Alexander (1976, 1989), Farlow (1981), and Thulborn (1982).

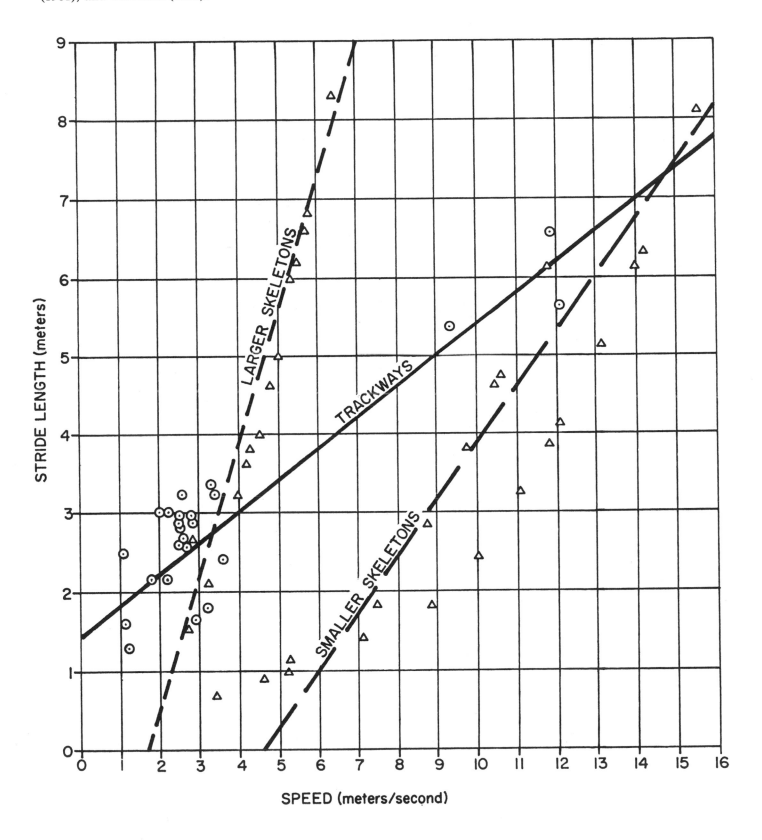

For comparison, the following list gives maximum speeds of several modern animals:

Animal	Maximum Speed (Meters/Second)
Cheetah	31
Pronghorn antelope	27
Lion	22
Fox	18
Zebra	17
Greyhound	17
Rabbit	15
Giraffe	14
Cat	13
Elephant	11
Human	10
Black mamba snake	9
Squirrel	5
Chicken	4
Spider	0.5
Giant tortoise	0.1

REQUIREMENTS

Time

45 minutes

Materials

- Stride measurements from previous activities
- Walk, trot or run determinations from table 9.2
- Figure 9.10 prepared as a handout for each student and as an overhead transparency
- Table 9.4 as a handout for each student

Grouping

Individuals

DIRECTIONS

1. Distribute a copy of figure 9.10 to each student. Figure 9.10 is a graph showing data collected by three researchers who calculated dinosaur speed using trackway and skeletal information. Evidence from trackways is plotted as circles; data from skeletons are plotted as triangles. The solid and dashed lines indicate the average speed per stride length, based on trackway information (solid line), skeletal information for larger dinosaurs (short-dash line), and skeletal information for smaller dinosaurs (long-dash line). The information suggests that agreement between skeletal and trackway data is poor and that animal size may have much to do with speed determinations.

2. Distribute a copy of table 9.4 to each student.

3. Have students complete table 9.4 (stride length, student speeds, and determination of walk, trot, or run for the classroom trackways have been determined in earlier activities, and students will merely need to transfer the data).

4. Referring to the left axis of the graph in figure 9.10, which plots stride length, students will need to determine the speed of the animals in the classroom trackways and enter the numerical value on their table. Start at the left side of the graph with the stride length the student has determined, move across the graph to the right to "Trackways" line, then determine where it falls on the speed scale. Similar comparisons can be made using skeletal data.

5. They will then need to determine whether that speed is close to the maximum speed of the animal. If they determined that their track was that of a walking animal, then the speed is not close to maximum. For a running animal, the determined speed will probably be near the maximum speed.

6. Can the student walk or run faster than the indicated dinosaur? The students have already determined their walking and running speeds and stride lengths. They can plot their data on the graph with the dinosaur data for comparison. Have students present their findings in a class discussion or short essay.

Table 9.4

Speed

NAME_____ PERIOD____DATE _____

TRACK	Stride Length (m)	Speed (m/sec)	WALK (W) TROT (T) RUN (R)	STUDENT SPEED	
				WALK (m/sec)	RUN (m/sec)

EXTENSIONS

1. All of the activities in this chapter on trackways are closely related. Students can be asked to use the data acquired from the various activities as the basis for a report or portfolio. By adding data from library or other sources, comparisons can be made between modern animals and dinosaurs.

2. Many references to dinosaur track-site discoveries include detailed maps of those track sites. From such maps more advanced students could determine such data as

   a. predator-to-prey ratios.

   b. the ratio of small (juvenile) to large (adult) animals.

   c. how the herd behaves (are juveniles in the center, or do they walk on the perimeter?).

REFERENCES

Alexander, R. McNeill. 1976. "Estimates of Speeds of Dinosaurs." *Nature* 261, no. 5,556: 129-130.

Alexander, R. McNeill. 1989. *Dynamics of Dinosaurs and Other Extinct Giants*. New York: Columbia University Press.

Alexander, R. McNeill. 1991. "How Dinosaurs Ran." *Scientific American* 264, no. 4: 130-136.

Farlow, James O. 1981. "Estimates of Dinosaur Speeds from a Trackway Site in Texas." *Nature* 294, no. 5,843: 747-748.

Thulborn, Richard A. 1982. "Speeds and Gaits of Dinosaurs." *Paleogeography, Paleoclimatology, Paleoecology* 38: 227-256.

SUGGESTED READING

Bakker, Robert T. *The Dinosaur Heresies*. New York: Zebra Books, 1986.

Lockley, Martin. *Tracking Dinosaurs*. Cambridge: Cambridge University Press, 1991.

Paul, Gregory S. *Predatory Dinosaurs of the World*. New York: Simon & Schuster, 1988.

Thulborn, Richard A. "The Gaits of Dinosaurs." In *Dinosaur Tracks and Traces*, edited by David M. Gillette and Martin G. Lockley. Cambridge: Cambridge University Press, 1989.

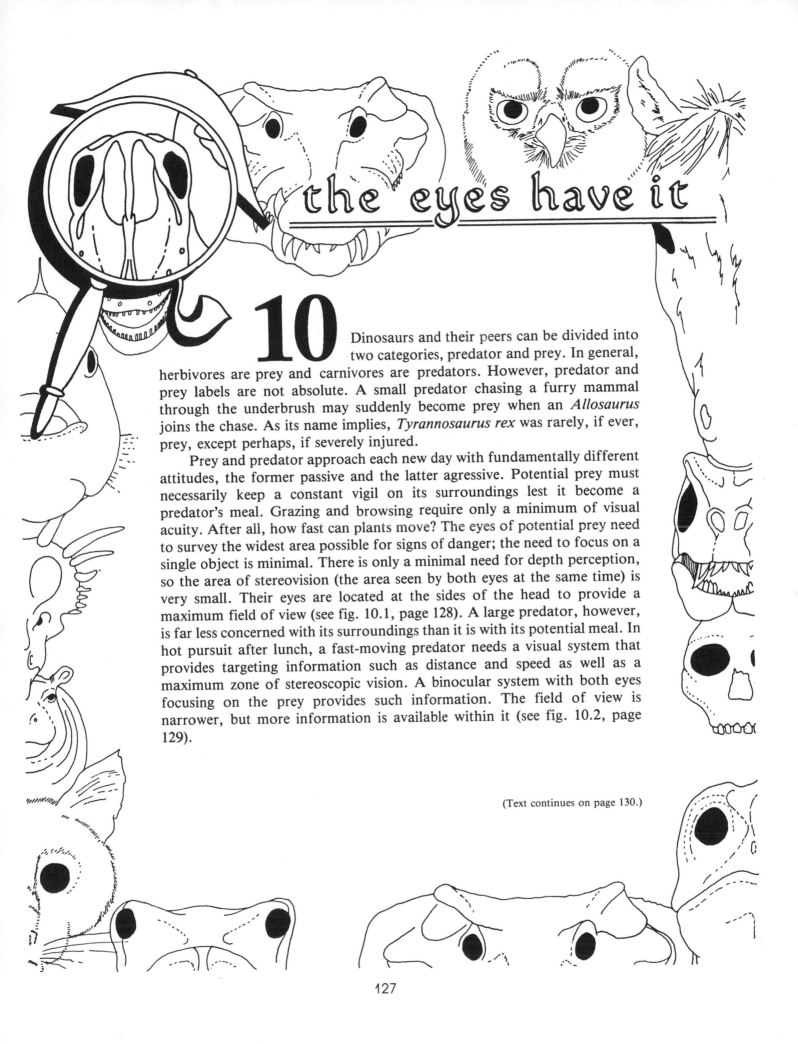

the eyes have it

10

Dinosaurs and their peers can be divided into two categories, predator and prey. In general, herbivores are prey and carnivores are predators. However, predator and prey labels are not absolute. A small predator chasing a furry mammal through the underbrush may suddenly become prey when an *Allosaurus* joins the chase. As its name implies, *Tyrannosaurus rex* was rarely, if ever, prey, except perhaps, if severely injured.

Prey and predator approach each new day with fundamentally different attitudes, the former passive and the latter agressive. Potential prey must necessarily keep a constant vigil on its surroundings lest it become a predator's meal. Grazing and browsing require only a minimum of visual acuity. After all, how fast can plants move? The eyes of potential prey need to survey the widest area possible for signs of danger; the need to focus on a single object is minimal. There is only a minimal need for depth perception, so the area of stereovision (the area seen by both eyes at the same time) is very small. Their eyes are located at the sides of the head to provide a maximum field of view (see fig. 10.1, page 128). A large predator, however, is far less concerned with its surroundings than it is with its potential meal. In hot pursuit after lunch, a fast-moving predator needs a visual system that provides targeting information such as distance and speed as well as a maximum zone of stereoscopic vision. A binocular system with both eyes focusing on the prey provides such information. The field of view is narrower, but more information is available within it (see fig. 10.2, page 129).

(Text continues on page 130.)

Fig. 10.1. Examples of animals with (mostly) nonstereovision. Eyes are set to the sides of the head, with only a small amount of overlap of field of view. Adapted from Lambert.

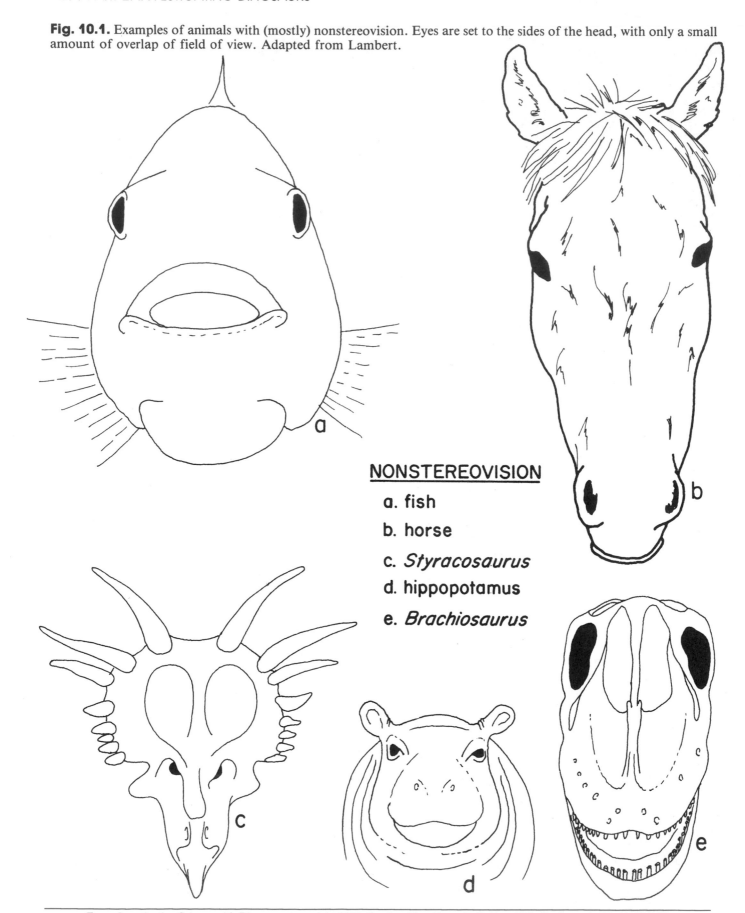

NONSTEREOVISION

a. fish

b. horse

c. *Styracosaurus*

d. hippopotamus

e. *Brachiosaurus*

Fig. 10.2. Examples of animals with stereovision. Eyes are set in the front of the head. Fields of view are narrowed, but the zone of stereovision is expanded. Figures 10.2a and 10.2e adapted from Lambert; figure 10.2b adapted from Bakker.

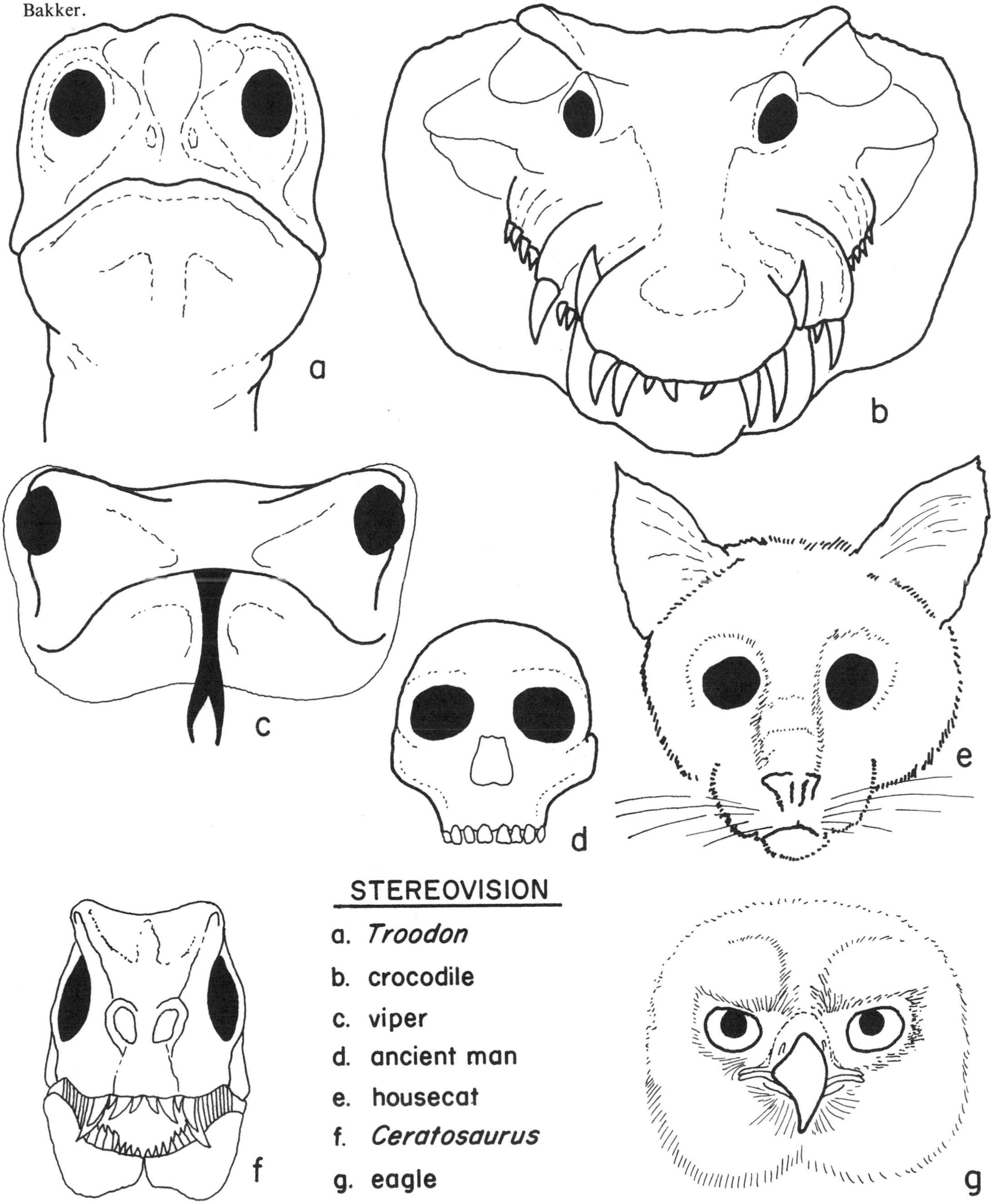
a
b
c
d
e
STEREOVISION
a. *Troodon*
b. crocodile
c. viper
d. ancient man
e. housecat
f. *Ceratosaurus*
g. eagle
f
g

★ ★ ★

ACTIVITY: WHERE DO YOUR EYES LOOK?

Two ways visual systems can be defined are by size of field of view and the zone of stereoscopic vision. Animals have different visual systems to suit their individual needs. Birds, for instance, utilize a broad range of visual systems (see fig. 10.3). An owl is a predator and requires a relatively narrow field of view but a broad area of stereoscopic vision. The woodcock, more worried about being prey, has only a very narrow zone of stereoscopic vision but an exceptionally large field of view. The shape and location of its eyes gives the woodcock a virtually unlimited field of view, the next best thing to having eyes in back of its head. The sparrow has some of each—a fairly broad stereoscopic field for targeting insects and a broad field of overall vision. In this activity students will be able to chart the area their eyes see; they literally will be able to see what they see.

REQUIREMENTS

Time

45-90 minutes

Materials

- 1 large sheet of paper (at least 11" × 17") per team

- Pencils

- Protractor

Fig. 10.3. Comparison of fields of view and zones of stereovision for different birds. The predatory owl has the narrowest field of view but the widest zone of stereovision. The woodcock is a wary species that has an extraordinary field of view but a very small zone of stereovision. The sparrow is intermediate, having a fairly wide zone of stereo-scopic vision for catching insects but a broad field of view for defense.

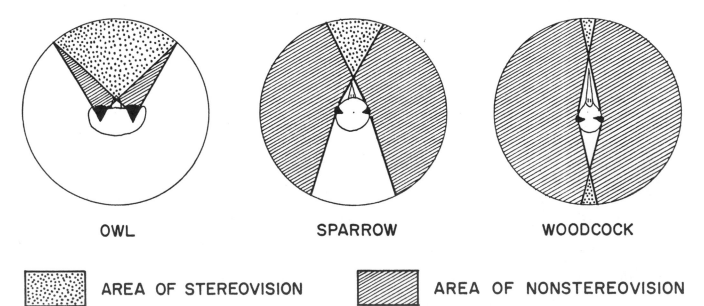

OWL   SPARROW   WOODCOCK

▨ AREA OF STEREOVISION   ▨ AREA OF NONSTEREOVISION

- Tape
- Colored pencils
- Ruler
- Handouts of figure 10.4 for students

Grouping

Pairs

DIRECTIONS

1. Describe the concepts *field of view* and *stereoscopic vision*. Explain to students that this activity will allow them to determine their individual fields of view and zones of stereoscopic vision. There is no correct answer to this activity, and findings may differ among students.

2. Each pair will designate a "student 1" and "student 2."

3. Have student 1 place the large piece of paper on a desk surface and tape it in place.

4. Have student 2 draw an arrow in the middle of the paper as shown in figure 10.4a.

5. Using a large compass or by measuring, student 1 should draw a semicircle 15 inches in diameter with its center at the base of the arrow (see fig. 10.4a).

6. Have student 2 place his or her chin on the desk surface on the base of the arrow, with head and eyes facing straight ahead in the direction of the arrow.

7. The activity will be done with one eye open at a time; for the first part the left eye should be closed.

8. Starting 12 inches (30 centimeters) in front of the nose of student 2, student 1 will hold a pencil, so it rests on the semicircle. Student 1 should move the pencil to student 2's left until student 2 indicates it can no longer be seen. It should be stressed to the students that they must not follow the pencil with their eyes; they must always look straight ahead.

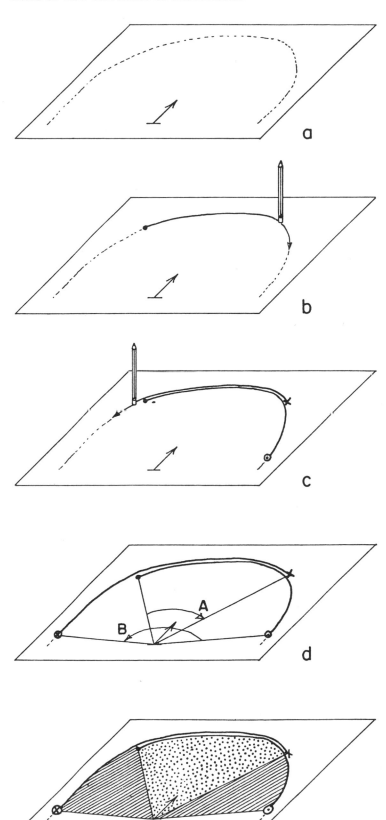

Fig. 10.4. Diagram of procedures for establishing students' fields of view and zones of stereovision.

9. At the point where student 2 can no longer see the pencil, student 1 will mark the paper with a filled-in circle, placed on the semicircular line as shown in figure 10.4b.

10. Student 1 should now move the pencil along the semicircle towards the right until student 2 again signals that it is not visible. Student 1 should mark this point with a dot and a circle as shown in figure 10.4c.

11. Repeat the procedure with the right eye closed and mark the paper as shown (see fig. 10.4c).

12. The completed sheet should look like figure 10.4d.

13. Draw the lines shown to the four points on the paper (fig. 10.4d).

14. Measure the angle of the zone of stereoscopic vision by using the protractor to find angle A.

15. The field of view can be measured by the protractor as angle B.

16. Repeat this exercise *on the same sheet of paper*, with students 1 and 2 switching places. Use different colors and symbols to mark the four points for the second student.

17. What are the angles? Are they the same for both students? Which type of bird has the system of vision most like man's (refer to fig. 10.3)?

★ ★ ★

ACTIVITY: WHAT THE EYES REVEAL

Animal eyes can indicate whether an animal is primarily a prey or predator species and whether the animal is nocturnal (active at night, like an owl) or diurnal (active during the day). Like a camera lens, which must be wide open to take pictures in low light, the eyes of nocturnal animals (such as owls, tigers, many monkeys, and even alligators) are large and round, utilizing all the minimal light available. Anyone who has ever tried to catch a housefly knows how easily a moving object is detected by the fly. Flies have what are known as compound eyes. Each eye produces several images of the surroundings, providing a broad field of view and excellent motion detection. Targeting information is not necessary, but collision (and predator) avoidance is. Other animals have similar specialized optical systems.

REQUIREMENTS

Time

Several library periods (in school or as outside research)

Materials

No special materials

Grouping

Individuals

DIRECTIONS

1. Discuss how different types of animals require eyes that do different things (compare the *Tyrannosaurus* with the housefly). Ask the class for input about animals that live in water or are nocturnal: How do their visual needs differ?

2. Students will need to prepare a report about visual systems of pairs of adversarial animals: for example, lions and antelope, sharks and sea lions, lizards and insects, owls and mice, man and a specific animal during hunting season (deer or bear), bears and fish, fish and insects, bats and insects. They might also study conditions under which eyes do not provide any real advantage (bats, cave fish, and tunneling insects and animals).

3. In the report, students will need to describe the two systems, how they work, under what conditions they favor one animal over the other, and which one is most effective. It is necessary to illustrate the report.

4. This activity can be done using school library resources over several periods or as an outside activity. Students should be encouraged to use periodicals as well as encyclopedias. In addition, many audio-visual resources are available on the subject of eyes and visual systems. These would make valuable additions to class presentations of the report.

ACTIVITY: SEEING LIKE THE DINOSAURS

Students can gain an appreciation of predator-prey visual systems by preparing paper-bag headpieces with appropriate eye holes to simulate dinosaur visual systems. The ratio of predators to prey among dinosaurs is unclear, but Robert Bakker (1986, 385) suggests between 1 percent and 5 percent predators in some dinosaur populations. Comparisons vary depending upon how the number is calculated, and the ratio is either much higher than (Bakker 1986, 385) or comparable to (Lockley, personal communication) that found among animals on the modern African plains. What this means is that among a group of approximately 30 students in a classroom there will be only one or two predators. All others in the class will be prey animals.

REQUIREMENTS

Time

45-90 minutes; possibly some time at home or in art class

Materials

Per student:

- 1 large paper supermarket bag
- Scissors
- Colored pencils, markers, or crayons to decorate bag (see "Extensions" for elaborate masks)
- Books about dinosaurs and modern animals
- Large indoor or outdoor area

Grouping

Individuals and whole class

DIRECTIONS

1. Discuss animal eye placement with students in terms of how an animal needs to see. Does it merely need to be aware of another animal's movement, or does it need to be able to have more definitive information for targeting?

2. In a population of large modern animals there would be fewer than 5 percent predatory animals. By analogy, this would be one "predatory animal" per class. To make this activity work better, select four students to be predatory animals per class. The remainder of the class will be prey.

3. Distribute materials to students. The paper bags will be used to make predator and prey headpieces as shown in figure 10.5.

4. Predator headpieces will have eye holes cut in the front (see fig. 10.5a). This gives predators a narrower field of view but also permits binocular vision and enhanced depth perception.

5. Prey headpieces will have eye holes cut on the sides of the bag toward the front (see fig. 10.5b), expanding the field of view but sacrificing depth perception and stereovision.

6. Once the students have the holes cut, they can decorate their bags to resemble their favorite appropriate dinosaur, predator or prey.

7. Once all headpieces have been completed, students can play dinosaur and be taken outdoors or moved to a large indoor area.

Fig. 10.5. Eyehole placements in the predator and prey headpieces. Figure 10.5a shows a predator headpiece, and figure 10.5b shows that of the prey.

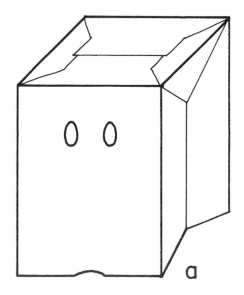 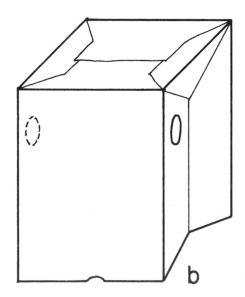

8. Scatter easily findable objects around in the area you select. Pencils might work well indoors; something larger will work better outdoors. Provide enough objects so that each student will be able to recover several. Explain to students that the items they are looking for are food, and they must try to recover as much as possible. Then turn them loose. Predators, with superior binocular vision and depth perception, should be able to recover far more than prey. Prey might be able to see more at a distance but will have a harder time actually retrieving the items. Try to have as many students as possible switch roles. Students should be able to develop a sense of the difference in the visual systems.

9. Divide the class into the same number of groups as there are predatory animals, approximately four. Each group will consist of one predator and approximately one quarter of the prey. In the large activity area have the predatory animals try to catch the prey in their same group. *Instruct students not to run*: because prey are visually restricted, running could be hazardous. Again, try to have as many students as possible switch roles.

10. When activities 8 and 9 have been completed, ask students to write a one- or two-page report explaining the differences in the two visual systems and how each gives the respective animals an advantage or disadvantage.

EXTENSIONS

This activity may be done in connection with an art class, where headpieces may be made more elaborate or fanciful using such materials as papier mâché. The only constraint is to maintain the correct type of eye placement for the predator or prey selected.

★ ★ ★

REFERENCES

Bakker, Robert T. 1986. *The Dinosaur Heresies*. New York: Zebra Books.

Lockley, Martin. 1991. *Tracking Dinosaurs*. Cambridge: Cambridge University Press.

SUGGESTED READING

Lambert, David. *The Dinosaur Data Book*. New York: Avon Books, 1990.

Norman, David. *The Illustrated Encyclopedia of Dinosaurs*. New York: Crown, 1985.

Peterson, Roger Tory. *The Birds*. Life Nature Library. New York: Time Life, 1968.

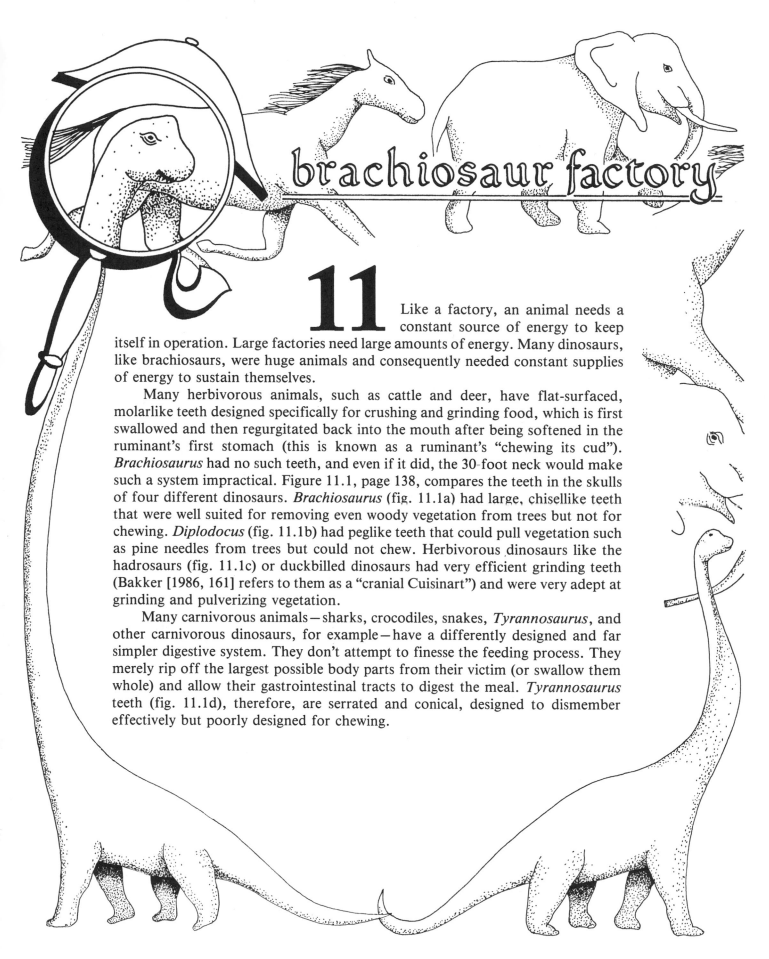

brachiosaur factory

11

Like a factory, an animal needs a constant source of energy to keep itself in operation. Large factories need large amounts of energy. Many dinosaurs, like brachiosaurs, were huge animals and consequently needed constant supplies of energy to sustain themselves.

Many herbivorous animals, such as cattle and deer, have flat-surfaced, molarlike teeth designed specifically for crushing and grinding food, which is first swallowed and then regurgitated back into the mouth after being softened in the ruminant's first stomach (this is known as a ruminant's "chewing its cud"). *Brachiosaurus* had no such teeth, and even if it did, the 30-foot neck would make such a system impractical. Figure 11.1, page 138, compares the teeth in the skulls of four different dinosaurs. *Brachiosaurus* (fig. 11.1a) had large, chisellike teeth that were well suited for removing even woody vegetation from trees but not for chewing. *Diplodocus* (fig. 11.1b) had peglike teeth that could pull vegetation such as pine needles from trees but could not chew. Herbivorous dinosaurs like the hadrosaurs (fig. 11.1c) or duckbilled dinosaurs had very efficient grinding teeth (Bakker [1986, 161] refers to them as a "cranial Cuisinart") and were very adept at grinding and pulverizing vegetation.

Many carnivorous animals—sharks, crocodiles, snakes, *Tyrannosaurus*, and other carnivorous dinosaurs, for example—have a differently designed and far simpler digestive system. They don't attempt to finesse the feeding process. They merely rip off the largest possible body parts from their victim (or swallow them whole) and allow their gastrointestinal tracts to digest the meal. *Tyrannosaurus* teeth (fig. 11.1d), therefore, are serrated and conical, designed to dismember effectively but poorly designed for chewing.

Fig. 11.1. Types of teeth of various dinosaurs. Figure 11.1a shows a *Brachiosaurus* skull, 11.1b a *Diplodocus* skull, 11.1c a hadrosaur skull, and 11.1d a *Tyrannosaurus* skull.

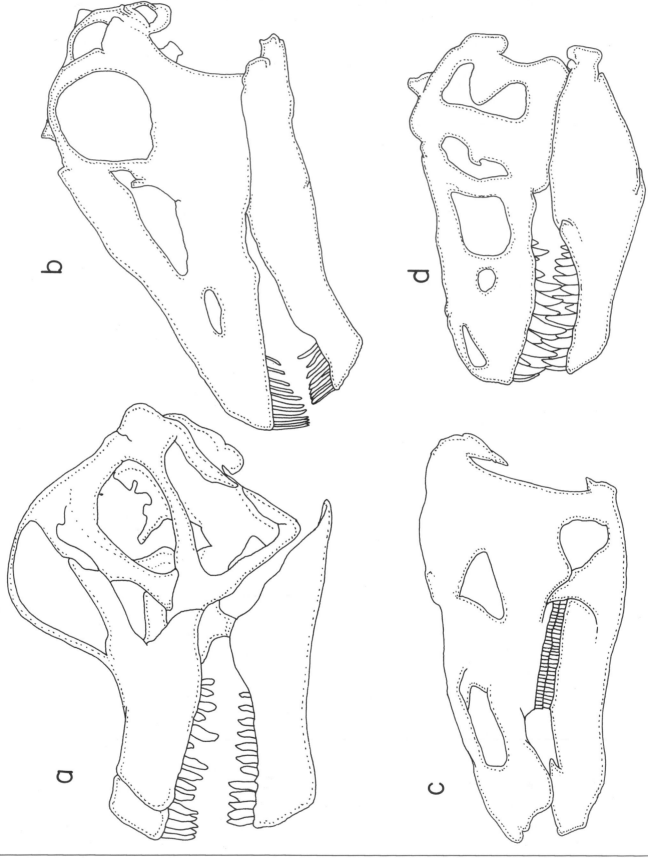

In humans most of the work done to make digestion more efficient is accomplished by the teeth. Canines, incisors, and molars are all designed for specific jobs. Chewing prepares food for digestion by crushing and pulverizing. There was reason behind your mother's advice to chew your food at least 10 times before swallowing.

★ ★ ★

ACTIVITY: DIFFERENT TEETH FOR DIFFERENT JOBS

Among the dinosaurs, one species had a dental design similar to humans: *Heterodontosaurus* (see fig. 11.2). As its name ("reptile with mixed teeth") indicates, the animal had a mixture of tooth types: incisors, canines, and molars. As in the human mouth, each tooth type was designed to accomplish a certain task. At the conclusion of this activity, students will recognize the importance of the different types of teeth.

REQUIREMENTS

Time

5-10 minutes

Materials

1 carrot circle or 2-inch piece of celery per student

Grouping

Individuals

Fig. 11.2. Lower part of the skull of *Heterodontosaurus*, showing the different types of teeth.

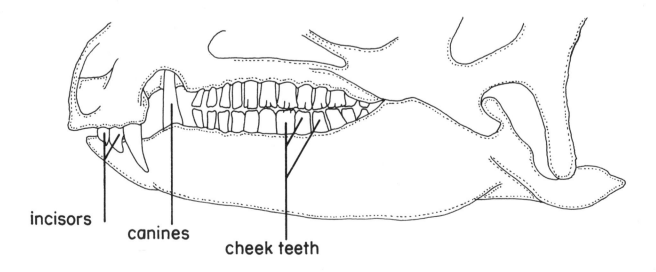

DIRECTIONS

1. Caution students not to do anything with the food until they receive instructions from you.

2. Give one carrot or celery piece to each student.

3. Ask them to bite it in half. When done, discuss with them which teeth they used to cut it with. They should have used the front teeth, the *incisors* (the name means "to cut").

4. Now ask them to chew it up as completely as possible. They should use the teeth toward the back of the mouth on both sides, the *molars*. The word *molar* comes from the Latin word for millstone, the large stone used for grinding corn or flour in a mill.

5. Explain to students that the third type of tooth humans have is called the cuspid or canine tooth, located between the incisors in the front of the mouth and the molars in the back. The canines are conical in shape and, in carnivores such as tigers and bears, are used to tear and hold chunks of food. The tusks of the elephant and the fangs of the extinct saber-tooth tiger are canine teeth. As the human diet has evolved to include a balance of meat and nonmeat foods, our canine teeth (named for those found in wolves and dogs), have become less prominent. Pure carnivores such as *Tyrannosaurus* had a mouth full of canine teeth.

6. Explain to students that the smaller the food pieces, the more efficiently chemical digestion can occur in the stomach and intestines. Ask students which teeth were more effective at making small pieces. They should say molars.

EXTENSION

To show how smaller particles can be digested more quickly than large particles, use ice. Place equal weights of shaved ice, ice cubes, and a single ice block in a bowl in the room. Because of the greater surface area, the shaved ice will melt more quickly; masticated food particles, because they have more surface area, are more easily broken down by gastric juices.

⊠ ⊠ ⊠

An elephant is an eating machine. Everything about its body is designed to process sufficiently large quantities of food to sustain its bulk. Everything about its large head serves as a food gathering machine. The trunk grabs plant material and pushes it into the large mouth, where large tooth surfaces efficiently grind the plant material into easily digestible pulp. Its gastrointestinal tract incorporates an enlarged rear portion of the colon, in which contained material can be acted upon by enzymes and microbes for efficient digestion, like a fermenting vat (Bakker 1986, 172). A *Brachiosaurus* had a much larger body than an elephant, yet it had a proportionately small head for its body size (see fig. 11.3). In addition, its head had none of the food gathering and processing machinery of the elephant. To put this into perspective, the head of a horse is approximately the same size as the head of a *Brachiosaurus*, yet the horse head supplies food for only an 800-pound body; a *Brachiosaurus* head of the same size supplied a 40,000-to-60,000-pound body (50 to 75 times larger). To put it another way, if the horse-head-length-to-body-weight ratio were kept consistent for *Brachiosaurus*, the dinosaur's head would have to have been 150 to 200 feet long. *Brachiosaurus* obviously had to evolve a different manner of processing food before digestion.

Like that of the elephant, the body shape of the *Brachiosaurus* suggests the presence of a fermenting vat: an enlarged area of the colon toward the rear end of the animal that fostered the complete digestion of food. Unlike the elephant, however, the teeth of *Brachiosaurus* were incapable of crushing or grinding the food to prepare it for digestion. How, then, was efficient digestion accomplished?

Fig. 11.3. Elephant, horse, and *Brachiosaurus* drawn with approximately the same body size. The head of the *Brachiosaurus* is proportionately smaller than the other two, suggesting a slightly different function: it did not chew.

Clues to the digestion system of large herbivorous dinosaurs comes from birds and crocodiles: neither has teeth to chew its food. Anyone who has ever had a parakeet can confirm the importance of putting gravel in the cage. The birds swallow the gravel and keep it in their gizzard, a muscular pocket in the digestive tract. As the muscles cause the walls of the gizzard to move, the contained gravel crushes the food. Parakeets are small birds and use small gravel. The gizzards of larger birds like ostriches may contain two handfuls of pebbles. Crocodiles are even larger animals and use proportionately larger rocks (crocodiles may also use these rocks as ballast). Much like rocks in a stream, these gizzard stones, or *gastroliths*, become very smooth and rounded.

Reasonably strong evidence exists that large dinosaurs like brontosaurs and brachiosaurs also had gizzard stones, probably several fist-size rocks capable of efficiently crushing and grinding ingested food. The large dinosaurs pulled vegetation as needed with their thin, peglike teeth, and rather than waste valuable energy on chewing, swallowed the food. The gizzard "chewed" as they walked. It is a far more efficient system because these dinosaurs could ingest new food as they "chewed" the old food.

★ ★ ★

ACTIVITY: HOW DO WE DO IT?

The process of grinding and crushing with gizzard stones can be simulated.

REQUIREMENTS

Time

20-30 minutes

Materials

- 2-liter plastic pop bottle with cap
- Handful of rounded pebbles, the largest that will fit into the bottle
- Pieces of lettuce or grass
- 1/2 cup of water
- Large strainer or colander
- Large bowl or bucket

Grouping

Whole class

DIRECTIONS

1. Discuss the absence of grinding and crushing teeth in the *Brachiosaurus* and *Brontosaurus*. Discuss with students how these dinosaurs might have pulverized their food.

2. Tell them they will demonstrate an option.

3. Place pebbles, water, and vegetables in the bottle and put the cap on tightly.

4. Pass the bottle around the room, allowing each student to shake it 15 to 20 times.

5. After all students have had the opportunity to shake the bottle, have students form a circle.

6. Place the colander over the bowl or bucket and pour out the bottle contents. The vegetables will be crushed. Discuss how they have been pulverized without being chewed.

EXTENSIONS

1. Students can try this experiment with other vegetables or plant materials at home—carrots, celery, tree leaves—and compile a list of how many shakes it takes to pulverize different materials. A class list can be compiled, with each student contributing the results of an individual effort.

2. A library research project to investigate how man uses similar grinding processes can be performed as a group project. Different kinds of grinding and crushing mills are used to process flour or metal ores. Mortar and pestle are used in many civilizations to powder grains. Wind and water mills use large grindstones to do the same thing.

3. To enhance the simulations, add dilute acids (5 percent hydrochloric, for instance) to the bottle and allow to stand for various time periods to study the chemical effects of the acid solution as well as the physical effects of pulverization.

4. Students can use "how-it-works" books to investigate different kinds of crushing or milling machines. Audiovisual resources of industrial processes might be available from industry sources.

★ ★ ★

REFERENCES

Bakker, Robert T. 1986. *The Dinosaur Heresies*. New York: Zebra Books.

SUGGESTED READING

Norman, David. *The Illustrated Encyclopedia of Dinosaurs*. New York: Crown, 1985.

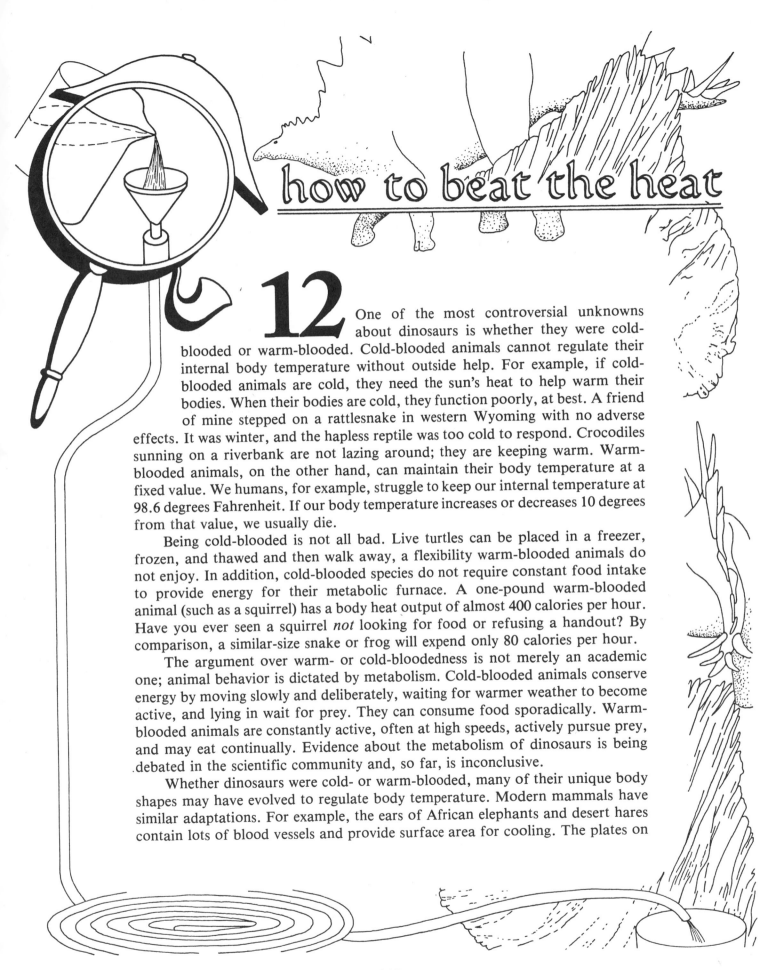

how to beat the heat

12 One of the most controversial unknowns about dinosaurs is whether they were cold-blooded or warm-blooded. Cold-blooded animals cannot regulate their internal body temperature without outside help. For example, if cold-blooded animals are cold, they need the sun's heat to help warm their bodies. When their bodies are cold, they function poorly, at best. A friend of mine stepped on a rattlesnake in western Wyoming with no adverse effects. It was winter, and the hapless reptile was too cold to respond. Crocodiles sunning on a riverbank are not lazing around; they are keeping warm. Warm-blooded animals, on the other hand, can maintain their body temperature at a fixed value. We humans, for example, struggle to keep our internal temperature at 98.6 degrees Fahrenheit. If our body temperature increases or decreases 10 degrees from that value, we usually die.

Being cold-blooded is not all bad. Live turtles can be placed in a freezer, frozen, and thawed and then walk away, a flexibility warm-blooded animals do not enjoy. In addition, cold-blooded species do not require constant food intake to provide energy for their metabolic furnace. A one-pound warm-blooded animal (such as a squirrel) has a body heat output of almost 400 calories per hour. Have you ever seen a squirrel *not* looking for food or refusing a handout? By comparison, a similar-size snake or frog will expend only 80 calories per hour.

The argument over warm- or cold-bloodedness is not merely an academic one; animal behavior is dictated by metabolism. Cold-blooded animals conserve energy by moving slowly and deliberately, waiting for warmer weather to become active, and lying in wait for prey. They can consume food sporadically. Warm-blooded animals are constantly active, often at high speeds, actively pursue prey, and may eat continually. Evidence about the metabolism of dinosaurs is being debated in the scientific community and, so far, is inconclusive.

Whether dinosaurs were cold- or warm-blooded, many of their unique body shapes may have evolved to regulate body temperature. Modern mammals have similar adaptations. For example, the ears of African elephants and desert hares contain lots of blood vessels and provide surface area for cooling. The plates on the back of *Stegosaurus* (see fig. 12.1) are the unique feature of the animal, giving it its name, "roofed reptile." The function of the plates has been discussed since their discovery more than 100 years ago. Differing opinions still run rampant. The most commonly postulated functions include sexual display, armor, and body temperature regulators (thermoregulators). On the basis of the physical evidence, thermoregulation seems the most plausible explanation.

The plates have been studied in great detail, from the inside to the outside. Once cut open, the interior structure of the plates is an open network, like a honeycomb, providing a series of passageways for the movement of blood from the body into the plates and back (much like a car radiator). The exterior surface of the plates (see fig. 12.2) has many grooves, which again suggest the presence of blood vessels. The plates have been examined in wind tunnels, and their shape has been found to be an excellent way to dissipate heat. Based upon such evidence many researchers suggest that plates allowed the animal to efficiently control its body temperature. Sails on the backs of *Ouranosaurus* and *Spinosaurus* may have acted as similar mechanisms.

When *Stegosaurus* needed to raise its body temperature, it would stand sideways to the sun (see fig. 12.1a), exposing the maximum surface area of both its body and the plates to solar radiation (the area of the plates possibly exceeded 50 percent of the body's surface area). In addition *Stegosaurus* would increase the amount of blood flowing through the plates to absorb and disperse as much heat as quickly as possible to the rest of the body. When it needed to minimize heat gain, it would face away from the sun, shading its head and brain, exposing only the edges of the plates to the sun (see fig. 12.1b) and reducing blood flow to the plates. Horses behave in a similar fashion. On cold, sunny days they stand broadside to the sun to absorb as much solar radiation as possible. In cold, windy, or stormy weather they orient themselves with their heads facing downwind, minimizing the surface area exposed to wind chill.

★ ★ ★

ACTIVITY: BLOOD TEMPERATURE

Blood vessels contained within the body are generally protected from the outside environment. Under certain circumstances, however, it is beneficial to allow the blood to be heated or cooled by the animal's surroundings. In this activity students will simulate solar heating of a stegosaur's blood and understand how effectively the mechanism can work. Water will replace blood, and rubber tubing will represent the vessels circulating through the plates. The tubing lengths indicated may seem long, but many stegosaur plates can be three to four feet long and four feet high. This activity will work much better outside on a warm, sunny day, but it can be done indoors using a heat source such as floodlights. The important thing is to make sure the tubing has been effectively heated by whatever heat source is selected.

REQUIREMENTS

Time

90 minutes

Materials

- Rubber tubing (available from auto supply stores) in various diameters and lengths (4', 6', 8')
- Water (room temperature) 100-200 milliliters per trial
- Clear tubing (used in fish tanks)
- Small-necked funnels (used for perfume bottles)
- Small beakers or containers with pouring spout to hold water for pouring into tubing (one per team)

Fig. 12.1. Two views of *Stegosaurus*. Figure 12.1a shows the side view, representing the greatest surface area of animal exposed to sun to maximize heat gain. Figure 12.1b shows the end view, representing the smallest surface area of animal exposed to sun to reduce heat gain.

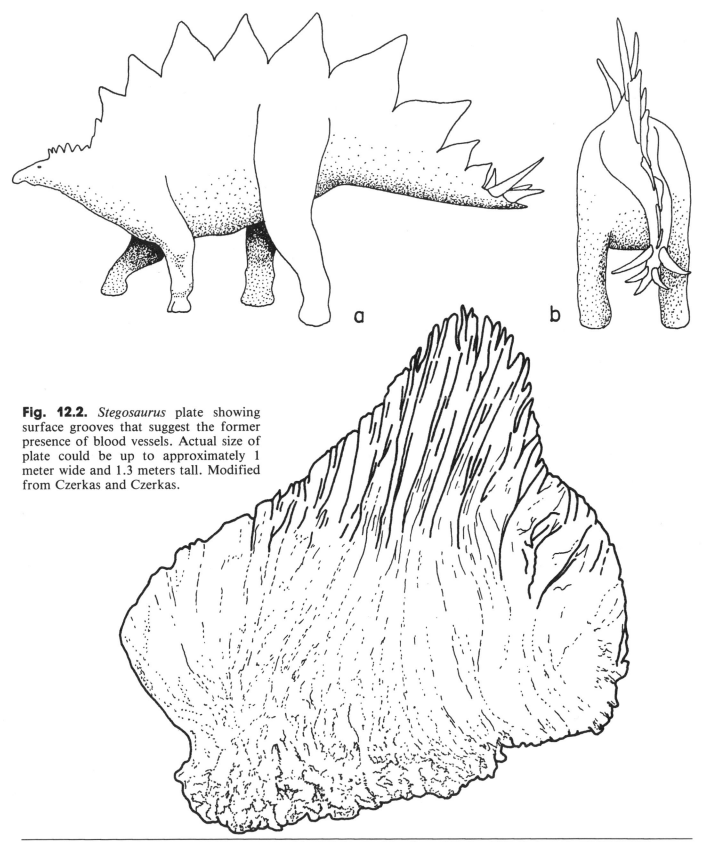

a

b

Fig. 12.2. *Stegosaurus* plate showing surface grooves that suggest the former presence of blood vessels. Actual size of plate could be up to approximately 1 meter wide and 1.3 meters tall. Modified from Czerkas and Czerkas.

Fig. 12.3. Assembly instructions for the activity on solar heating and blood circulation.

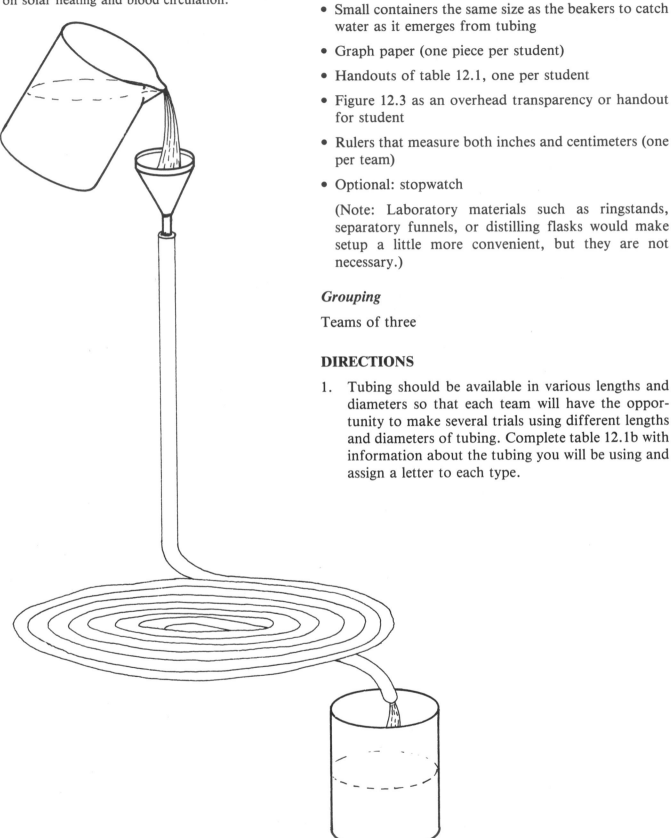

- Thermometers (one per team)

- Small containers the same size as the beakers to catch water as it emerges from tubing

- Graph paper (one piece per student)

- Handouts of table 12.1, one per student

- Figure 12.3 as an overhead transparency or handout for student

- Rulers that measure both inches and centimeters (one per team)

- Optional: stopwatch

  (Note: Laboratory materials such as ringstands, separatory funnels, or distilling flasks would make setup a little more convenient, but they are not necessary.)

Grouping

Teams of three

DIRECTIONS

1. Tubing should be available in various lengths and diameters so that each team will have the opportunity to make several trials using different lengths and diameters of tubing. Complete table 12.1b with information about the tubing you will be using and assign a letter to each type.

Table 12.1

NAME_____ PERIOD_____ DATE _____

Other team members_____

TABLE 12.1a

tubing type	outside diameter in.	outside diameter mm.	inside diameter in.	inside diameter mm.	description
A					
B					
C					
D					
E					

TABLE 12.1b

Trial	water temperature starting °F	°C	ending °F	°C	change °F	°C	tubing type see below	length of tubing in.	cm.	volume of water oz.	ml.	flow time sec.
1												
2												
3												
4												
5												
6												
7												
8												
9												
10												

2. Have each team obtain the following:

> water
>
> funnel
>
> 2 containers
>
> selected piece of tubing
>
> thermometer
>
> 3 pieces of graph paper
>
> 3 copies of table 12.1

3. Set the equipment up as shown in figure 12.3, coiling the tubing as tightly as possible. Note: for the activity to work effectively, the tubing must be as hot as possible.

4. The team should have a holder/pourer (who is responsible for holding up the funnel and tubing and pouring water into the funnel), a temperature taker (responsible for setup and reading the temperature of the water before it enters the tubing and after it exits the tubing), and a recorder (who must measure the tubing and record data on table 12.1a). Each member of the team will rotate through all positions during the trials.

5. Table 12.1a should be filled in with data collected as each trial is completed.

6. Data from table 12.1a can be graphed in many different ways:

> temperature change vs. tubing length
>
> temperature change vs. tubing diameter
>
> temperature change vs. tubing thickness

7. If a stopwatch is available, fluid flow rates can also be examined and related to tubing dimensions and temperature increases.

EXTENSIONS

1. Many mathematical relationships can be examined in the heating process. If the tubing doubles in diameter, does it carry twice the liquid? Does thin tubing heat more efficiently? What are the implications for *Stegosaurus*? Does the evidence suggest it had many small blood vessels or only a few large vessels? Which system would provide better heat collection and distribution? Does the thickness of the rubber of the tubing make any difference? Would clear tubing (like that used in fish tanks) work as well? Why or why not?

2. This activity might be used as a springboard to examine solar collectors. Students can be asked to research the materials and methods used in solar collectors. How are they similar to or different from those found in *Stegosaurus*? Using the type of materials listed in this activity, ask students to build a model of a device to heat water for a backyard swimming pool using solar power only. Plans for small model solar collectors are available in many science activity books such as Megan Stine *et al.*, *Smithsonian Institution Science Activity Book* (New York: GMG, 1987).

3. Recent work using isotopes shows that the difference between the temperature of the core of the body (measurable in the armpits and mouth) and extremities (surfaces of the fingers) is much greater in cold-blooded reptiles than in warm-blooded animals. Using thermometers, student teams can determine differences in their own core and surface temperatures. Veterinarians or zoos might be contacted to provide information about cold-blooded animals.

4. "Fins" of aluminum foil placed in a container of water so they stick up above its surface can be used to model *Stegosaurus* plates. If hot water is placed in the container, the fins should radiate heat and increase the rate of cooling. If the container is placed in the sun and filled with cold water, the fins should provide heating. Experimentation will be necessary to find the most efficient shape of container and shape and material of fins.

5. Through an activity in *The Big Beast Book* Jerry Booth (1988) examines one of the advantages of dinosaur size (the larger the animal the slower body heat is lost).

★ ★ ★

REFERENCES

Booth, Jerry. 1988. *The Big Beast Book: Dinosaurs and How They Got That Way*. Boston: Little, Brown.

SUGGESTED READING

Benton, Michael J. *On the Trail of the Dinosaurs*. New York: Crown, 1989.

Czerkas, Sylvia J., and Stephen A. Czerkas. *Dinosaurs: A Global View*. New York: Mallard Press, 1991.

Norman, David. *The Illustrated Encyclopedia of Dinosaurs*. New York: Crown, 1985.

Storey, Kenneth B., and Janet M. Storey. "Frozen and Alive." *Science* 255, no. 9 (1990): 92-97.

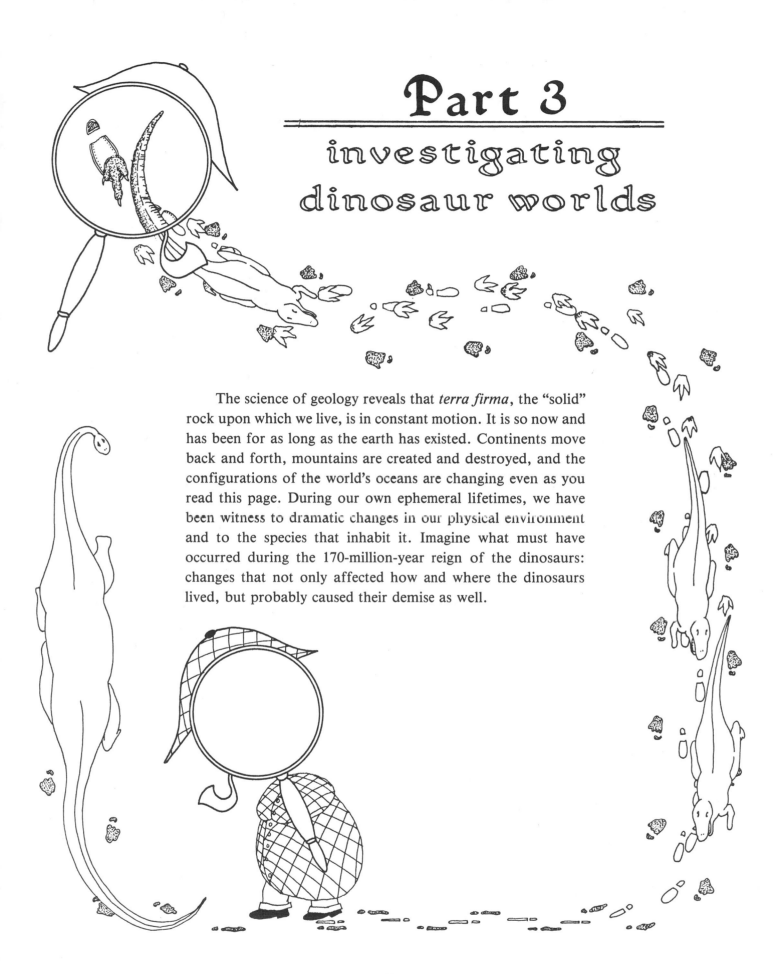

Part 3

investigating dinosaur worlds

The science of geology reveals that *terra firma*, the "solid" rock upon which we live, is in constant motion. It is so now and has been for as long as the earth has existed. Continents move back and forth, mountains are created and destroyed, and the configurations of the world's oceans are changing even as you read this page. During our own ephemeral lifetimes, we have been witness to dramatic changes in our physical environment and to the species that inhabit it. Imagine what must have occurred during the 170-million-year reign of the dinosaurs: changes that not only affected how and where the dinosaurs lived, but probably caused their demise as well.

its age is relative

13 We know that dinosaurs existed on earth for approximately 165 million years, and we also know that all dinosaurs did not live at the same time. Species appeared, others became extinct, and new ones filled their niche. In short, some dinosaurs were older than others. Relative age compares the age of one thing against the age of another; it does not provide a specific span of time. The actual age is not being discussed, so it is not known whether the objects are 25 years old or 125 million years old, only that one is older or younger than the other. When students line up according to height, they are arranged by relative size. Their actual heights have not been measured, but it is still possible to state that one student is taller or shorter than another.

★ ★ ★

ACTIVITY: RELATIVE MEASUREMENT

Ask students to line up by height to demonstrate relative size. Explain that heights have not been measured, so that absolute, or actual, heights are not known. They are now arranged by relative height: each student is taller or shorter than the one next to him or her. *Relative* means that one is being compared to another. Next, arrange students by relative age, using their birth dates. Again explain that they do not know how old each student is, only that he or she is older than the person on one side and younger than the person on the other.

★ ★ ★

When geologists examine rock layers that are close to one another, it is generally easy to determine which is older or younger from the self-evident *law of superposition*. This law states that in a normally deposited sequence of rock layers, each layer is older than the one immediately above. Imagine a stack of books on a desk. The book resting on the desk had to have been placed there first, so it is the "oldest." It has been there longer than the book that rests on top of it. The "youngest" book, therefore, sits on top of the stack. In general, the oldest layer of the sequence is on the bottom and the youngest on the top.

This system works well when all the layers can be seen touching one another. What happens, however, if there is a need to compare the layers in New York with those in, let's say, California, or even further afield, in Europe? Seeing where the layers touch becomes difficult or impossible, so the geologist needs additional information. The additional information comes in the form of fossils—not just any fossils, but unique types called *index fossils*.

Consider the clam, or pelecypod. Clams live in only a certain natural environment: shallow water. You never find a clam naturally occurring in a forest. Clams have existed on earth for almost 500 million years, the first ones appearing long before dinosaurs ever evolved. Trying to use the presence of clam fossils to help separate the layers of sediment that were deposited in shallow water would be impossible because clams would appear in all of them. On the basis of clam fossils, you would not be able to determine which specific layer you were looking at and, therefore, which layer was older or younger than the one next to it. The only thing a clam fossil would tell you is that the rock layer in which it was found was deposited in shallow water. But what if there were a very special clam that had some unique feature different from all other clams? And what if that clam lived all over the world at only a certain time in geologic history? Now, whenever you found that unique clam fossil you would know you were examining the same rock layer, and the layer immediately above it would be younger than the layer immediately below it. That special clam is an index fossil, and there are many different types of these. An index fossil can be thought of as something that occurs only during, and therefore identifies, a particular time span, is easily recognizable, and is widespread. A commemorative souvenir of the 1992 summer Olympics in Barcelona, for example, could serve as an "index fossil," provided the souvenir was buried at the time of the games: Such souvenirs are found worldwide, are easily recognizable, and represent a particular event. By comparing the index fossil clam to other index fossils, it is possible to determine which layers around the world are the same and, finally, which are older or younger than others.

✮ ✮ ✮

ACTIVITY: HOW DO THEY CONNECT?

Knowing there is a sequence of rock layers in one place and a similar sequence of rock layers somewhere else does not allow a scientist to say with certainty which layers are the same or which are the oldest or youngest. It is the index fossils within those layers that indicate to scientists which layers are the same. Unless the sequence has somehow been overturned by tectonic activity, the older fossils will be found below the younger ones. In this activity students will use index fossils to see which layers correlate and, ultimately, to determine the age sequence of the layers.

REQUIREMENTS

Time

45-90 minutes

Materials

For each student:

- Copies of figures 13.1 through 13.3

- Drawing pencil with eraser

- 2 colored pencils

Grouping

Individuals

DIRECTIONS

1. Distribute copies of figure 13.1, page 158, to students. The two columns represent sequential layers of rocks in two different parts of the world: New England and the British Isles (point these out on a map or globe). The geology of both of these areas is similar in many ways and provides a source of evidence for plate tectonics and the theory that the continents of Europe and North America were once joined.

2. Tell students their job is to show which layers from New England correlate with, or are the same as, the appropriate layers in the British Isles. Have them take one of their colored pencils and connect the layers as they think appropriate and determine the age sequence of the layers. Students may be frustrated by this because there is so much uncertainty, but that is precisely the point! With the information they have available, it is impossible to determine the age sequence of the layers and, in all probability, they will arrive at different answers. At this point they cannot determine the correct answer. On the back of figure 13.1, have them list (by alphabet letter) the sequential age of the rock layers. The youngest layer should be at the top, the oldest at the bottom. If two layers are the same age, connect them with a hyphen as follows:

   A - H

   B - J

   C - K

   D - L

   E - M

   F - N

   G - P

   Because the students are bound to ask, letters *I* and *O* were purposely omitted to avoid confusion with the numerals 1 and 0.

3. List the different age sequences determined by the students on the board or an overhead transparency for all to see. Discuss the differences with the class. As long as the law of superposition is adhered to, any interpretation is valid; the older layer is always below. In the natural world this can be complicated when layers are turned upside-down by tectonic activity; for purposes of this activity, no such complications exist.

4. Ask students what would help them determine which layers are the same. Answers might include being able to follow the sequential layers from one place to another. Hopefully, someone will suggest finding the same plants or animals in the same layer.

Fig. 13.1. Blank columns of rock strata for students to correlate.

NAME_____ PERIOD_____DATE_____

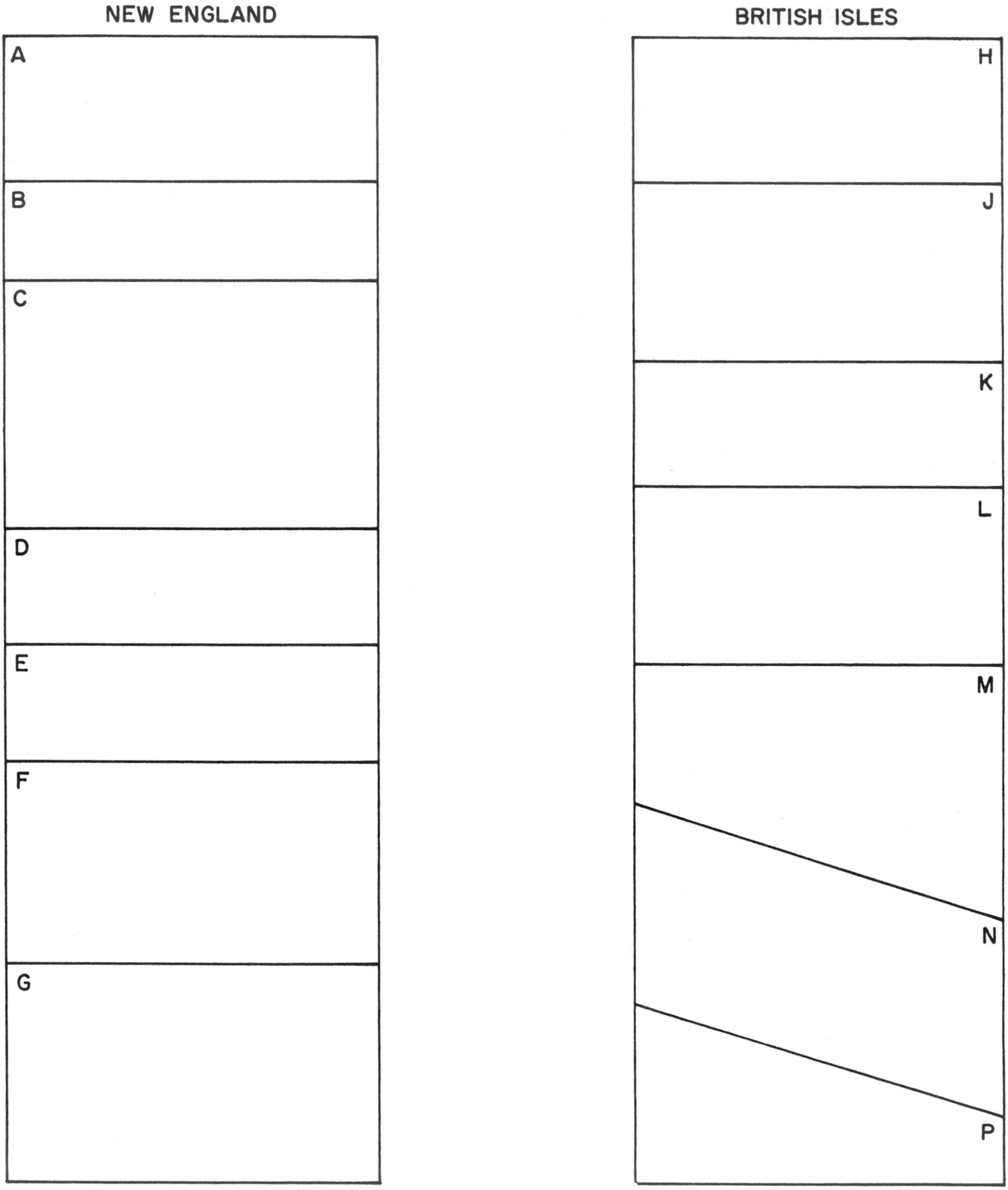

NEW ENGLAND

A
B
C
D
E
F
G

BRITISH ISLES

H
J
K
L
M
N
P

5. Introduce the concept of index fossils, emphasizing that they are different from other fossils.

6. Give students copies of figure 13.2, page 160. Ask them not to write on the handouts. Tell them figure 13.2 shows the index fossils found in these rock layers.

7. Students should determine which fossils are found in which layer(s) and draw the fossil(s) in the appropriate layer(s) on figure 13.1.

8. Once the fossils are all drawn, the students should use a different color to correlate the layers. Again, on the back of figure 13.1 they should list the age sequence of the layers next to the original sequence they made. Students should now all have the same sequence. The correct sequence follows:

A

B - H

C - J

D - K

E - L

M

F - N

G - P

Layer G - P is the oldest, and layer A is the youngest. Some layers are not continuous from one sequence to the other because they might never have been deposited or because they have been worn away by erosion. Without the fossils, the correlations would have been impossible to determine.

Figure 13.3, page 161, is the completed diagram showing all the fossils and the correct correlation based upon the fossils. It can be prepared as an overhead transparency for class discussion.

EXTENSIONS

1. Ask students to think about what future "index fossils" might be for different periods in history. An "index fossil" for the 1950s might be the hula hoop, for the 1980s, a souvenir from a particular rock music group or a particular Nintendo game. This project might include library research (old magazines, catalogs) or discussions with parents or grandparents. Period or historical photographs can also be considered.

2. The science of examining rock layers is called *stratigraphy*, a discipline of geological science that developed in Europe in the late eighteenth and early nineteenth centuries. Advanced classes could study the development of the worldwide rock sequences that are now recognized.

3. Universities and local geographic or geological societies should be able to provide information about the stratigraphy in your area. Field trip opportunities are often included.

(Text continues on page 162.)

Fig. 13.2. Index fossil data showing the fossils and the layers of rock in figure 13.1 in which they are found.

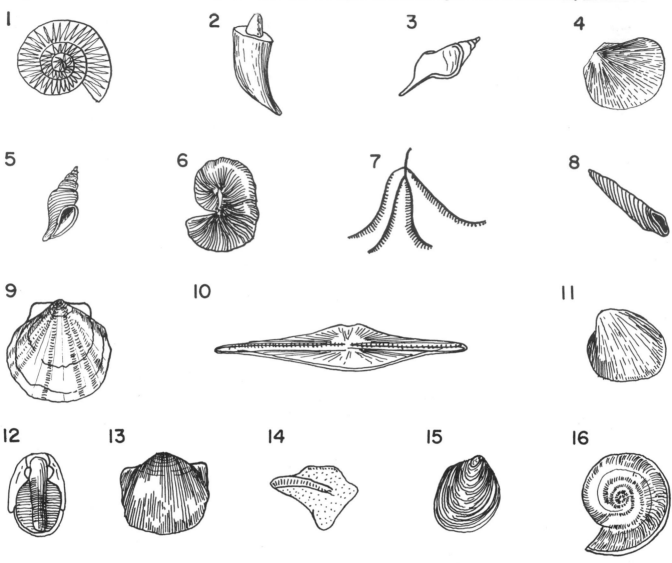

INDEX FOSSIL NUMBER	FOUND ONLY IN LAYER LETTER(S)	INDEX FOSSIL NUMBER	FOUND ONLY IN LAYER LETTER(S)
1	D, K	9	A
2	M	10	F, N
3	B, H	11	H
4	E, L	12	G, P
5	A	13	M
6	C	14	N
7	G	15	C, J
8	D, K	16	L

Fig. 13.3. Columns of rock strata as they should be completed by students to show index fossils and correlation of layers.

NAME_____PERIOD_____DATE_____

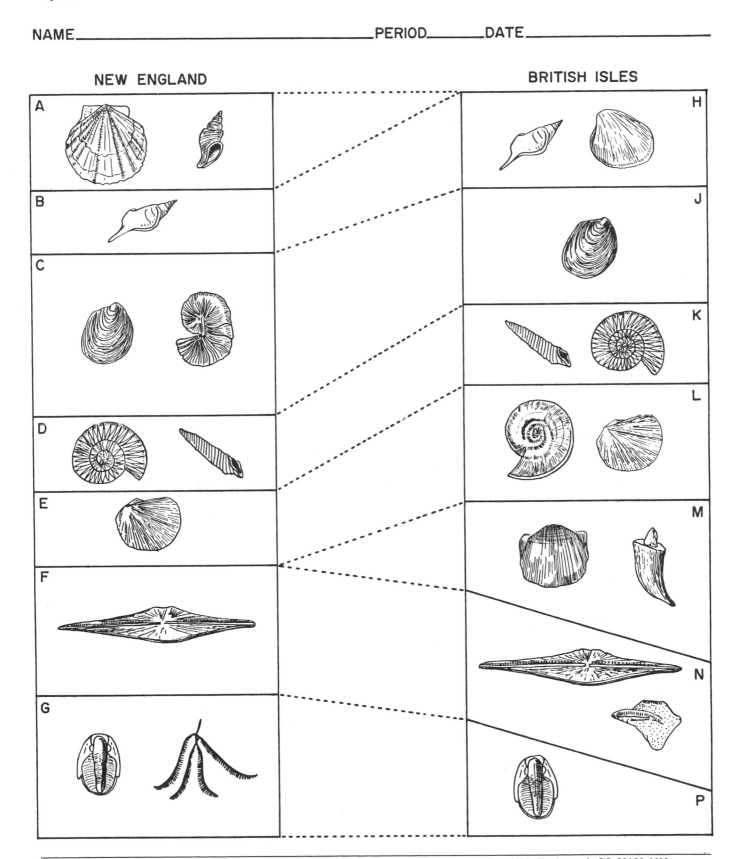

NEW ENGLAND

BRITISH ISLES

SUGGESTED READING

Dunbar, Carl O., and John Rodgers. *Principles of Stratigraphy*. New York: John Wiley and Sons, 1957.

Moore, Raymond C., Cecil G. Lalicker, and Alfred G. Fischer. *Invertebrate Fossils*. New York: McGraw-Hill, 1952.

Newman, William L. *Geologic Time*. Denver, Colo.: U.S. Geological Survey, 1991.

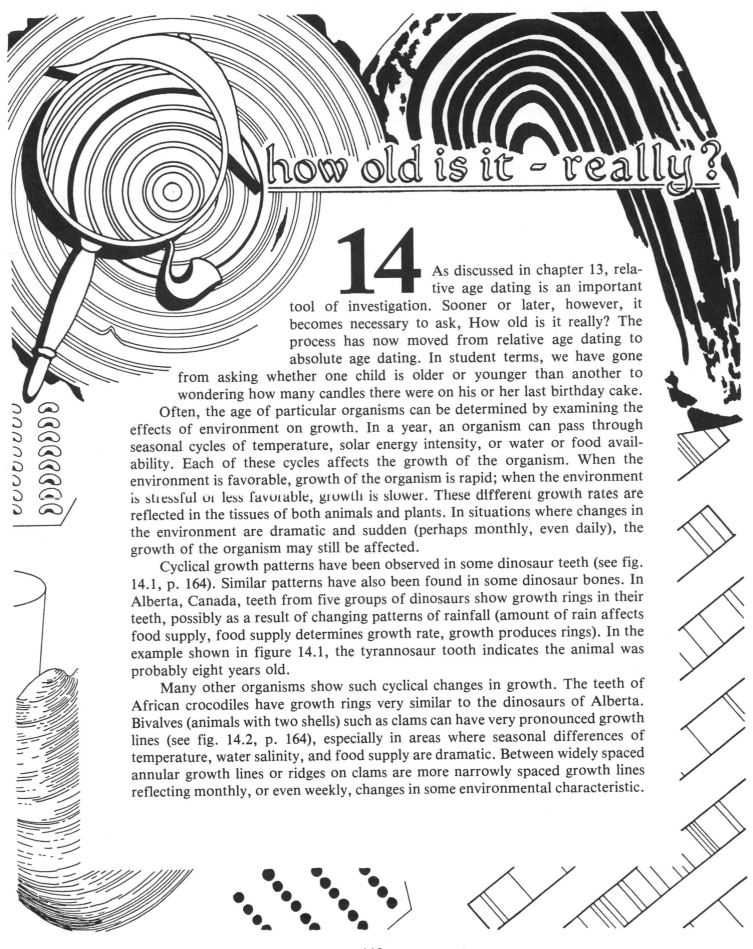

how old is it - really?

14

As discussed in chapter 13, relative age dating is an important tool of investigation. Sooner or later, however, it becomes necessary to ask, How old is it really? The process has now moved from relative age dating to absolute age dating. In student terms, we have gone from asking whether one child is older or younger than another to wondering how many candles there were on his or her last birthday cake.

Often, the age of particular organisms can be determined by examining the effects of environment on growth. In a year, an organism can pass through seasonal cycles of temperature, solar energy intensity, or water or food availability. Each of these cycles affects the growth of the organism. When the environment is favorable, growth of the organism is rapid; when the environment is stressful or less favorable, growth is slower. These different growth rates are reflected in the tissues of both animals and plants. In situations where changes in the environment are dramatic and sudden (perhaps monthly, even daily), the growth of the organism may still be affected.

Cyclical growth patterns have been observed in some dinosaur teeth (see fig. 14.1, p. 164). Similar patterns have also been found in some dinosaur bones. In Alberta, Canada, teeth from five groups of dinosaurs show growth rings in their teeth, possibly as a result of changing patterns of rainfall (amount of rain affects food supply, food supply determines growth rate, growth produces rings). In the example shown in figure 14.1, the tyrannosaur tooth indicates the animal was probably eight years old.

Many other organisms show such cyclical changes in growth. The teeth of African crocodiles have growth rings very similar to the dinosaurs of Alberta. Bivalves (animals with two shells) such as clams can have very pronounced growth lines (see fig. 14.2, p. 164), especially in areas where seasonal differences of temperature, water salinity, and food supply are dramatic. Between widely spaced annular growth lines or ridges on clams are more narrowly spaced growth lines reflecting monthly, or even weekly, changes in some environmental characteristic.

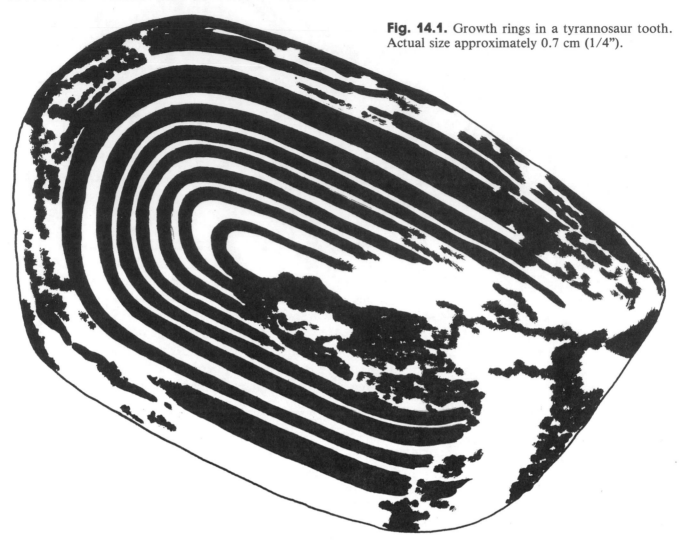

Fig. 14.1. Growth rings in a tyrannosaur tooth. Actual size approximately 0.7 cm (1/4").

Fig. 14.2. Growth patterns on a bivalve shell. This is a common clam, *Venus mercenaria*. Modified from Moore, Lalicker, and Fischer.

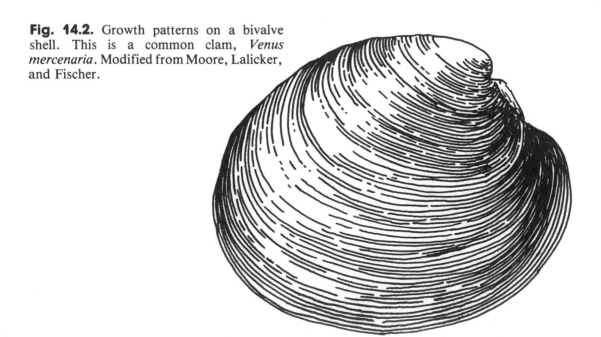

Horns of sheep and antelope show annual rings resulting from growth during only one season. Probably the most well-known example of cyclical tissue growth is tree rings. Their study is called *dendrochronology*. Cross sections of the trunk can be cut from dead trees, but live trees require more careful treatment. A thin cylinder (3/16" [4.5 mm]—about as thick as macaroni) is cut and removed from the tree by a special boring instrument that leaves the tree undamaged.

Like the dinosaurs and crocodiles, the growth of trees is affected by many environmental conditions. When conditions are favorable during the spring (plenty of water and sunlight), trees grow rapidly and produce a wide, light-colored ring. As water supplies become short, temperatures rise, and the trees are under stress (during the summer), the bands become narrower and darker. A year is represented by a combination of one light and one dark band. Because the present year is known, it is a simple matter to count the bands of the tree inward from the bark to determine the absolute age of the tree (see fig. 14.3).

Fig. 14.3. Cross section of a tree showing growth rings and what a sample and enlarged core would look like.

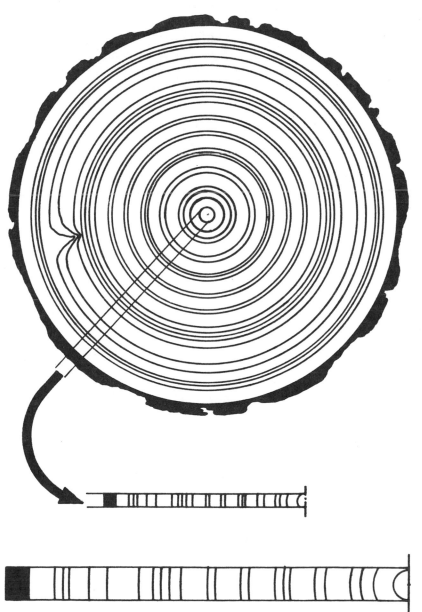

All factors affecting the growth of trees are recorded in its rings: climatic variation, forest fires, landslides (causing the trees to tilt), floods, hurricanes, and man's activities. (Some of these events of relatively short duration may cause a short-term change in growth and thus create a tree ring, which can complicate the annual dating pattern.) It is possible to determine when ancient civilizations cut trees down for use in their homes. Because the rings represent both time and environment, a history of the area in which a tree grew can be determined. By combining the evidence from many different trees, a history covering a large area and long time period can be uncovered. In California, for example, a continuous chronology has been determined for the past 7,507 years.

★ ★ ★

ACTIVITY: IT'S WRITTEN IN THE TREES

Each sample of the rings of a tree reveals history (droughts, forest fires) recorded while that tree was alive. As trees die and new trees grow, comparing samples taken from one tree with those from others (a process called cross-dating) allows the reconstruction of a history spanning a much greater time period than one tree could reveal. For example, four successive drought years would be recorded in a tree by four very close growth rings. A tree that died immediately after that fourth dry year would have those four close rings near the bark, on the outside. A tree which began to grow just prior to the dry years would have the four closely spaced rings near the center. By comparing samples from the two trees and matching the ring patterns of the four drought years, the history recorded in the rings of the two trees can be added together to make a continuous time line (see fig. 14.4). Figure 14.4 shows tree rings from two trees, each of which is less than 20 years old, yet cross-dating of the two samples allows construction of a 33-year history. This same procedure makes it possible to determine when log cabins were built in a forest.

In the following activity, students will use cross-dating to complete an almost-200-year history of the area from which these (fictional) tree samples were taken.

Fig. 14.4. Two cores from different trees showing how cross-dating can be used to create a time span greater than that represented by a single tree.

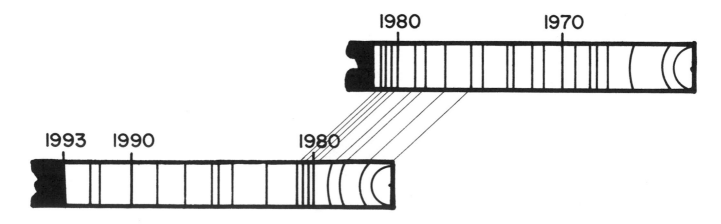

REQUIREMENTS

Time

45-90 minutes

Materials

Per pair:

- Scissors
- Handouts of figures 14.5 and 14.6
- Clear tape for each team
- Paper adding machine tape (48"/120 cm)
- Small metric/English ruler

Grouping

Pairs (may also be done individually)

DIRECTIONS

1. Make certain the students understand the technique of cross-dating. Use an overhead transparency of figures 14.3 and 14.4 to help clarify any questions they may have.

2. Divide the class into pairs.

3. Each pair should have scissors, tape, a copy of figures 14.5 and 14.6 and adding machine tape.

4. Explain to the class that figure 14.5, page 168, represents samples taken from 10 trees in a forest. Discuss with them which sample is the oldest (the innermost, which has the small circle to the right) and the youngest (the outermost, which has the bark at the far left). The date at the inner edge of the bark is 1993.

5. Tell the class they are research scientists studying this forest, and they must reconstruct the history of the area by cross-dating the tree-ring samples.

6. To construct their time line, they must cut apart the samples, correlate them correctly, tape them to each other (one above the other like stairs) so that the matching tree rings can be seen, and then tape them to the adding-machine tape. **(FOR TEACHER INFORMATION: THE CORRECT SEQUENCE OF RECONSTRUCTION IS [OLDEST TO YOUNGEST] B, E, H, C, J, G, D, I, A, F.)**

7. When the time line is completed, have students answer the following questions:

   a. The two blackened areas represent burned parts of the trees caused by forest fires. In what years did the forest fires occur? **(ANSWERS: 1907, 1834)**

   b. Closely spaced lines indicate years of stress, such as drought, for the trees. In what periods were there four or more consecutive years of drought? **(ANSWERS: 1945-1948, 1913-1917, 1855-1860, 1836-1839, 1826-1829, 1815-1819, 1801-1804)**

   c. How many years are represented by the time line? **(ANSWER: 193 years)**

Fig. 14.5. Core samples taken from 10 trees to be used in cross-dating.

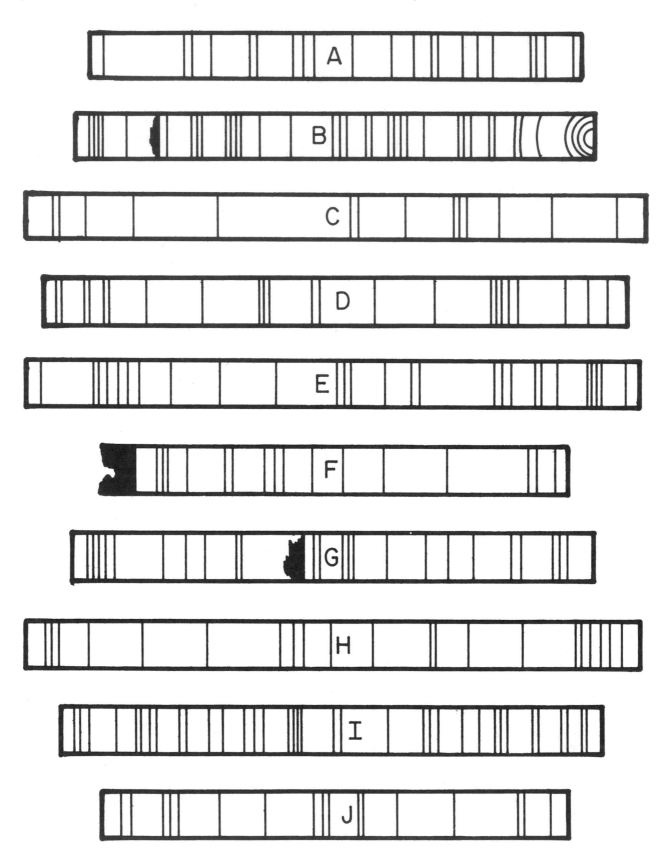

d. What is the diameter of the tree represented by your time line in inches and in centimeters? **(ANSWER: 91½"; 232 cm)**

e. In what year did the trees grow the most? **(ANSWER: 1878)**

f. Locate the year of your birth on the time line and mark it with a B.

g. Locate when your school building was constructed on the time line and mark it with an S.

h. Figure 14.6 is a sample taken from a log that formed part of the wall of an old cabin in the woods. When was that cabin built? **(ANSWER: 1847)**

Fig. 14.6. Tree-ring core sample from a log cabin wall.

i. Students have measured the radius and determined the diameter of the tree and know how old it is. Have them calculate the growth rate of the tree trunk in inches per year and centimeters per year. **(ANSWERS: 0.47" per year; 1.2 cm per year)**

8. Evaluations may be done by displaying all time lines in the classroom and having students give each time line a grade (use the consensus), or the teacher may give each a grade.

EXTENSIONS

1. Students may be given time outside the classroom to research dates to add to their time line. Individuals or teams may be assigned specific topics, such as world, American, or state history; sports; scientific discoveries; or famous inventions. Appropriate illustrations would enhance the completed time line.

2. If available, actual tree cross sections would be wonderful to use as an introduction to the activity. Firewood suppliers are an excellent source of small logs that can be cut into slices for student samples. A generous technical arts staff might be persuaded to do the cutting.

3. An excellent resource for tree-ring information is the Laboratory of Tree Ring Research, University of Arizona, Tucson, AZ 85721.

★ ★ ★

Annual growth rings and lines are found not only in living organisms. In northern climates, abundant water present during the summer carries a mix of sediment (sand, silt, and clay) that ultimately settles on lake bottoms. During the winter, when the lakes are frozen, only very fine, darker colored material slowly settles to the lake bottom. The two different layers (coarser on the bottom, fine at the top) represent an annular cycle and are called *varves*. Studies in Scandinavia based on varves date the presence of the last glacier in southern Sweden at 13,500 years ago. Similar studies in Wyoming determined that a lake existed there for between 5 and 8 million years. Varves can only be used in local areas, and attempting to determine the age of something very old, like the earth, would be impossible using such a method.

Over the centuries, the determination of the age of the earth has generated a great deal of interest from both the scientific and religious communities. The methods used to date our planet analyze ocean salinity, loss of heat from the earth's interior, total thickness of the rocks around the world, radioactive decay, and biblical accounts of generations. Not unexpectedly, calculated ages of the earth varied, as is shown in table 14.1:

Table 14.1

Estimator	Date	Method	Estimated Age (in Years)
Archbishop Usher	1650	Bible/begats	6,000
Haughton	1878	thicknesses of rocks	200 million
Walcott	1893	heat flow	27.6 million
Lord Kelvin	1897	heat flow	20-40 million
Goodchild	1897	heat flow	704 million
Halley/Joly	1898	sea salt	250 million
Sollas	1900	heat flow	18.3 million

In the seventeenth century, the Bible was considered the preeminent authority on the world. It was logical, therefore, to use the Bible to determine the absolute age of the earth. Such an approach was taken by James Usher, archbishop of the Anglican Church of Armagh, Ireland, in 1650. His method of calculation is described in the following excerpt from *Inherit the Wind* by Jerome Lawrence and Robert E. Lee (1955, 85), in which Matthew Harrison Brady (a biblical scholar and prosecuting attorney based on William Jennings Bryant) is being questioned by Henry Drummond (an agnostic and defense attorney based on Clarence Darrow). It is 1925 in Dayton, Tennessee, at the trial of Betram Cates (based on John Thomas Scopes, the high school biology teacher who was placed on trial for violation of the Butler Act, a Tennessee law prohibiting the teaching in public schools of anything but the biblical account of man's creation). Having been denied permission to present scientific expertise to plead his case, Drummond turns to an incisive examination of the biblical scholar:

Brady

That rock is not more than six thousand years old.

Drummond

How do you know?

Brady

A fine Biblical scholar, Bishop Usher, has determined for us the exact date and hour of the Creation. It occurred in the year 4004, B.C.

Drummond

That's Bishop Usher's opinion.

Brady

It is not an opinion. It is literal fact, which the good Bishop arrived at through careful computation of the ages of the prophets as set down in the Old Testament. In fact, he determined that the Lord began the Creation on the 23rd [sometimes given as the 26th or 21st] of October in the Year 4004 B.C. at ... 9 A.M.!

Drummond

That Eastern Standard Time? Or Rocky Mountain Time? It wasn't daylight-saving time, was it? Because the Lord didn't make the sun until the fourth day!

Inherit the Wind is available in paperback. It was first presented as a play in 1955. The movie version of the play is available on videocassette, and television dramas were presented in 1965 and 1988. Some of the material presented in the play, book, movie, and television drama may be beyond the scope of fourth- to sixth-graders. The trial concerns the still-controversial issue of creationism versus evolution. In the mid-1980s for example, fundamentalists filed suit against the state of Tennessee because children in public schools were not being given the opportunity to learn creationism: apparently, the arguments have come full circle. Depending upon their potential market, textbooks often address the evolution/creation issues in different ways. Student comparisons of textbook approaches to the problem could generate classroom debates or creative writing exercises. Additionally, students could review magazine and newspaper articles about the evolution/creation debate.

The method commonly used today to determine the age of the earth is called *radiometric age dating* because of the use of the radioactive ("radio-") decay of certain elements to measure ("-metric") the passage of time. Consequently, absolute age dating is often used synonymously with radiometric age dating. *Radiometric* dating is often (and erroneously) used synonymously with *radiocarbon* dating. The former is the general term for using any radioactive element to measure time; the latter is used to describe the use of only radioactive carbon to measure time. Many other elements, in addition to carbon, are used.

In 1896 Henri Becquerel, a French scientist, discovered that naturally occurring elements (specifically, uranium) give off particles or rays. In so doing, he discovered radioactivity. As particles are given off from the original atoms, they change or decay into slightly different atoms called *isotopes*.

Atoms decay at different rates, and those differing rates of decay provide a means to obtain absolute ages for many objects. Atoms with slow rates of decay permit absolute dating of very old materials, such as the oldest rocks on earth. Relatively rapid decay rates permit age determinations for younger materials, such as campfires of Stone Age civilizations.

Decay rates are compared by determining the *half-life*, that is, the time it takes for half the amount of one isotope (atoms of the same element with slightly different components of the nucleus) to decay to another isotope. For example, carbon-14 is formed in the earth's atmosphere and is absorbed by living trees. Once the tree dies, the carbon-14 is no longer formed and begins to decay to another isotope, carbon-12. It takes 5,730 years for half of the original carbon-14 to change to carbon-12. As the dead tree gets older, the amount of carbon-14 decreases and the amount of carbon-12 increases. By comparing the amounts of the two isotopes, the age of the dead tree can be determined. Table 14.2, page 172, lists half-lives of several radioactive isotopes:

Table 14.2

Element	Half-Life
oxygen-14	71.0 seconds
plutonium-246	10.9 days
cobalt-60	5.26 years
carbon-14	5,730 years
chlorine-36	310,000 years
potassium-40*	1.28 million years
uranium-235	710 million years
uranium-238	4.51 billion years
vanadium-50	6,000,000,000,000,000 years

* used to date dinosaurs

ACTIVITY: HALF-LIFE CAN TELL IT ALL

In this activity, which has four parts—acquiring data, recording data, graphing data, and interpreting data—students will grasp the concept and utility of half-life. For purposes of this activity, beans will represent radioactive isotopes, with Type A beans decaying to Type B beans with a half-life of 1,500 years. Students will determine the age of a "bone" by comparing the amount of an original element (Type A beans) to the amount of the element produced by its decay (Type B beans). The ratio of the two bean types is a direct function of the age of the "bone." In the data table, students will enter appropriate numbers as they proceed through the activity, then graph the results of the activity to better understand the behavior of the two elements.

REQUIREMENTS

Time

45 minutes

Materials

Per pair:

- 2 different kinds (or colors) of beans (32 of each)
- 3 small paper cups (preferably nonwaxed)
- Pencil and one dark-colored marker
- Handouts and overhead transparencies of figures 14.7 and 14.8, pages 173 and 174

Grouping

Pairs

Fig. 14.7. Data table and graph for using half-lives to determine age.

NAME_____ PERIOD_____ DATE_____

DATA TABLE

	TYPE A BEANS REMAINING	TYPE B BEANS REMAINING	NUMBER OF HALF-LIVES	CALCULATED AGE (YEARS)
LIVING ANIMAL	_____	_____	_____	_____
TRIAL 1	_____	_____	_____	_____
TRIAL 2	_____	_____	_____	_____
TRIAL 3	_____	_____	_____	_____
TRIAL 4	_____	_____	_____	_____
TRIAL 5	_____	_____	_____	_____
TRIAL 6	_____	_____	_____	_____

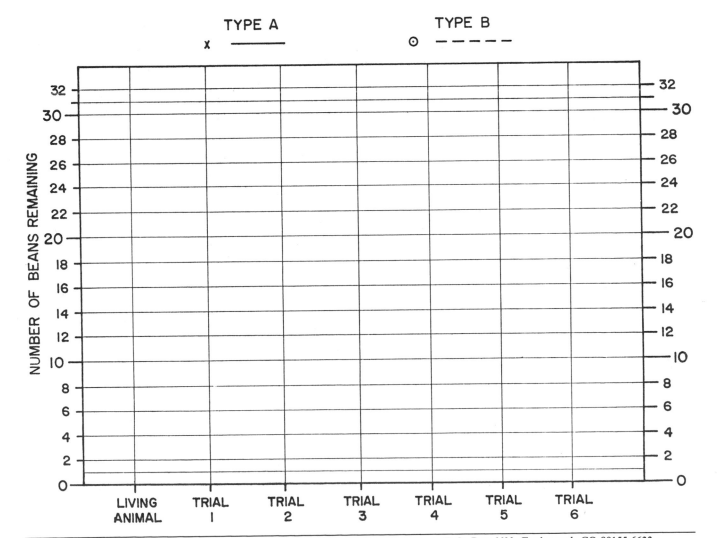

Fig. 14.8. Setup and procedures for simulating radioactive decay.

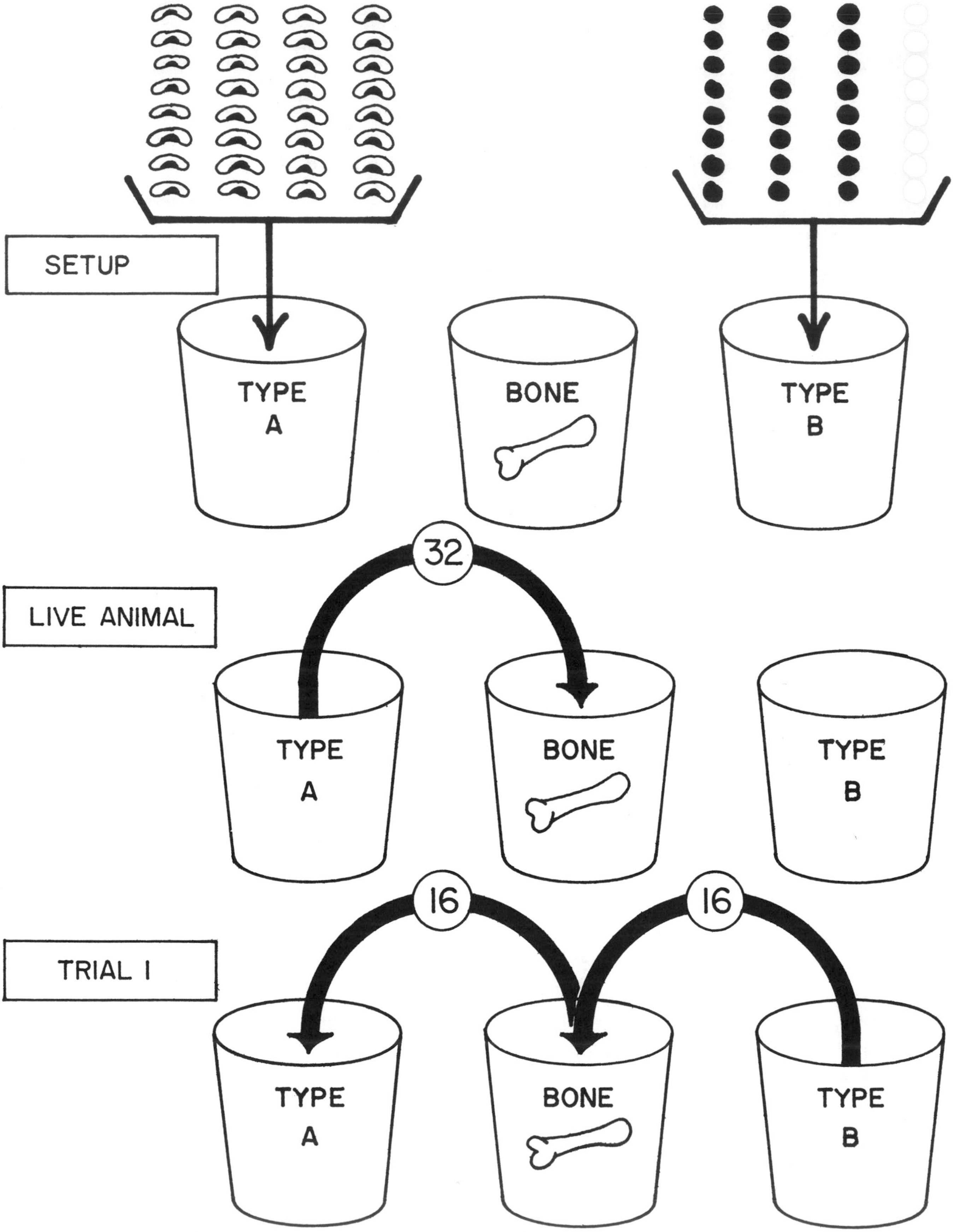

DIRECTIONS

1. Distribute both handouts and show overhead transparency of figure 14.7, explaining the data table and graph to students.

2. Label the paper cups as follows: "Type A," "Type B," and "BONE" (draw a bone on this cup).

3. Show overhead transparency of figure 14.8. Have each team put all beans of one kind in the cup marked "Type A" and all beans of the other variety in the cup marked "Type B" (see fig. 14.8, "Setup").

4. The living animal can only manufacture type A beans in its bones; move all 32 type A beans to the cup labeled "Bone" (see fig. 14.8, "Live Animal").

5. Fill in only the first three columns of the line "Living Animal" in the data table in figure 14.7 as follows: There are 32 type A beans remaining in the organism and zero type B beans. Because no decay or change of type A beans took place, no half-lives have passed; students should put a zero in the "Number of Half-Lives" column.

6. Tell students that the animal is now dead, and radioactive decay has begun. After each half-life, one half of the amount of the original element (type A beans) changes by radioactive decay to another element (type B beans). Each half-life reduction will be called a trial.

7. Trial 1 is the passage of one half-life; half of the type A beans have now decayed and changed into type B beans. Have students reflect this change by removing one half of the original 32 type A beans, placing them in the cup labeled "Type A" and replacing them in the cup marked "Bone" with the same number of type B beans (see fig. 14.8, "Trial 1"). At the conclusion of this trial, the "Bone" cup should still have 32 beans, but now there are 16 of type A and 16 of type B.

8. Students should now complete the first three columns of the "Trial 1" line of the data table in figure 14.7. (For teacher information, figure 14.9, page 176, shows a completed data table.)

9. Students should perform subsequent trials using the same procedures, replacing one half of the type A beans in the "Bone" cup with an equal number of type B beans, remembering that the number of total beans in the "Bone" cup must always be 32.

10. At the completion of each trial, students must complete the first three columns of the appropriate line on the data table.

11. Continue the process until trial 6 has been completed; the first three columns of the data table should now be completed. (You might want to collect the beans and cups now, rather than at the end of the lesson. Students will no longer need them, and the beans will be less likely to wander.)

12. Have students plot the "Living Animal" data on the graph, using the symbol for each bean type shown. Discuss with the students what the beginning points of each line should be: type A should begin at 32, type B at zero.

13. Discuss with students what they think the graph will look like when they plot each trial (remaining type A beans getting smaller and type B beans increasing; does the total number of beans change?).

14. Have students complete the graph using the data they entered on the data table.

Fig. 14.9. Figure 14.7 as it should look after completion by students.

NAME _____ PERIOD _____ DATE _____

DATA TABLE

	TYPE A BEANS REMAINING	TYPE B BEANS REMAINING	NUMBER OF HALF-LIVES	CALCULATED AGE (YEARS)
LIVING ANIMAL	32	0	0	NEW
TRIAL 1	16	16	1	1,500
TRIAL 2	8	24	2	3,000
TRIAL 3	4	28	3	4,500
TRIAL 4	2	30	4	6,000
TRIAL 5	1	31	5	7,500
TRIAL 6	½	31½	6	9,000

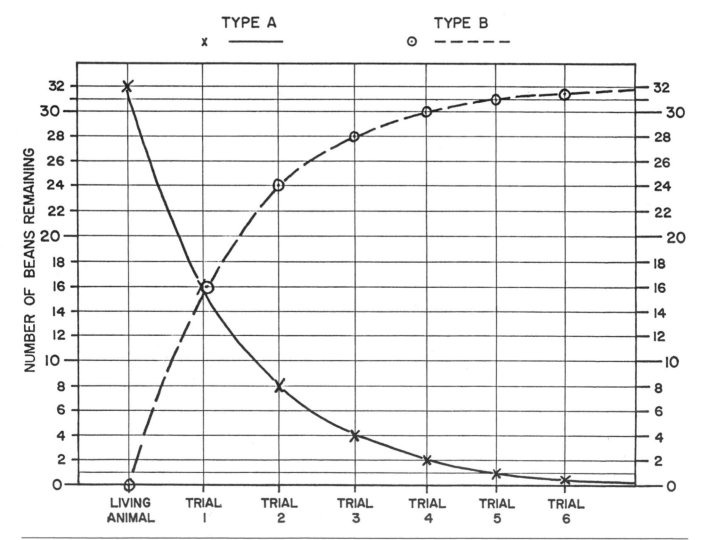

15. Discuss with the students what would happen with additional trials. Would they ever get zero type A beans (the original element)? (No.) If students have calculators, have them multiply 1/2 × 1/2, then 1/2 × the answer, and so on. They will obtain smaller and smaller numbers, but never zero. The fact that there is always some of the original type A element remaining allows very old objects to be dated.

16. Students can now determine the age of the "bone." The half-life of the original radioactive element (type A bean) has been determined to be 1,500 years.

17. Students should complete the last column of the data table. For purposes of this activity only one half of a type A bean has been determined to be remaining at the end of the trials. How old is the "bone"? **(ANSWER: 9,000 years)**

EXTENSIONS

1. Radioactivity has proven to be both a curse and a blessing for man. The class can be divided into groups to debate the virtues of radioactivity. Library resources could include periodical articles (the Chernobyl incident, new medical applications, nuclear power referenda, sterilization of dangerous insects to reduce populations), historical volumes (philosophical debates about the Manhattan Project by the scientists involved, aftermath of Hiroshima), and audiovisual materials. If many students will be researching the same project, both school and public libraries might be notified so that librarians can prepare completed searches for relevant articles, thus saving considerable frustration for students and wear and tear on librarians.

2. This activity can be made more complex by involving students in the study of an actual decay series (for instance, uranium-238 to lead-206) and the particles they generate.

3. Construction of a cloud chamber will allow students to actually "see" the radioactive particles being generated during the decay process. To make a classroom-type cloud chamber, place some alcohol and a radioactive source (such as radioactive earth or even the mantle of a Coleman gasoline lantern, which is impregnated with some radioactive material) in a container. Place the container on dry ice in a darkened room. The dry ice cools the alcohol vapor. When the radioactive source emits a particle, it travels through the vapor, leaving a small trail, like the vapor trail of a jet. If a flashlight is shined on the chamber, the trails are easily visible.

★ ★ ★

REFERENCES

Lawrence, Jerome, and Robert E. Lee. 1955. *Inherit the Wind*. New York: Bantam Books.

SUGGESTED READING

Andrews, J. T. "Recent and Fossil Growth Rates of Marine Bivalves, Canadian Arctic and Late Quaternary Arctic Marine Environments." *Paleogeography, Paleoclimatology, Paleoecology* 11 (1972): 157-176.

Curtis, Will. *The Nature of Things*. New York: ECCO Press, 1984.

Ferguson, C. W. "Concepts and Techniques of Dendrochronology." In *Scientific Methods in Medieval Archaeology*, edited by Rainer Berger. Berkeley, Calif.: University of California Press, 1970.

Harris, Miles F., Dale T. Hesser, J. Allen Hynek, William H. Matthews, III, Chalmer J. Roy, James W. Skehan, S.J., and Robert E. Stevenson. *Investigating the Earth*, 4th ed. Boston: Houghton Mifflin, 1973.

Holmes, Arthur. *Principles of Physical Geology*. New York: Ronald Press, 1965.

Lord, John. *Teaching About Energy*. Santa Monica, Calif.: Enterprise for Education, 1986.

Moore, Raymond C., Cecil G. Lalicker, and Alfred G. Fischer. *Invertebrate Fossils*. New York: McGraw-Hill, 1952.

Panati, Charles. *Panati's Extraordinary Endings of Practically Everything and Everybody*. New York: Harper & Row, 1989.

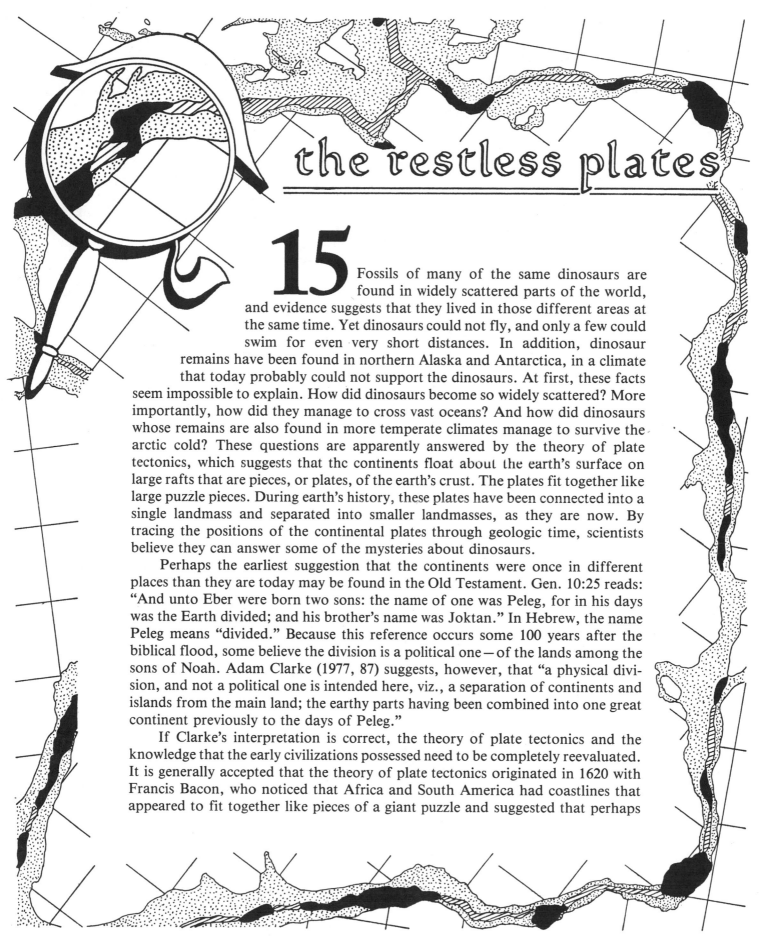

the restless plates

15 Fossils of many of the same dinosaurs are found in widely scattered parts of the world, and evidence suggests that they lived in those different areas at the same time. Yet dinosaurs could not fly, and only a few could swim for even very short distances. In addition, dinosaur remains have been found in northern Alaska and Antarctica, in a climate that today probably could not support the dinosaurs. At first, these facts seem impossible to explain. How did dinosaurs become so widely scattered? More importantly, how did they manage to cross vast oceans? And how did dinosaurs whose remains are also found in more temperate climates manage to survive the arctic cold? These questions are apparently answered by the theory of plate tectonics, which suggests that the continents float about the earth's surface on large rafts that are pieces, or plates, of the earth's crust. The plates fit together like large puzzle pieces. During earth's history, these plates have been connected into a single landmass and separated into smaller landmasses, as they are now. By tracing the positions of the continental plates through geologic time, scientists believe they can answer some of the mysteries about dinosaurs.

Perhaps the earliest suggestion that the continents were once in different places than they are today may be found in the Old Testament. Gen. 10:25 reads: "And unto Eber were born two sons: the name of one was Peleg, for in his days was the Earth divided; and his brother's name was Joktan." In Hebrew, the name Peleg means "divided." Because this reference occurs some 100 years after the biblical flood, some believe the division is a political one—of the lands among the sons of Noah. Adam Clarke (1977, 87) suggests, however, that "a physical division, and not a political one is intended here, viz., a separation of continents and islands from the main land; the earthy parts having been combined into one great continent previously to the days of Peleg."

If Clarke's interpretation is correct, the theory of plate tectonics and the knowledge that the early civilizations possessed need to be completely reevaluated. It is generally accepted that the theory of plate tectonics originated in 1620 with Francis Bacon, who noticed that Africa and South America had coastlines that appeared to fit together like pieces of a giant puzzle and suggested that perhaps the continents had moved. Even that hypothesis, however, could not have been arrived at without the mapping efforts of the earlier great navigators: Vasco da Gama, Vasco de Balboa, Eric the Red, Amerigo Vespucci, Henry Hudson, and Sir Francis Drake. Science evolves. Those navigators, in turn, could not have succeeded without the tools of navigation and the knowledge of oceanography developed by their predecessors in the ancient world of the Mediterranean and the Middle East.

Fig. 15.1. Map showing the fit of the continental landmasses of North America, South America, Africa, and Europe. Adapted from a computer-generated map by Sir Edward Bullard in 1969.

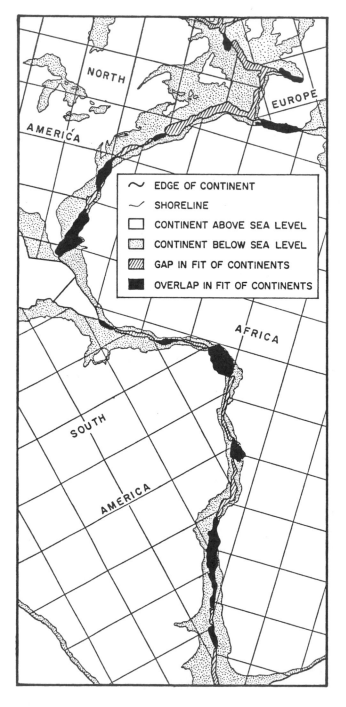

In the late 1800s an Austrian geologist noticed strong similarities in the rock sequences on different continents of the southern hemisphere, and he proposed that the lands of that hemisphere all once formed a single continent, Gondwanaland (named after a geological province in India). In 1908 American geologist F. B. Taylor first suggested a mechanism for movement of the continents. In 1910 Alfred Wegener went one step further. Based upon data from both fossils and rocks, he proposed that all continents were joined at one time as a single supercontinent called Pangea and discussed mechanisms by which the movement could have occurred. The debate about continental drift was off and running, and it continues today. In the 1960s and early 1970s, research done mainly in the ocean basins suggested that the continents themselves did not float around like rafts upon the earth's surface. Instead, the earth's outer layer (the crust) was broken into large plates, like a broken shell on the outside of an egg. The continents were part of those plates, which float upon an inner layer of the earth, sometimes separating, and sometimes colliding.

This new theory, the theory of plate tectonics, provided a great deal of excitement in the geological sciences. It not only suggested that the entire surface of the earth was in constant motion, but it incorporated volcanic activity, earthquakes, and the formation of mountain chains as well. Many details still need explanation (that is why it is still only a theory), but the theory of plate tectonics is widely accepted today.

Anyone looking at the Atlantic Ocean will sooner or later be struck by the fact that the bulge in the northeastern coastline of South America appears to fit nicely into the hollow of the coastline of the west coast of Africa (see fig. 15.1). When this proposed fit was rigorously examined, it was found to be fairly good, but not exact. The examination, which caused scientists to examine the edge of the continents, raised the question, "Where *is* the edge of the continent?" Maps and globes usually show the edge of the landmass where it contacts the ocean. That makes sense, except that sea level is not always the same. As the glaciers advanced across the continents tens of thousands of years ago, sea level was hundreds of feet lower than it is today. Does that mean the continents were much larger than they are today? As the sea rises and falls, does a continent become smaller or bigger? Scientists recognized that to examine how continents fit together, they would need to find a mappable, physical edge that did not depend upon the changing level of water in the ocean basins. The side of the continent is usually a gentle slope going from shallow water to the deeper water of the ocean basins (continental slope). Scientists generally agree that the actual edge of the continent occurs at the midpoint of this slope. The fit of the continents was fair when the shoreline of the continents was used but improved dramatically when the midpoint of the continental slope was used (see fig. 15.1). Figure 15.2 shows a cross section of the edge of a continent. Most exercises involving fitting pieces of the continental puzzle use the midpoint of the continental slope.

Fig. 15.2. Cross section of the edge of a continent or landmass showing how the edge is determined. Actual slopes are much gentler than those shown.

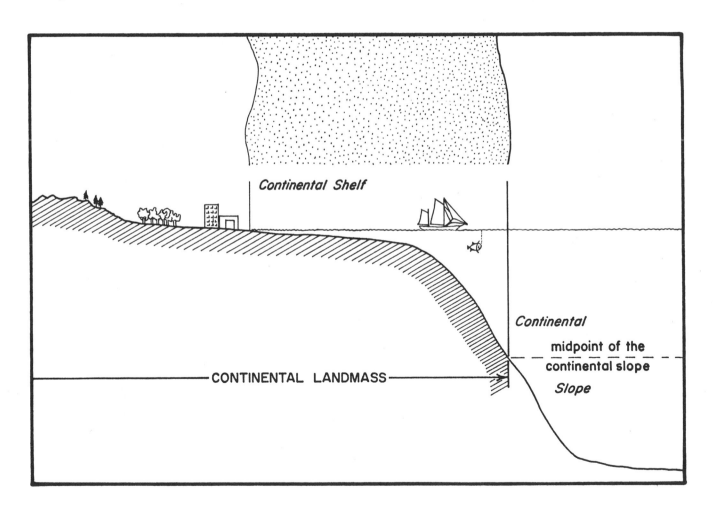

⊠ ⊠ ⊠

ACTIVITY: A 100-MILLION-YEAR-OLD PUZZLE

Dinosaurs are only one of the many sources of evidence suggesting the landmasses of the earth might have moved. Other evidence comes from the movements of glaciers in the southern hemisphere, the ages of groups of rocks in various places, fossils, and, of course, the physical fit of the continents. In this activity students will be able to incorporate the different types of evidence for plate movement to reconstruct how the earth may have appeared approximately 100 million years ago, during the Age of Reptiles, when the dinosaurs dominated the land areas of the earth.

REQUIREMENTS

Time

90-135 minutes

Materials

Per pair:

- Handouts of figures 15.3 and 15.4

- Figure 15.5 as an overhead transparency or as handouts for each team

- Scissors

- Clear tape or glue

- Globe or world map

- Letter-size envelope per team

Grouping

Pairs

DIRECTIONS

1. Introduce students to the concept of continental movement and plate tectonics by showing figure 15.1. Show the landmasses involved on a globe to indicate their present positions. Discuss the apparent fit of the four continents. Do they fit well? How can this fit be explained?

2. Distribute materials to students.

3. Figure 15.3 is a drawing of a blank globe. Have students hold it so the crossed lines are vertical and horizontal. What does the horizontal line represent (the equator, zero latitude)? If the drawing showed the Atlantic Ocean, what might the vertical line be (the Prime, or Greenwich, Meridian, zero longitude)?

4. Figure 15.4, page 184, is a drawing of all the large landmasses of the world and the way scientists think they appeared 100 million years ago. Have students cut around the outlines as closely as possible and put the pieces in the envelope as they complete cutting them.

5. Figure 15.5, page 185, is the legend explaining the symbols on figure 15.4. Students should refer to it as they complete the activity.

Fig. 15.3. Reference grid ("blank globe") upon which to assemble the landmasses in figure 15.4. The horizontal line is the equator and the vertical line is the Prime (Greenwich) Meridian.

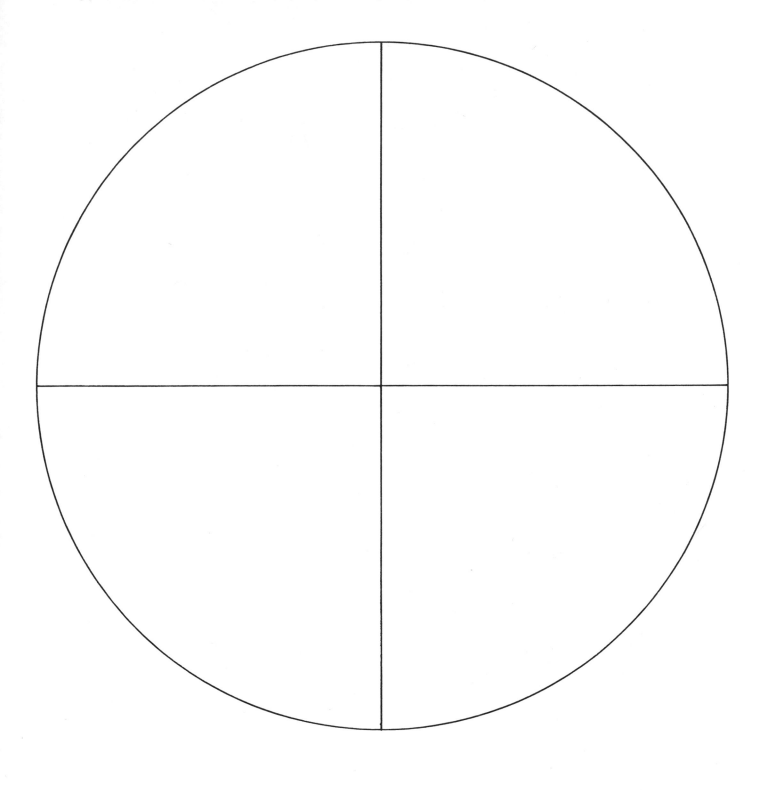

(Answer is on page 186.)

Fig. 15.4. Shape of the landmasses as they appeared approximately 100 million years ago. Adapted from Czerkas and Czerkas.

Fig. 15.5. Legend of symbols shown in figure 15.4.

①	South America	sauropods (if drawn as outline, presence is unconfirmed)	
②	Europe		
③	Africa	stegosaurs	
④	Greenland	lystrosaurs	
⑤	India	400	age of rocks (millions of years)
⑥	Madagascar		
⑦	North America	G	similar glacial deposits
⑧	Australia		direction of glacier movement
⑨	Asia		landmass below sea level
⑩	Antarctica		landmass above sea level

6. Using all the evidence found on the continental landmasses (refer to figure 15.5) and the way landmasses appear distributed today as a guide, students should try to reconstruct the way the landmasses were arranged 100 million years ago. Caution the students not to glue or tape anything in place until they are certain of its position.

7. Once students believe the landmasses are in the correct positions, they should tape or glue them securely to figure 15.3. The answer is on page 186.

8. As a means for evaluation, teams can prepare a written or oral report explaining their reconstruction and what evidence led to their conclusions.

EXTENSIONS

1. Questions about climates in Alaska and Antarctica at the time of the dinosaurs can be discussed. It is generally considered the dinosaurs lived in warm climates, yet fossil remains are found in Antarctica. How can this be explained? Students should investigate the movements of the plates and recognize that plates move not only east-west but also north-south. India was once located near Antarctica, and Antarctica was once much closer to the equator. As the plates moved, their climates changed.

2. The movement of dinosaurs across land bridges and among continents hundreds of millions of years ago has a corollary in human settlement: movement of peoples (and many animal species) from Asia to North America occurred along a land bridge across the Bering Sea from what is now Russia to what is now Alaska. Landmass movements are also responsible for isolation of the unique animal species in Australia.

3. To test Clarke's biblical theory, students might investigate the Old Testament as a history book. Try to discover ways in which the scientists and explorers of the time might have been aware of the configuration of the continents. It is not as far-fetched as you may think. The Greeks were aware, for instance, that all the oceans were connected, and in Egypt in approximately 200 B.C., Eratosthenes determined the circumference of the earth, and came surprisingly close, using a crude geometric procedure.

Answer to figure 15.3 with 15.4.

Before concluding this discussion of continents, it is interesting to examine which bodies of land are considered continents and which are not. Most books list seven continents, defined as a major or large landmass. I have always had problems with this list of continents. For example, even though Europe and Asia form a single landmass, they are apparently "separated" into two continents by the north-south-trending Ural Mountains, putting half of Russia in Europe and half in Asia. Applying this same criterion to other large landmasses, South America should be two continents because of the north-south-trending Andes Mountains. North America should be three, roughly split into thirds by the Appalachian Mountains in the East and the Rocky Mountains in the West.

In addition, geomorphically, North and South America are continuous; a physical connection exists from the northernmost parts of Alaska to the Straits of Magellan, just north of Tierra del Fuego. So how (and why) was it split into two continents? Geography textbooks describe the separation point of North and South America as the Panama Canal; if the canal did not exist, would they be one continent? The country of Panama not only spans two oceans, but two continents as well. Similarly, Asia and Africa were continuous until the Suez Canal was built. If canals were critical to continental demarcation, northern Germany and Denmark would be separate from Europe because of the Kiel Canal. Humans have incredible power: they can not only split submicroscopic atoms but, apparently, gigantic continents, too.

Greenland is never considered a continent, apparently because it is not large enough. This is often confusing to people because on many maps, Greenland looks considerably larger than either Antarctica or Australia and approximately the same size as South America. The only reasonably accurate portrayal of the Earth is a globe; all maps have inherent inaccuracies. Frequently, the maps in classrooms are based on a Mercator projection. Such maps accurately portray landmass sizes at the equator but enlarge masses at dramatically increasing rates toward the poles. Distortion at the poles is so bad that Mercator projections do not even show the northern and southern extremes of the globe. The result is that Greenland is distorted to look much larger than it is, and Antarctica appears merely as a partially visible strip across the bottom of the map.

Another oddity in the way continents are designated is that India is often called a subcontinent. India could be considered separated from Asia by the Himalaya Mountains (the same criterion that separates Asia from Europe), but this would make India a continent all by itself. Finally, if an island is a landmass surrounded by water, then all individual continents and combinations of continents (such as Asia-Africa) are islands.

Definitions of continents do not provide a measure of how large an area must be before it is considered a continent, only that it must be large. The areas of the various landmasses discussed follow:

Landmass	Size (in Square Miles)
Asia	17,153,000
Africa	11,677,000
North America	9,420,000
South America	6,870,000
Antarctica	5,100,000
Europe	3,825,000
Australia	2,968,000
India	1,266,595
Greenland	837,000

Greenland is smaller than the others, but 837,000 square miles is still large. It appears as though a landmass needs to contain at least 1 or 2 million square miles before it is considered a continent. Greenland is considered merely the world's largest island. But isn't Australia a larger island? Apparently, if it is larger than 1 million square miles, it is not an island. But if a landmass is totally surrounded by water, the definition says that it is an island. The definitions should be amended. An island might be redefined as "a landmass of an area less than 1 million square miles completely surrounded by water." The nature of a continent is still somewhat ambiguous. The definition might read, "a landmass exceeding 1 (or 2) million square miles, *sometimes* separated from an otherwise continuous landmass by either a mountain range or canal."

⊠ ⊠ ⊠

ACTIVITY: DEFINE A CONTINENT

Students are usually given a list of the continents, which is accepted as truth. In the following activity students will develop their own definitions of continents.

REQUIREMENTS

Time

45-90 minutes

Materials

- Writing materials
- Library or media center
- World wall map in classroom

Grouping

Pairs

DIRECTIONS

1. Discuss the concept and definition of continents as presented in this chapter. Have students look at the world map and discuss which landmasses might be considered continents. *Do not give them the conventional list of continents!*

2. Tell them they work for a group of people writing a geography textbook. Each pair's job is to determine what a continent is, to make a list of the continents, and to explain why the landmasses on their list are continents and why other landmasses are not.

3. The report should be two pages in length and will be read aloud to the class. The list of continents should be put on the board at the beginning of the presentation. The remainder of the class will be a "jury of geographers" that must question the decisions and ask for explanations.

EXTENSION

The appearance of the continents is determined to a large extent by the map projection used. During discussions of continents, map projections can be introduced and student teams can be assigned different projections to research, explaining both their uses and the problems inherent in each.

⊠ ⊠ ⊠

REFERENCES

Clarke, Adam. 1977. *Clarke's Commentary*. Nashville, Tenn.: Abingdon Press.

SUGGESTED READING

Czerkas, Sylvia J., and Stephen A. Czerkas. *Dinosaurs: A Global View*. New York: Mallard Press, 1991.

Harris, Miles F., Dale T. Hesser, J. Allen Hynek, William H. Matthews, III, Chalmer J. Roy, James W. Skehan, S.J., and Robert E. Stevenson. *Investigating the Earth*, 4th ed. Boston: Houghton Mifflin, 1973.

Hurley, Patrick M. "The Confirmation of Continental Drift." In *Continents Adrift, Readings from Scientific American*. San Francisco: W. H. Freeman, 1972.

Leet, L. Don, and Sheldon Judson. *Physical Geology*. New York: Prentice Hall, 1971.

Sarton, George. *A History of Science*. New York: John Wiley & Sons, 1952.

Tarling, Don, and Maureen Tarling. *Continental Drift*. Garden City, N.Y.: Anchor Books, 1971.

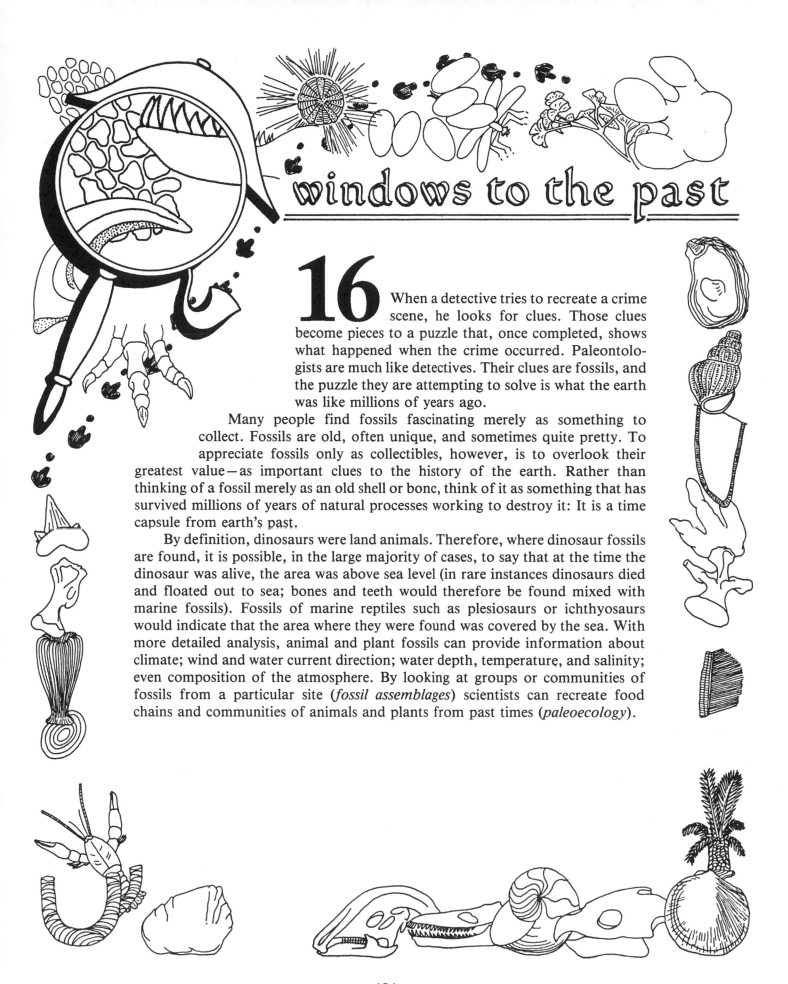

windows to the past

16

When a detective tries to recreate a crime scene, he looks for clues. Those clues become pieces to a puzzle that, once completed, shows what happened when the crime occurred. Paleontologists are much like detectives. Their clues are fossils, and the puzzle they are attempting to solve is what the earth was like millions of years ago.

Many people find fossils fascinating merely as something to collect. Fossils are old, often unique, and sometimes quite pretty. To appreciate fossils only as collectibles, however, is to overlook their greatest value—as important clues to the history of the earth. Rather than thinking of a fossil merely as an old shell or bone, think of it as something that has survived millions of years of natural processes working to destroy it: It is a time capsule from earth's past.

By definition, dinosaurs were land animals. Therefore, where dinosaur fossils are found, it is possible, in the large majority of cases, to say that at the time the dinosaur was alive, the area was above sea level (in rare instances dinosaurs died and floated out to sea; bones and teeth would therefore be found mixed with marine fossils). Fossils of marine reptiles such as plesiosaurs or ichthyosaurs would indicate that the area where they were found was covered by the sea. With more detailed analysis, animal and plant fossils can provide information about climate; wind and water current direction; water depth, temperature, and salinity; even composition of the atmosphere. By looking at groups or communities of fossils from a particular site (*fossil assemblages*) scientists can recreate food chains and communities of animals and plants from past times (*paleoecology*).

★ ★ ★

ACTIVITY: WHAT'S FOUND WHERE?

Different plants and animals are found in different environments. By discussing several different environments, students will understand how environments can be represented by the plants and animals inhabiting them.

REQUIREMENTS

Time

Approximately 30 minutes

Materials

Blackboard or overhead projector

Grouping

Six groups, two for each environment

DIRECTIONS

Ask students to name things that live in the following environments: land, beach, and ocean, and list them on the board. Discuss how these environments might be represented by fossils (for instance, a fish or dinosaur might be represented by a fossil bone or tooth, a clam by a fossilized shell or burrow, or a pine tree by a fossilized pine cone or petrified wood). At the end of this activity, students should understand the relationship between the living organism, the environment, and the fossil remains. Examples of what students might suggest follow:

Land

Modern	Fossil
trees	leaf impressions, petrified wood, roots
forest animals	bones, teeth, footprints, coprolite, skin
alligators	teeth, parts of skin
fresh-water fish	teeth, scales
soil or dirt	rocks showing old soils

Beach

Modern	Fossil
crabs	shells, claws
clams	shells, burrows
sand	sandstone

Ocean

Modern	Fossil
sharks, whales	bones, teeth
turtles	shells
sea urchins	shells
clay	shale

★ ★ ★

ACTIVITY: WHERE CAN I SEE THE SEA?

Understanding how the pieces of the fossil puzzle fit together allows the paleontologist to imagine the earth as it was millions of years ago. Introduce the activity to the students by telling them that they are all paleontologists and have found many different fossils. Based upon those fossils, they will have to draw a map showing what environments were present in a certain area more than 70 million years ago. (Note: This activity will use drawings of fossils. When available, actual fossils should be used to replace the drawings. In an ideal case, only actual fossils would be used. See the list of fossil sources at the end of this chapter.)

REQUIREMENTS

Time

45-90 minutes

Materials

- Prepared grid with one grid space for each student (see fig. 16.1, page 194) and one copy for each student
- Fossil figures and descriptions (see figs. 16.2, 16.3, and 16.4, pgs. 195-197), enlarged if possible, cut apart and placed on individual 3" × 5" cards, one card for each student. (duplicates can be made as needed to accommodate a larger class)
- Watch or clock that indicates seconds
- Blue, yellow, and green colored pencils for each student
- Pencil with eraser for each student

Grouping

Whole class

DIRECTIONS

Part 1: Filling in the Grid. At the outset, students will sit at their regular seats. At predetermined intervals (1½ to 2 minutes) students will move to the next seat according to a planned sequence determined by the teacher. This seat switching will be repeated until each student has had the opportunity to sit in every seat.

(Directions continues on page 198.)

Fig. 16.1. Blank grid for fossil puzzle activity.

THE FOSSIL PUZZLE

Name_____   Date_____

1	2	3	4	5
6	7	8	9	10
11	12	13	14	15
16	17	18	19	20
21	22	23	24	25
26	27	28	29	30

Fig. 16.2. Fossils for grid spaces 1 through 10. Modified from Moore, Lalicker, and Fischer.

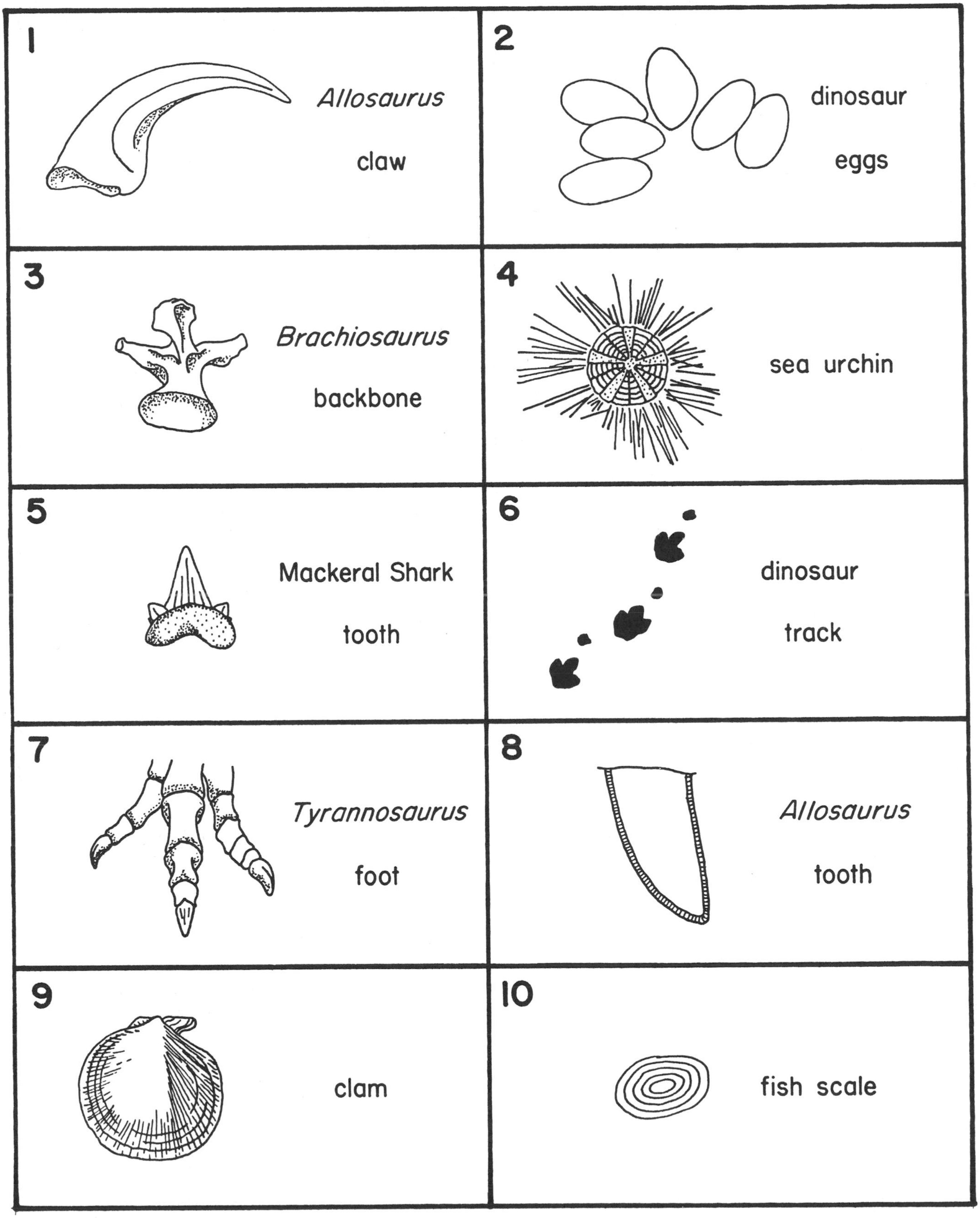

1 *Allosaurus* claw	**2** dinosaur eggs
3 *Brachiosaurus* backbone	**4** sea urchin
5 Mackeral Shark tooth	**6** dinosaur track
7 *Tyrannosaurus* foot	**8** *Allosaurus* tooth
9 clam	**10** fish scale

Fig. 16.3. Fossils for grid spaces 11 through 20. Modified from Moore, Lalicker, and Fischer.

11 	tyrranosaur jaw	12 	cycad tree
13 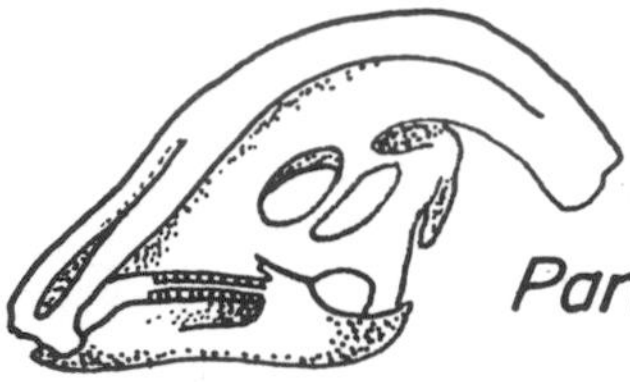	*Parasaurolophus* skull	14 	burrows
15 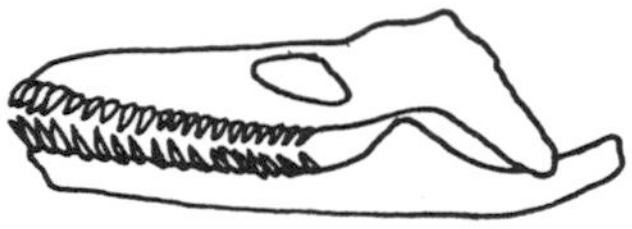	plesiosaur skull	16 	ginkgo tree
17 	dinosaur footprint from China	18 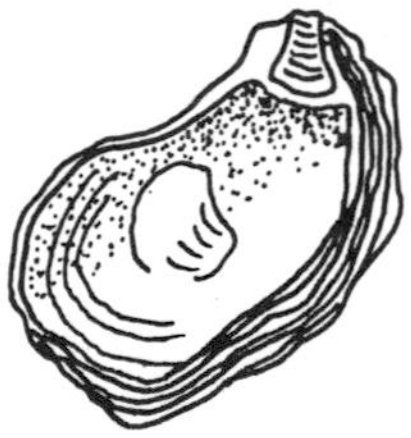	oyster
19 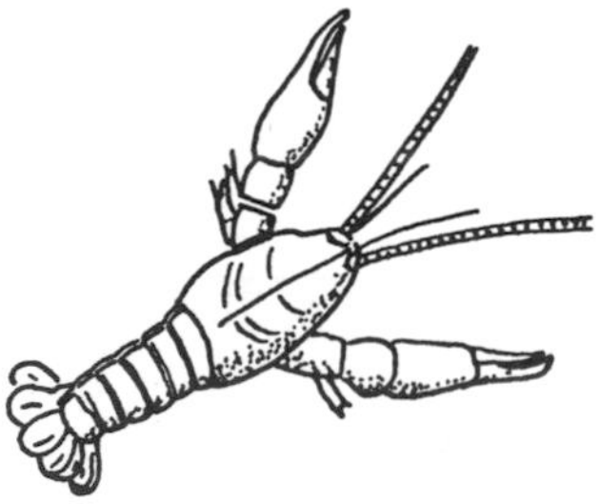	lobster	20 	nautilus

Fig. 16.4. Fossils for grid spaces 21-30. Modified from Moore, Lalicker, and Fischer.

21 	*Triceratops* leg bone	22 	*Stegosaurus* plate
23 	marine snail	24 	coral
25 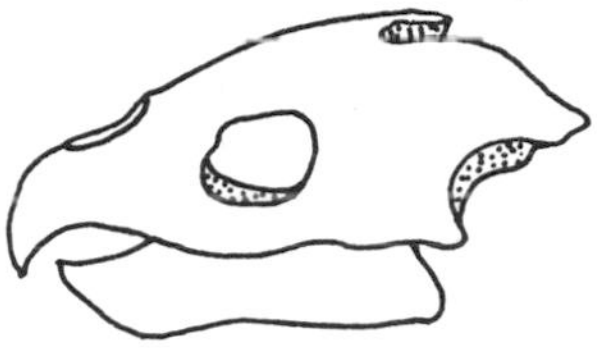	marine turtle skull	26 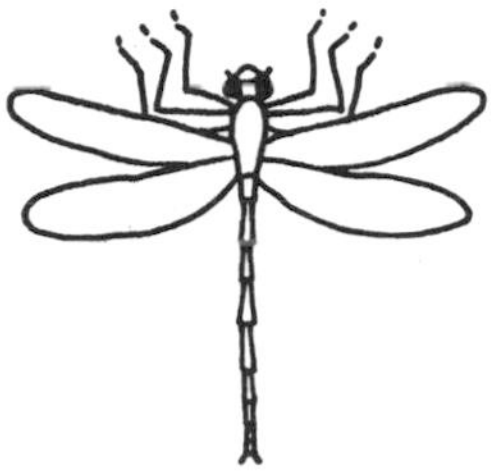	dragonfly
27 	dinosaur skin design	28 	dinosaur footprint in sand
29 	Tiger Shark tooth	30 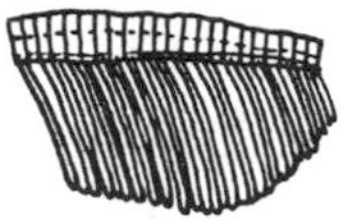	ichthyosaur skeleton

1. Have all students stand to one side or the back of the room. Each student should have a pencil and eraser.

2. Place one of the fossil figures face down at each seating position.

3. Explain to students what will be happening: "In front of each seat is a card showing a fossil, a description, and a number. It is now face down. Do not turn them over until I ask you to do so. When I ask you to return to your seats, go to your regular seat but do not touch the card in front of you."

4. Have students return to their seats.

5. When students are seated, give one of the blank grid sheets (fig. 16.1, page 194) to each student and have them fill in their names and the date.

6. Explain a grid; show figure 16.1 on the overhead projector.

7. Ask students to turn over the card in front of them and give them the following directions: "Each space on the grid has a number, and each card has a number. Find the space on your grid that has the number to match the card. In that space draw the picture of the fossil found on the card and write the name of the fossil underneath it. You will be moving from one seat to another until all the grid spaces are filled. You will only have two minutes to fill in the grid and move to the next seat, so it is important to pay attention, draw quickly, and concentrate on what you are doing."

8. Draw the plan of seating changes on the board and tape arrows to the desks or tables so students know which seat to move to next.

9. Use the first move as practice. Tell the students what signal you will use to indicate it is time to move (e.g., say "Go," blow a whistle, or ring a bell). Make certain they understand what is expected of them before continuing.

10. Have students proceed until all the grid spaces are filled in with a drawing of the fossil and its name (see fig. 16.5, which shows the completed grid).

Part 2: Interpreting the Grid. Once the grid is completed, the students should use dots and hatch marks to separate the different types of environments (see fig. 16.6, page 200). Show examples of how to do this on the board. Discuss which fossils might indicate which environments, as in the first activity in this chapter. The normal sequence would have any fossils indicating a beach found in between those of the ocean and the land. For this part of the activity, students may work as individuals or pairs. Working in groups of more than two becomes difficult. Students should color their filled-in grids as follows: boxes with land fossils, green; beach fossils, yellow; and sea fossils, blue.

Allow students to discuss their own interpretations and their reasons for separating environments. Make an overhead transparency of the solution (fig. 16.6) and show it to the class, placing it on top of the transparency of figure 16.5, after you have graded the papers. Discuss with students any different interpretations they may have.

EXTENSIONS

1. If actual fossils are used, some time should be taken to explain their ages and types.

2. Assign different environments to students (individually or in small groups) as subjects to research in the library. Their task is to identify as many "fossils" as possible that might be found 50 million years from now. They should also describe other things that might indicate that particular environment; e.g., sand dunes on a desert.

Fig. 16.5. Completed grid for fossil puzzle activity. To be prepared as an overhead transparency.

THE FOSSIL PUZZLE

Name_____ Date_____

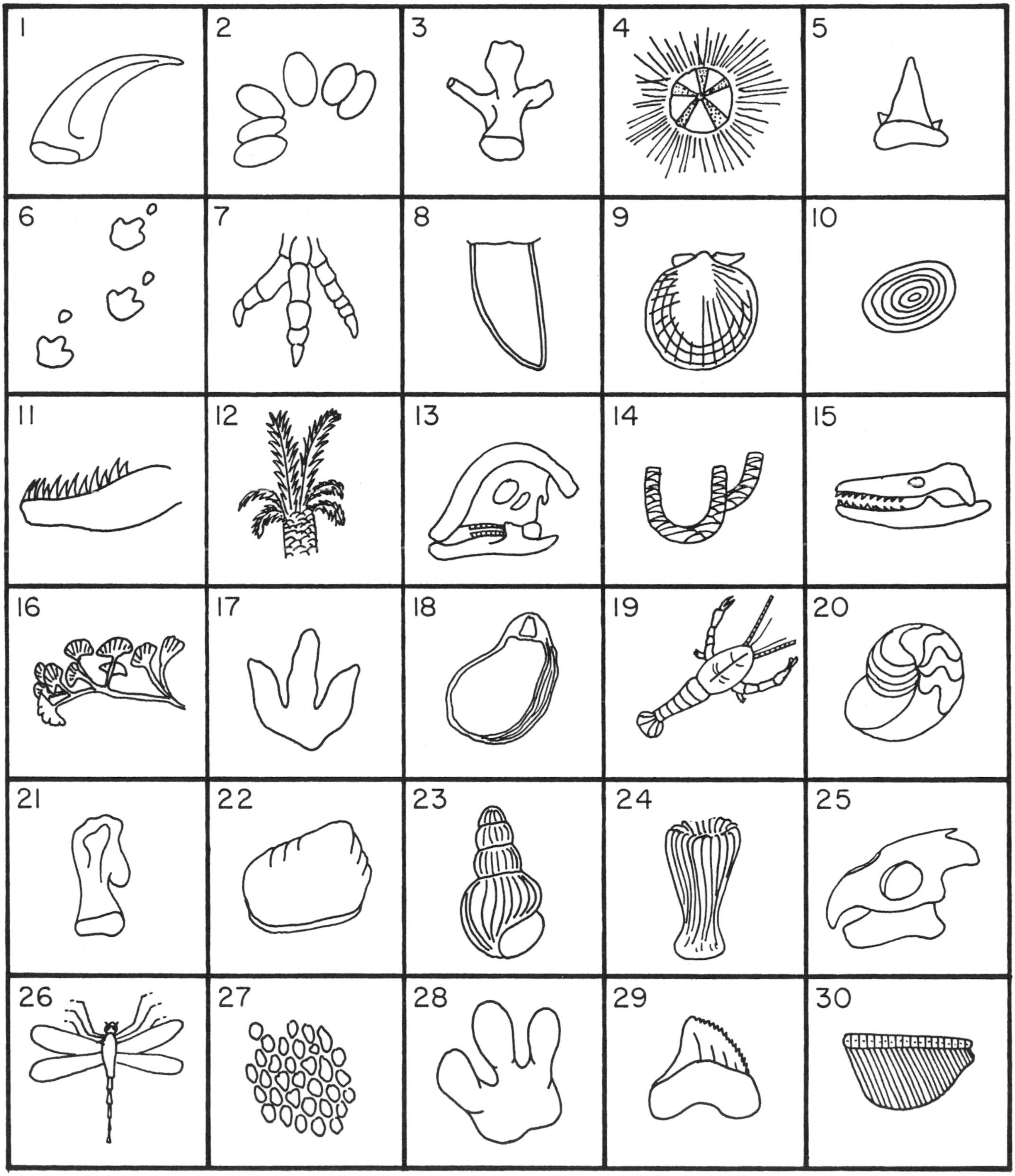

Fig. 16.6. Markings to indicate different environments for the fossil puzzle grid. To be prepared as an overhead transparency to be placed on top of the transparency of figure 16.5.

INTERPRETATION

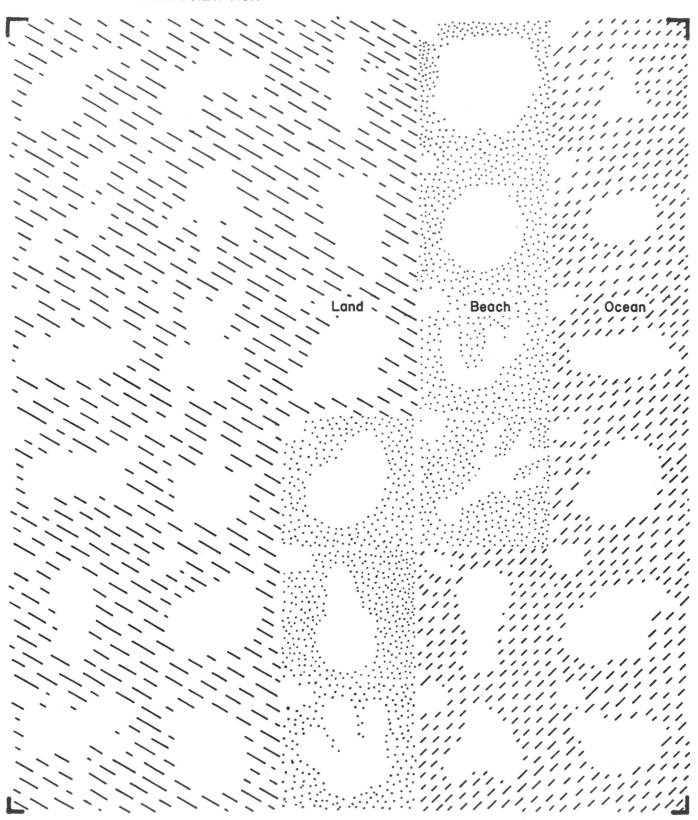

3. Research different animals to see how they are adapted to their environments (e.g., flippers for animals at sea, webbed feet for aquatic birds).

★ ★ ★

RESOURCES

The U.S. Geological Survey in Denver, Colorado, has hands-on fossil kits available for loan. The hundreds of fossils contained in the kit represent a broad spectrum of organisms, from plants to dinosaurs. For information contact the U.S. Geological Survey Library GEO Center at (303) 236-1015 (Denver, Colorado). The Colorado School of Mines also has fossil kits for loan. Information can be obtained by calling the Geology Museum of the Colorado School of Mines at (303) 273-3823 (Golden, Colorado).

Other fossil sources might be state government geological surveys, local universities, high school earth science or geology departments, or clubs of amateur collectors. Often, such clubs congregate at fossil or mineral shows where specimens are on display and for sale. State geological survey departments are also excellent sources of free or inexpensive publications about where to find fossils in your area. Local rock shops (frequently with a large fossil inventory) are often owned by education-minded entrepreneurs who can be quite generous, either with small gifts or loans.

SUGGESTED READING

Lockley, Martin. *Tracking Dinosaurs*. Cambridge: Cambridge University Press, 1991.

Moore, Raymond C., Cecil G. Lalicker, and Alfred G. Fischer. *Invertebrate Fossils*. New York: McGraw-Hill, 1952.

Norman, David. *The Illustrated Encyclopedia of Dinosaurs*. New York: Crown, 1985.

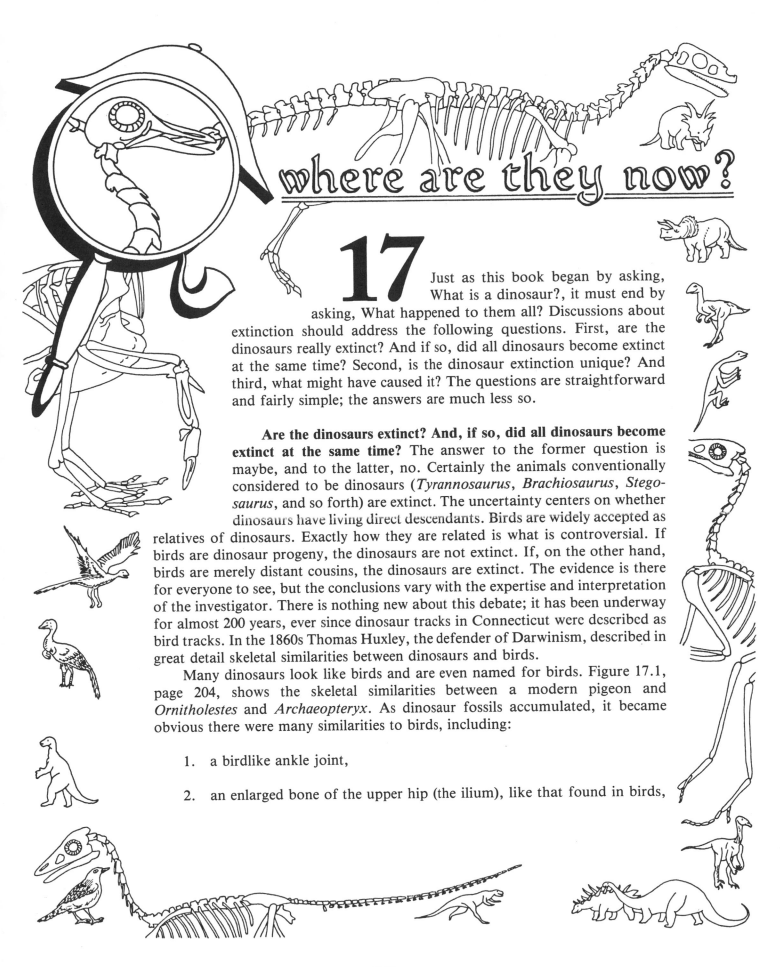

where are they now?

17 Just as this book began by asking, What is a dinosaur?, it must end by asking, What happened to them all? Discussions about extinction should address the following questions. First, are the dinosaurs really extinct? And if so, did all dinosaurs become extinct at the same time? Second, is the dinosaur extinction unique? And third, what might have caused it? The questions are straightforward and fairly simple; the answers are much less so.

Are the dinosaurs extinct? And, if so, did all dinosaurs become extinct at the same time? The answer to the former question is maybe, and to the latter, no. Certainly the animals conventionally considered to be dinosaurs (*Tyrannosaurus*, *Brachiosaurus*, *Stegosaurus*, and so forth) are extinct. The uncertainty centers on whether dinosaurs have living direct descendants. Birds are widely accepted as relatives of dinosaurs. Exactly how they are related is what is controversial. If birds are dinosaur progeny, the dinosaurs are not extinct. If, on the other hand, birds are merely distant cousins, the dinosaurs are extinct. The evidence is there for everyone to see, but the conclusions vary with the expertise and interpretation of the investigator. There is nothing new about this debate; it has been underway for almost 200 years, ever since dinosaur tracks in Connecticut were described as bird tracks. In the 1860s Thomas Huxley, the defender of Darwinism, described in great detail skeletal similarities between dinosaurs and birds.

Many dinosaurs look like birds and are even named for birds. Figure 17.1, page 204, shows the skeletal similarities between a modern pigeon and *Ornitholestes* and *Archaeopteryx*. As dinosaur fossils accumulated, it became obvious there were many similarities to birds, including:

1. a birdlike ankle joint,

2. an enlarged bone of the upper hip (the ilium), like that found in birds,

Fig. 17.1. Comparisons of dinosaur and bird skeletons drawn comparable size. Modified from Norman.

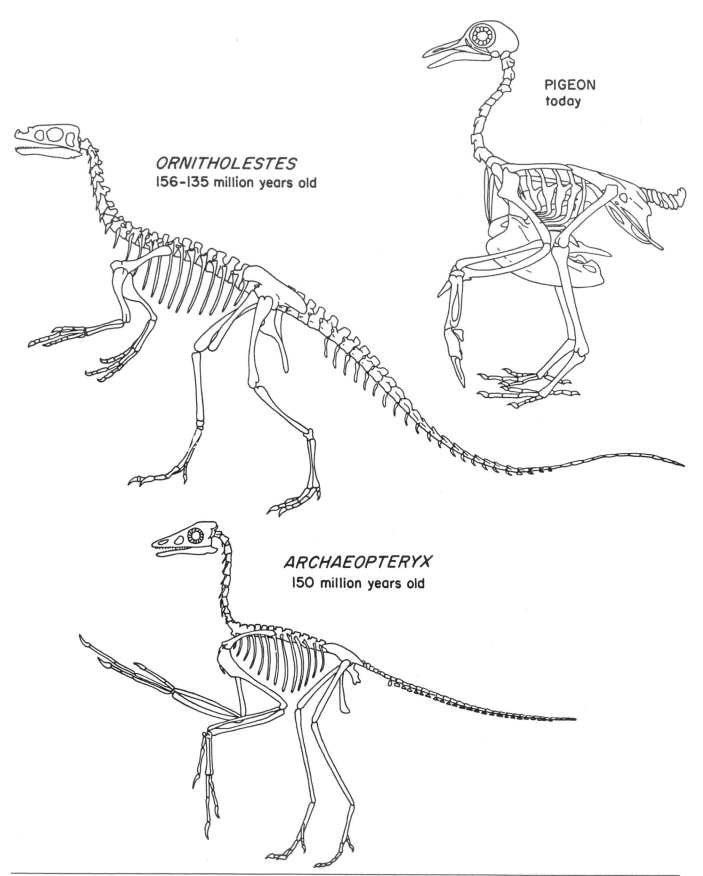

PIGEON
today

ORNITHOLESTES
156-135 million years old

ARCHAEOPTERYX
150 million years old

3. a birdlike hind foot (three toes pointing forward, fourth pointing backward),

4. a birdlike body shape and bipedal movement,

5. air sacs in the vertebrae,

6. a backward-pointing pubic bone, characteristic of the ornithischians, and

7. similarities in the bony structures of the "hand."

Two critical birdlike features, however, are noticeably missing: feathers and the collarbone, or wishbone. Both are characteristic features of birds—without them, birds cannot fly. In 1861 a discovery in a German quarry seemed to provide the missing link. An animal fossil similar to a reptile but with feathers and a collarbone was discovered in 150-million-year-old Jurassic rocks. This fossil creature was named *Archaeopteryx* (meaning "ancient wing") and apparently confirmed the link between birds and dinosaurs. Or did it? If *Archaeopteryx* was the link between modern birds and dinosaurs, how could it be older than many of the dinosaurs that resembled birds? If it was a direct link, descendants of *Archaeopteryx* would have appeared more and more like birds and less and less like dinosaurs. To make matters even more confusing, in 1983 Sankar Chatterjee, a paleontologist working in Texas, found bones of an animal he claims is a bird. It was found in rocks 225 million years old and was named *Protoavis* ("early," or "prebird") and seems more birdlike than *Archaeopteryx*. If *Archaeopteryx* was transitional between reptiles and birds, how could something even more like a bird be 75 million years older? Based upon interpretations of the available evidence, two schools of thought have evolved (see fig. 17.2, p. 206). Those that believe the newly discovered *Protoavis* is an ancestor of *Archaeopteryx* believe dinosaurs and birds branched separately from the evolutionary tree; they may have evolved from a common root of primitive reptiles, but the birds did not evolve from the dinosaurs (see fig. 17.2a). To students of this school, the dinosaurs are extinct. The second school has not accepted what they believe is the ambiguous evidence of *Protoavis* and instead believe that dinosaurs, *Archaeopteryx*, and birds all had common dinosaur ancestors that lived approximately 240 million years ago (see fig. 17.2b). Students of this second school believe dinosaurs are not extinct, that they are being fed sunflowers in backyards and lighting on statues all over the world. Which school is correct? No one is certain. Are the dinosaurs extinct? Maybe, maybe not. Birds are related to the dinosaurs somehow. Dinosaur descendants may be chirping outside your window at this moment.

The Age of Dinosaurs lasted from 245 to 66 million years ago. Many believe that all dinosaurs appeared at its beginning and the same species, all of which still existed, became extinct at the end. Figure 17.3, page 207, is a graph of the time distribution of 141 genera of dinosaurs studied by David Norman. Each vertical bar represents the time span of one dinosaur genus. Four well-known genera, *Tyrannosaurus*, *Triceratops*, *Stegosaurus*, and *Diplodocus* are indicated respectively by letters A, B, C, and D. Although the dinosaurs dominated the earth for almost 165 million years, animals like *Stegosaurus*, *Triceratops*, *Diplodocus*, and even *Tyrannosaurus* existed on earth for only about 10 million years each. During their reign on earth, dinosaur genera evolved and became extinct with surprising regularity.

Robert Bakker (1986, 193) presents the case that many of the dinosaur extinctions that occurred before the end of the Age of Dinosaurs had to do with changes in the vegetation available. Figure 17.4, page 208, shows the direct relationship between types of vegetation that flourished and groups of dinosaurs that flourished. For instance, sauropods were larger, taller dinosaurs (like brontosaurs) that fed on taller trees. As the taller trees diminished in number, so did the sauropods. Similarly, flowering plants evolved in the Cretaceous, and with them, the dinosaurs that fed low to the ground, such as the horned dinosaurs and ankylosaurs. Carnivorous dinosaurs evolved to reflect changes in their food supply, the herbivores.

(Text continues on page 209.)

Fig. 17.2. Two interpretations of bird-dinosaur relationships based upon recent discoveries. Modified from Zimmer.

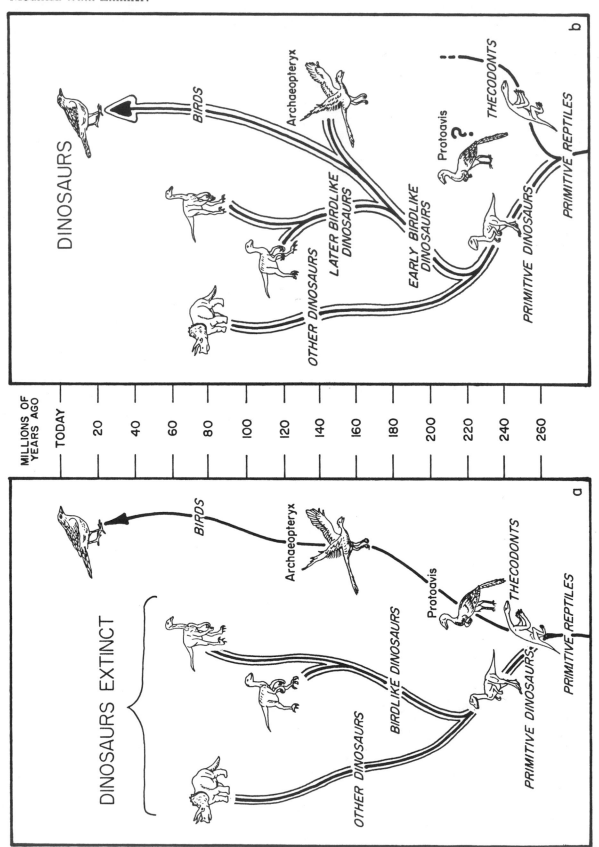

Fig. 17.3. Graph showing appearance and disappearance of 141 dinosaur genera in the Age of Dinosaurs. The height of the bar represents the time the genus existed. Data from Norman.

A = *Tyrannosaurus*

B = *Triceratops*

C = *Stegosaurus*

D = *Diplodocus*

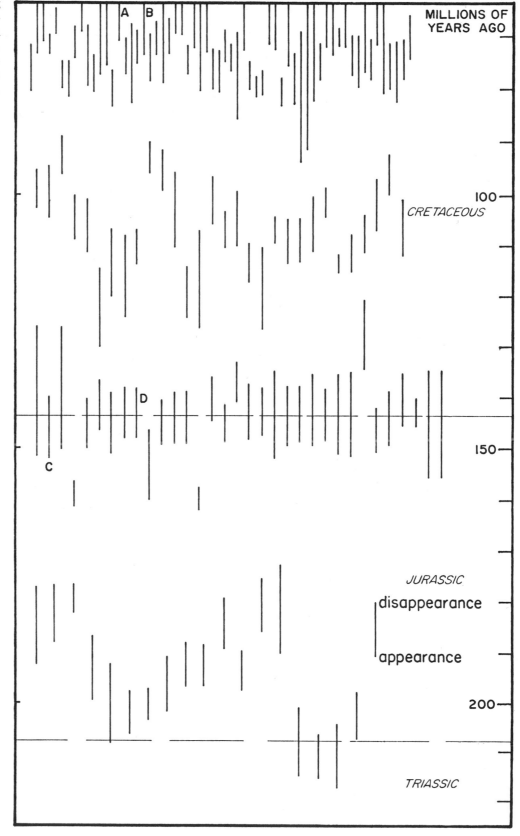

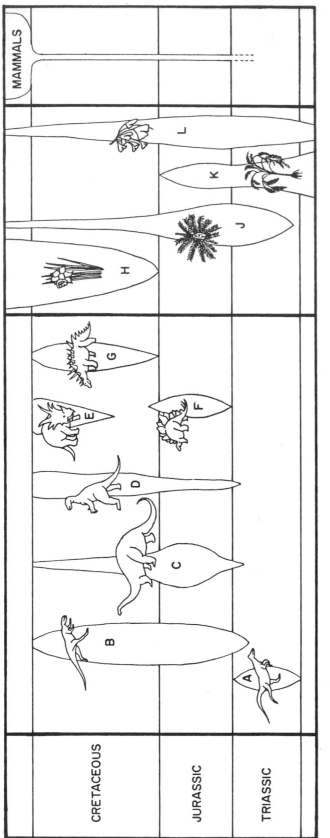

Fig. 17.4. Relative abundances of dinosaur groups, plants, and mammals. Modified from McAlester.

A = Thecodonts
B = Theropods
C = Sauropods
D = Ornithopods
E = Horned Dinosaurs
F = Stegosaurs
G = Ankylosaurs
H = Flowering plants
J = Cycads
K = Seed ferns
L = Gingkoes

The changes in vegetation did not occur in a vacuum. Bakker (179-198) believes the evolution of flowering plants was accelerated by the dinosaurs themselves. That may be true, but some credit for changes in the flora must be given to global climatic changes, repositioning of continents, and the changes that occurred in the shape of the earth's crust. Just as the complete extinction of the dinosaurs may have been influenced by these occurrences, so some of the intermediate dinosaur extinctions may have also been caused by them.

Is the dinosaur extinction unique? Extinctions are as much a part of the history of life on earth as is the appearance of new species. The type of extinction that affected the dinosaurs is called a *mass extinction*. What may surprise many readers is that it was one of the smaller mass extinctions. Figure 17.5 shows a graph of the number of families of marine organisms living on the earth at various times.

Fig. 17.5. Graph of families of marine animals showing five mass extinctions. The numbers represent the percentage of families of marine animals killed during the extinction. Modified from Kaufman and Mallory and Raup and Sepkoski.

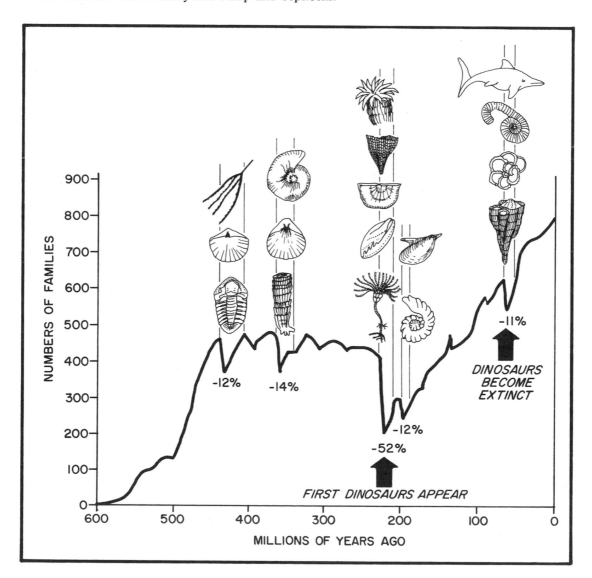

Marine organisms provide excellent information about extinctions because they have existed on the planet longer than land organisms and when they die, they fall to the bottom of the sea, where fossil preservation is better than on land. The animals pictured are characteristic of those that perished during the extinction. The graph shows that during the dinosaur extinction (approximately 66 million years ago), only 11 percent of the families of marine organisms became extinct; that is the smallest of the five major mass extinctions indicated. By comparison, at the end of the Permian period (245 million years ago, just before the beginning of the Age of Dinosaurs), more than half of the number of living families of marine animals died—that is devastation! Approximately 10,000 years ago, during the Pleistocene epoch (the Ice Ages), approximately 50 percent of the large mammals worldwide perished during another major extinction, this one possibly exacerbated by the hunting practices of ancient man.

What might have caused the dinosaur mass extinction? Theories about the causes of the dinosaur extinction are almost as numerous as those investigating the extinction. In 1963 a university professor listed 46 reasons for the extinction; more have appeared since then. Some theories are more credible than others. Among the least accepted and most difficult to prove are the following:

- The bodies of dinosaurs were so awkward the animals could no longer live or breed.

- Carnivores ate all the herbivores, then starved to death.

- Dinosaur eggs were eaten by the mammals, who were becoming increasingly successful.

- Rapidly evolving flowering plants contained high concentrations of chemicals that poisoned the dinosaurs.

- Dinosaurs succumbed to an epidemic.

- Dinosaurs died of senility.

- Dinosaurs died because the lowest members of the oceanic food chain (the phytoplankton) died.

- Butterflies and moths ate so many plants that the herbivores all died; the carnivores died soon after.

- Dinosaurs developed cataracts, became blind, and were unable to reproduce.

- "Lack of even standing room for the dinosaurs in Noah's Ark" (my personal favorite), in other words, overcrowding or overpopulation.

More generally accepted theories, all with their share of critics, incorporate some sort of change in global climate (either hotter or colder). Most recent theories of global climate change have focused on a thin layer of clay found in several places around the world that has been determined to be coincident with the extinction of the dinosaurs. That clay layer, called the *boundary clay* because it marks the Cretaceous-Tertiary boundary, is anomalously enriched in a dense, metallic element, iridium—as much as 160 times that which is found in the rocks immediately above and below it. Iridium is rare in the earth's crust, but intraterrestrial sources (some volcanoes) and extraterrestrial sources (asteroids) can have high concentrations of this element. These sources of iridium support two current extinction theories. The catastrophists believe an asteroid impact created a huge dust cloud on earth that reduced (or raised) global temperatures and caused catastrophic extinctions. Recent discoveries of a 65-million-year-old impact crater in the Yucatán Peninsula of Mexico have provided strong support for the catastrophists. The vulcanists believe the iridium was generated by volcanic activity, which created clouds of ash, shielding the earth from the sun and reducing (or raising) global temperatures.

Other scientists believe the key lies in dramatic changes that were taking place in the earth's crust at about the same time as the extinctions. Mountains were being formed; continents were moving; sea levels were dropping dramatically as continental landmasses rose; volcanic activity, resulting from this turmoil, generated ash clouds; and this all combined to reduce (or raise) atmospheric temperature and change rainfall patterns as well. These theories are too complex to discuss here; for further information, consult the "Suggested Reading" list at the end of this chapter. The bottom line is that no one really knows, and the significance of the evidence is still being debated. As Leonard Krishtalka (1989, 26) writes, "the trail is 65 million years cold and the geologic fingerprints are smudged."

It is interesting to theorize what life on earth might be like had this mass extinction not occurred. Birds are, arguably, dinosaur descendants. What if not only the birds but all other members of the dinosaur group were present on earth today? How would we *Homo sapiens* be different? How would we behave? Dinosaur investigators such as R. McNeill Alexander (1991, 136) have speculated about how human behaviors might have compared with those of the dinosaurs: "We could have strolled alongside a walking sauropod or tyrannosaur, keeping up with it without difficulty.... I think I am probably fast enough to outrun a pursuing tyrannosaur but, perhaps fortunately, I am unlikely to have a try." Other authors have envisioned the interaction of dinosaurs and man (or mammals) quite differently. Many scenarios can be conjured. Two extreme views are those provided by Dougal Dixon (1988) and James Gurney (1992).

In his book *The New Dinosaurs: An Alternative Evolution*, Dixon portrays a world in which dinosaurs never became extinct; they continued to evolve and maintain their dominance over all other land animals, including mammals. Tyrannosaurs, whose earlier extinction removed them from the earth just as they were gaining prominence, now flourish and are the biggest meat-eating animals ever to have existed. Because Dixon's dinosaurs never became extinct, it follows that mammals never achieved dominance over the land: "And the mammals? They began in the Triassic period as small insectivorous creatures. By the end of the Cretaceous they were still small insectivorous creatures. They have no opportunity to expand and diversify, and they are small insectivorous creatures to this day" (Dixon 1988, 12). In short, major changes in mammalian evolution never occurred, and man never evolved.

Gurney's premise is that dinosaurs still exist, or rather did exist on the island of Dinotopia in the 1860s. On Dinotopia, man and dinosaur coexist symbiotically. Dinosaurs serve as nannies to protect human children at play. Humans act as "midwives" when dinosaurs lay eggs, and they help nurture the newborn. Dinosaurs act as scribes, recording history with a unique alphabet of footprint characters. Humans build outhouses within which dinosaurs deposit their excrement, and human "copro carters" collect and transport the dung for use as fertilizer. Dinosaurs help people complete tasks, not as beasts of burden like the Asian elephant, but as willing partners. Dinotopia is "a land where dinosaurs and humans live together in peaceful interdependence. The dinosaurs appreciate the skills and liveliness of *Homo sapiens*, and the humans benefit from the wisdom and gentleness of the very much older species" (Gurney 1992, jacket copy). Both of these books are fanciful explorations of the possibilities. There can be many others.

★ ★ ★

ACTIVITY: WHAT IF?

The scenarios just presented, that humans never evolved or that humans and dinosaurs peacefully coexisted, are interesting explorations. They can be contrasted to a 1950s science fiction movie like *Gorgo*, in which a "*Gorgosaurus*" appears in Japan, and the entire military population is mobilized to kill the creature. Man's relationship to other animals with whom we share the planet can change dramatically through only short periods of time. We are the only animal to make other species extinct by direct annihilation (for example, the passenger pigeon), yet we pass laws to protect endangered creatures (like the American alligator).

In this activity students can speculate within the "what if" framework about dinosaurian and non-dinosaurian topics alike:

1. What if dinosaurs had not evolved? What animals might have evolved in their place? Would birds exist today? Would man exist? Would he be different (after all, he might have evolved some 60 million years earlier than he did)?

2. What if the Loch Ness monster were proven to be a plesiosaur and captured? What should we do with it — try to breed it with some other animal? Dissect it to learn as much as we can, killing it in the process? Place it in an aquarium and charge money for public viewing, risking the health of the animal?

3. What if the theme park in Michael Crichton's *Jurassic Park* (1991) in which living dinosaurs are reconstructed from fossil DNA, is a reality and a promoter wants to establish a series of such parks worldwide? How can the public be protected? Should such parks be encouraged? What can we learn about dinosaurs from such places?

4. What if genetic control of dinosaurs is possible; should dinosaurs be crossbred like dogs to improve certain features: small tyrannosaurs to act as watchdogs, friendly *Compsognathus* to act as seeing-eye dinosaurs?

REQUIREMENTS

Time

At least 45 minutes

Materials

Library resources

Grouping

Individuals or pairs

DIRECTIONS

1. Students, either individually or in pairs, should select a "what if" topic.

2. After researching the topic, students should prepare a written report (including illustrations). Length of the report will depend upon grade level.

3. The report should be presented to the class.

EXTENSION

The "what if" concept could be tied to historical events. For example, a class might be given the assignment, What if the Panama Canal was never constructed? What kinds of world events might have changed? How would the development of the United States have been different? Other questions might be tied to current or natural events: What if a strong hurricane (or earthquake, tsunami) were to strike your city? How would it be affected? Students could research the topic with emergency preparedness offices or organizations like the American Red Cross.

★ ★ ★

In discussing the question of dinosaur extinction, the following topic may come up: Are extinctions necessarily bad? Extinctions are part of the natural development of organisms and so cannot really be considered good or bad. Extinction caused by man's actions, however, may be considered outside the natural order of things and is therefore harmful or unnatural. Certainly extinctions are a boon neither to the organisms becoming extinct nor to those organisms dependent upon the extinct species. On the other hand, the void left by the disappearing animals or plants provides an ecologic niche that other existing—or new—organisms quickly fill.

The most dramatic worldwide extinction seen in the fossil record occurs near the beginning of the Triassic period (approximately 245 million years ago). During that extinction, more than half (52 percent) of the families of animals that lived in the oceans became extinct (see fig. 17.5). The record is less complete on land, but the timing coincides with the global drying trend described by McLoughlin (1979, 27), which ultimately created the ecologic niche into which the dinosaurs evolved. The dinosaurs disappeared (unless birds are their descendants) because of global extinction, but the same process created the opportunity for their appearance in the first place. For instance, if *Allosaurus* had not become extinct, *Tyrannosaurus rex* might not have evolved. Figure 17.4 shows the relationship between the dinosaurs and the mammals. During the 165-million-year reign of the dinosaurs on land, the mammalian presence was certainly minimal. Immediately after the dinosaur extinction, the mammal presence increased dramatically and quickly. Coincidence? Probably not. What is more likely is that the dominance of dinosaurs in the food chain suppressed mammal evolution and populations. That dominance disappeared with the dinosaurs themselves, and the mammals emerged as the preeminent large land animal, a position they still enjoy today. We are mammals. If *Tyrannosaurus* still dominated the land, how far would humans have progressed? I suspect not very far.

The actions of man as an agent of extinction certainly are bad. Man has caused extinctions directly, as a result of hunting, and indirectly by drastically changing both the physical characteristics of natural environments (draining wetlands, clear-cutting forests) and the chemical nature of these environments (acid rain, air and water pollution, pesticides) and by the ignorance of natural systems. During World War II a tree snake from New Guinea managed to hitchhike in an airplane to Guam, where it had no natural predators. That snake has virtually destroyed bird life on Guam and has become a dangerous pest to the human population. It is now threatening the Hawaiian Islands. In 1681 the first extinction of a bird—the dodo—was documented. Since then, 75 more species of birds have been declared extinct. At least one third of these extinctions can be directly attributed to man's hunting or destruction of habitat. Intentionally and inadvertently, man evidently is responsible for more plant and animal extinctions than any other organism in the history of the planet. The following statistics are truly frightening:

> In the past 2,000 years man has exterminated 2 percent of known mammals, more than half of those since 1900.

> Since approximately 1800, the rate of extermination by man has increased 5,000 percent.

> At current trends, 2,000,000 species of animals will be extinct by 2050.

Such numbers may be exaggerated by those trying to promote their cause; exaggerated or not, the problem is very real.

The U.S. Department of the Interior, Fish and Wildlife Service publishes an annual listing of endangered and threatened wildlife and plants. In 1989, 833 animals and 206 plants were on the list; two years later the list increased to 894 animals and 255 plants. In July 1991 the list contained 336 mammals, 241 birds, 108 reptiles, 19 amphibians, 100 fish, 11 snails, 43 clams, 10 crustaceans, 23 insects, 3 arachnids, 255 plants. These numbers are increasing at a distressing rate. Even more alarming is that in 1991 seven species of plants and animals disappeared from the earth forever. Fortunately, man has the ability to do something about it.

★ ★ ★

ACTIVITY: IS IT TOO LATE TO HELP?

The impact of man upon the earth and its organisms is under constant review by the press, as well it should be. Student awareness of such events is important.

REQUIREMENTS

Time

Several class periods; outside class time

Materials

Library materials, newspapers, periodicals; other current sources of information

Grouping

Individuals or groups

DIRECTIONS

These directions are purposely vague to allow for teacher discretion. The intent of this activity is to make students aware of current events affecting plant and animal populations on the planet. This can be accomplished by submission of a weekly article that students have found in a periodical; by submission of a library research paper with a particular focus (cutting down the rainforest, activities of zoos, poaching in Africa); through student involvement with organizations (National Wildlife Federation, Greenpeace, U.S. Fish and Wildlife Service); by organizing and sponsoring a neighborhood discussion and debate with invited speakers; or through a class project to foster a wildlife habitat in the state, neighborhood, or school grounds (perhaps a bird sanctuary).

★ ★ ★

The wonderful, and at the same time frustrating, thing about science is that "evidence" can provide more controversy than solutions. Experts look at a unique clay layer deposited at the end of the Cretaceous period. Half acclaim it as proof positive of an asteroid impact; the other half are convinced it is of earthly volcanic origin. Two groups of paleontologists evaluate a bone discovery in Texas. Half pronounce it is proof that the birds are evolutionary successors of the dinosaurs; the other half proclaim the bones are too ambiguous to prove anything. Cold climates are proposed as the agent of mass extinction at the end of the Cretaceous, yet during the Pleistocene ice ages, when glaciers covered large areas of the continents and sea level dropped several hundred feet, many animals prospered and migrated from Asia to North America. In the following activity, students will debate various issues relating to dinosaur extinction.

✶ ✶ ✶

ACTIVITY: THE GREAT DEBATE

What should be obvious about the discussions of extinction is that there are no absolutes. It is not even known for certain that the dinosaurs are extinct! Students will tackle the various arguments through the formats of classroom debates or mock trials.

By dividing the class into groups, different sides of the many controversial issues can be discussed. Students should be allowed outside time for research and class time for preparation of either presentations to be given to the class or trials of someone who proposed a theory. Such activities can be centered on issues such as the following:

Are the dinosaurs really extinct?

Is the bird evidence proof of dinosaur extinction?

What caused the extinction?

What good do extinctions produce, and how are extinctions harmful?

How has humankind caused extinctions, and what are we doing to help prevent extinctions?

By using newspapers and magazines, as well as books, research for these debates can be kept current.

Two groups of three or four can be assigned to opposite sides of an issue and debate them before the class. The remainder of the class can then vote on the issue or be asked to write a short summary of what they think and why. Have students alternate roles between debaters and voters.

Many students are deficient in research skills. The librarian might be asked to deliver a short lesson describing the research process and the resources available. Additional time could be spent on gathering and evaluating data, determining point of view, and preparing the final product. In addition to library materials, the following resources may be useful. The U.S. Department of the Interior, Fish and Wildlife Service publishes an annual list of endangered and threatened wildlife and plants. These are available free. Many state wildlife organizations are associated with Project Wild, an excellent source of information, speakers, ideas, and funds for wildlife projects.

✶ ✶ ✶

REFERENCES

Alexander, R. McNeill. 1991. "How Dinosaurs Ran." *Scientific American* 264, no. 4 (1991): 130-136.

Bakker, Robert T. 1986. *The Dinosaur Heresies*. New York: Zebra Books.

Crichton, Michael. 1991. *Jurassic Park*. New York: Ballantine Books.

Dixon, Dougal. 1988. *The New Dinosaurs: An Alternative Evolution*. Topsfield, Mass.: Salem House.

Gurney, James, 1992. *Dinotopia*. Atlanta, Ga.: Turner.

Krishtalka, Leonard. 1989. *Dinosaur Plots and Other Intrigues in Natural History*. New York: Avon Books.

McLoughlin, John C. 1979. *Archosauria: A New Look at the Dinosaur*. New York: Viking.

Norman, David. 1985. *The Illustrated Encyclopedia of Dinosaurs*. New York: Crown.

SUGGESTED READING

Alvarez, Walter, and Frank Asaro. "An Extraterrestrial Impact." *Scientific American* 263, no. 4 (1990): 78-84.

Charig, Alan. *A New Look at the Dinosaurs*. New York: Facts on File, 1983.

Chatterjee, Sankar. "Cranial Anatomy and Relationships of a New Triassic Bird from Texas." *Philosophical Transactions of the Royal Society of London*, Series B, 332, no. 1,265 (1991): 277-342.

Courtillot, Vincent E. "A Volcanic Eruption," *Scientific American* 263, no. 4 (1990): 85-92.

Erlich, Paul, and Ann Erlich. *The Causes and Consequences of the Disappearance of Species*. New York: Random House, 1981.

Gore, Rick. "Extinctions." *National Geographic* 175, no. 6 (1989): 662-699.

Hsu, Kenneth J. *The Great Dying*. San Diego, Calif.: Harcourt Brace Jovanovich, 1986.

Huxley, T. H. "On the Animals Which Are Most Nearly Intermediate Between Birds and Reptiles." *Geological Magazine* 5 (1868): 357-365.

Huxley, T. H. "Further Evidence of the Affinity Between the Dinosaurian Reptiles and Birds." *Quarterly Journal of the Geological Society of London* 26 (1870): 12-31.

Kaufman, Les, and Kenneth Mallory. *The Last Extinction*. Cambridge, Mass.: MIT, 1986.

Kerr, Richard A. "Huge Impact Tied to Mass Extinction." *Science* 257 no. 5,072 (1992): 878-880.

Manetti, William. *Dinosaurs in Your Backyard*. New York: Atheneum, 1982.

McAlester, A. Lee. *The History of Life*. Englewood Cliffs, N.J.: Prentice-Hall, 1968.

Panati, Charles. *Panati's Extraordinary Endings of Practically Everything and Everybody*. New York: Harper & Row, 1989.

Raup, David M., and J. John Sepkoski. "Mass Extinctions in the Marine Fossil Record." *Science* 215, no. 4,539 (1982): 1,501-1,502.

Swisher, Carl C., III, Jose M. Grajales-Nishimura, Alessandro Montanari, Stanley V. Margolis, Phillipe Claeys, Walter Alvarez, Paul Renne, Estebán Cedillo-Pardo, Florentin J-M. R. Maurasse, Garniss H. Curtiss, Jan Smit, and Michael O. McWilliams. "Coeval 40Ar/39Ar Ages of 65.0 Million Years Ago from Chicxulub Crater Melt Rock and Cretaceous-Tertiary Boundary Tektites." *Science* 257, no. 5,072 (1992): 954-958.

Zimmer, Carl. "Ruffled Feathers." *Discover* 13, no. 5 (1992): 44-54.

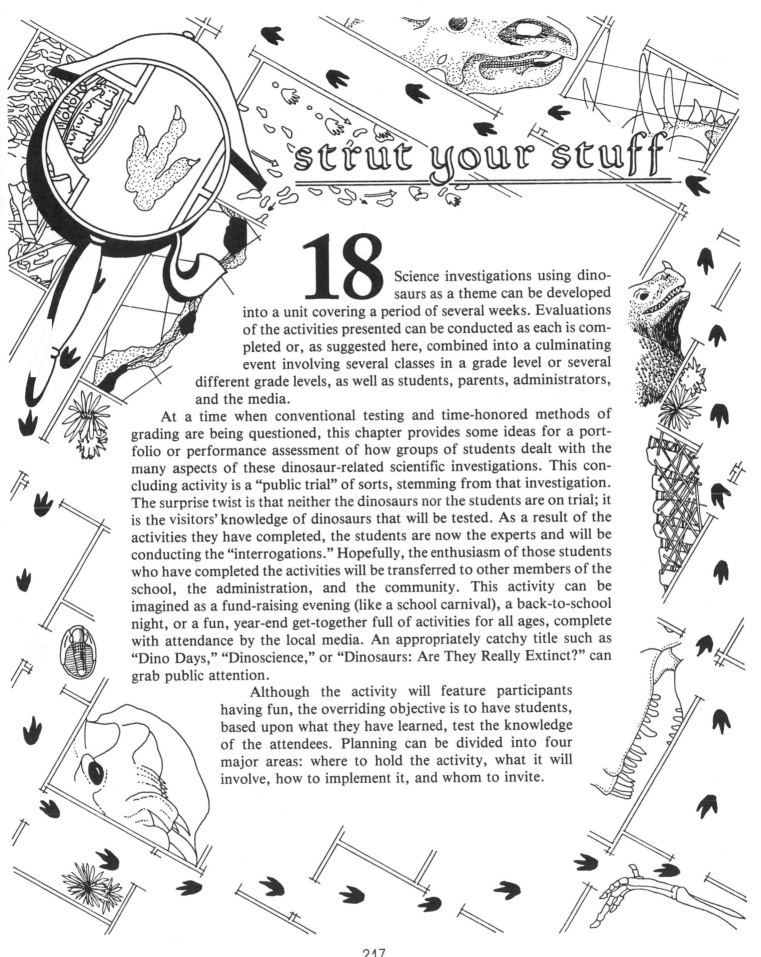

strut your stuff

18

Science investigations using dinosaurs as a theme can be developed into a unit covering a period of several weeks. Evaluations of the activities presented can be conducted as each is completed or, as suggested here, combined into a culminating event involving several classes in a grade level or several different grade levels, as well as students, parents, administrators, and the media.

At a time when conventional testing and time-honored methods of grading are being questioned, this chapter provides some ideas for a portfolio or performance assessment of how groups of students dealt with the many aspects of these dinosaur-related scientific investigations. This concluding activity is a "public trial" of sorts, stemming from that investigation. The surprise twist is that neither the dinosaurs nor the students are on trial; it is the visitors' knowledge of dinosaurs that will be tested. As a result of the activities they have completed, the students are now the experts and will be conducting the "interrogations." Hopefully, the enthusiasm of those students who have completed the activities will be transferred to other members of the school, the administration, and the community. This activity can be imagined as a fund-raising evening (like a school carnival), a back-to-school night, or a fun, year-end get-together full of activities for all ages, complete with attendance by the local media. An appropriately catchy title such as "Dino Days," "Dinoscience," or "Dinosaurs: Are They Really Extinct?" can grab public attention.

Although the activity will feature participants having fun, the overriding objective is to have students, based upon what they have learned, test the knowledge of the attendees. Planning can be divided into four major areas: where to hold the activity, what it will involve, how to implement it, and whom to invite.

Anticipating a large number of participants and the need for open space in which to operate, an area like a gymnasium would work very well for this culminating activity. Rather than a single large venue, it could also be held at several stations spread throughout the school (various classrooms, areas in the hallways).

During the unit, students investigated science using dinosaurs and discovered (1) that the study of dinosaurs is really a study of how science works, (2) that the study of dinosaurs is really a study of different types of science, (3) that there are many popularly held misconceptions about dinosaurs, (4) that discovering how we know what we know about dinosaurs was fun, (5) that the fact that a piece of information is in a book does not make it correct, (6) that what was a "fact" when parents were in school may be incorrect information today, and (7) that in many cases, the students know more about dinosaurs than their parents. During the event, students will facilitate the learning process as visitors travel through "Dinoworld" or "Mesozoicville" investigating how science works, using scientific methods to study dinosaurs and test their own knowledge. Students will be evaluating the knowledge of the visitors as the latter proceed through a series of activities. The visitors are the active participants; students act as guides, facilitators, and resident experts.

At stations placed around the gymnasium or the school building, visitors will participate in many of the activities the students completed earlier. As they test their knowledge of dinosaurs, participants will be returned to the Mesozoic environment in which the dinosaurs dominated the earth. Full-size dinosaur drawings from activities "They Can Be Really BIG" (page 31) or "Life-Size Skeletons" (page 76) can be appropriately placed to set the stage. For the more ambitious, full-size models of the animals can be built using large cardboard tubes and papier-mâché on wire frames. In art class, duplicates of pith helmets can be made out of papier-mâché. These helmets can be worn by both students and visitors to enhance the spirit of the event. Free-standing, historically correct vegetation can be constructed. Tall, large-diameter cardboard tubes (used as forms for poured concrete columns) can be decorated and used as tree trunks. Large potted palms may be borrowed from landscaping companies or offices for an evening. Strategic lighting can also heighten dramatic effects. Dry ice and fans (placed out of reach) can create atmosphere. Recordings of animal noises or primordial growls as background could effectively unnerve visitors.

Before entering "Dinoworld," visitors will be required to research their destination at the "Dinoworld" library and complete a "passport application" that tests their knowledge. Which animals are they likely to find? Which ones will be dinosaurs? Which ones do they need to fear? As visitors proceed through this Mesozoic world, they will do the following:

- Explore the different kinds of science that provide a better understanding of dinosaurs.

- Experience the excitement of discovery using the methods of science.

- Examine the history of dinosaur discoveries and dinosaur names; discover how we know how old they are.

- Come upon dinosaur tracks and investigate (under the guidance of the students) what kind of strange animal might have created them. How big was it? Could it run fast? Did it walk on two legs or four?

- Discover bones and teeth and try to determine whether they belong to the same animal — herbivore or carnivore.

- Find a safe refuge from carnivorous dinosaurs, using fossils as a clue to where an ocean might be. Scattered plant fossils, footprints, clams, and marine fossils can provide clues as to how a beleaguered visitor might escape to the sea.

- Explore the way dinosaurs lived — how they ate, kept cool, balanced, used their visual systems.

As they enter "Dinoworld," visitors should each be given a guide, which can be designed to resemble a passport. The passport should also include a worksheet for each activity that visitors must complete. As a visitor completes each activity, the passport can be stamped with a rubber stamp made by students. Before a visitor is allowed to leave, a certain number of activities must be stamped. Perhaps a prize can be awarded for the most activities completed, or various prizes can be designated for total number of activities completed (1 activity completed earns a dinosaur cookie, 5 a pencil topper, 10 a T-shirt).

Students have already received intensive training about science and dinosaurs. Visitors should include friends and families, nonparticipating faculty, administrators (who work in and outside of the school building), members of the community, and the media. The planning and execution can be overseen by students cooperating with a committee made up of teachers and parents (perhaps the PTSA could be involved). Many (or all) of the activities will previously have been completed in class, so new materials should not be necessary. At a time when the educational system needs to reinforce its credibility as an institution where children expand their horizons, this activity will provide a means to "strut your stuff!"

APPENDIX A
Activity Summary Chart

ACTIVITY NAME	Time required (minutes)	Student grouping	LIBRARY	READING	WRITING	LISTENING	DEBATING, DISCUSSION	MATHEMATICS, MEASURING	GRAPHING	MAPPING, GEOGRAPHY	DATA INTERPRETATION	DRAWING, ART	ACTIVE, MANIPULATIVE	OUTDOOR POSSIBILITIES	Page number
How Many Horns Are There?	180	C	✓			✓	✓			✓	✓				7
What Is It? (*Stegosaurus*)	45	1				✓				✓	✓				14
Which Is More Efficient?	20	1,C				✓						✓	✓		22
Charting the Dinosaurs	45+	var	✓					✓		✓					25
Books Can Be Wrong	45+	var	✓					✓		✓					28
They Can Be Really Big	45+	var	✓								✓	✓	✓		31
Why Did He Think It Was So Big?	25	1	✓				✓								44
Kangaroo?	45+	1	✓	✓						✓					49
What Does It Look Like?	90	1,2	✓								✓				56
Dictionary Search	45+	1	✓												57
Bone Assembly	90+	2	✓	✓		✓				✓		✓			64
Life-Size Skeletons	90+	var	✓							✓	✓	✓	✓		76
Arches Everywhere	hw	1	✓									✓			87
Neck and Tail Tales	45	1					✓					✓			91
The Angle Makes It Easy	90	2						✓				✓			94
Counterbalance	5	2										✓			100
Moment to Moment	45+	2					✓			✓		✓			102
How Did They Do That?	45	2,C								✓	✓	✓	✓		106
Trackway Interpretation	135	4								✓	✓	✓			107

220

Activity	Time required	Grouping	A	D	E	G	I	L	M	O	P	R	S	W	
How Fast Did They Do That?	135	2,C	✓						✓				✓	✓	110
Did They Walk, Trot, or Run?	45+	1,2							✓					✓	113
Can We Tell How Big They Were?	45	1							✓					✓	119
How Fast Did They Move?	45	1							✓			✓	✓		122
Where Do Your Eyes Look?	45+	2					✓		✓				✓		130
What the Eyes Reveal	45+	1	✓								✓	✓			132
Seeing Like the Dinosaurs	45+	1,C	✓								✓	✓	✓	✓	133
Different Teeth for Different Jobs	5	1											✓		139
How Do We Do It?	25	C	✓										✓	✓	142
Blood Temperature	90	3							✓			✓	✓	✓	146
Relative Measurement	5	C										✓			155
How Do They Connect?	45+	1	✓					✓			✓	✓			156
It's Written in the Trees	45+	2	✓					✓	✓		✓	✓	✓	✓	166
Half-Life Can Tell It All	45	2	✓			✓			✓		✓	✓	✓	✓	172
A 100-Million-Year-Old Puzzle	90+	2	✓		✓		✓					✓	✓		182
Define a Continent	45+	2	✓		✓							✓			188
What's Found Where?	20	var		✓				✓			✓				192
Where Can I See the Sea?	45+	C	✓					✓			✓	✓	✓		193
What If?	45+	1,2	✓	✓				✓				✓	✓		211
Is It Too Late to Help?	45+	var	✓		✓			✓				✓	✓	✓	214
The Great Debate	45+	var	✓	✓				✓				✓			215

Skill Legend

A = active, manipulative
D = drawing, art
E = debating, discussion
G = graphing
I = interpretation of data
L = library

M = mathematics, measuring
O = outdoor possibilities
P = mapping, geography
R = reading
S = listening
W = writing

Grouping

1,2,4 = number of students
C = entire class
var = various

Time required

approximate time needed to complete activities (in minutes)
hw = homework

APPENDIX B
Fossils
(Words in **bold** type will appear in the "Glossary.")

WHAT ARE FOSSILS?

Fossils are remnants or traces of organisms that lived in the past. The word comes from the Latin *fossilis*, meaning "dug up." Fossils can be divided into two categories: **body fossils** and **trace fossils**. Body fossils are part of the organism itself, such as clam shells, leaves, or, for dinosaurs, bones and teeth. Trace fossils are created by the activities of an organism, for example the burrow of a clam, or, for dinosaurs, footprints, nests, **gastroliths** (stomach stones), and **coprolites** (fossilized dung).

Before even a single bone can be displayed in a museum, a remarkable concatenation of coincidences has occurred. An organism died; the bone was protected from destruction by other animals and weather; it was buried further so the layer of sediment in which it was embedded was turned into rock; a portion of the rock layer was uplifted to the surface; erosion wore away the rock to expose the bone; someone found the bone and brought it to the museum. This process, in the case of dinosaurs, took at least 66 million years. Often, to create a single museum skeleton, this same process has to be repeated hundreds of times.

A similar string of luck is necessary to preserve footprints and trackways. Imagine a single dinosaur strolling along the beach at sunset, her feet barely avoiding the swashing surf, leaving a perfect, solitary trackway behind. If you have ever had a similar experience, you know that the chances of that set of footprints being there the next morning are not good. Wind, tides, rain, and the action of other animals all quickly erase or obscure what was clearly imprinted the night before. It is remarkable, therefore, that hundreds of dinosaur trackways have been documented around the world.

Compared to the amount of evidence that once existed, the fossilized material available today represents a very small portion. It is tribute to the **paleontologists** and **paleoichnologists** that so much has been learned about dinosaurs from the scant evidence available.

HOW ARE BODY FOSSILS PRESERVED?

There are several types of body fossils. The most important for scientists is the actual animal shell, wood, or bone, all still composed of the original material. After the original material is buried, however, water with dissolved minerals can move through spaces (or **pores**) in the rock. When it reaches the buried fossil, the minerals in the water can replace, fill in, or chemically change the original material of the fossil. The original shape and texture is preserved, but the composition may be quite different. Petrified wood is a well-known example of such a process. In certain cases, the water chemistry can actually dissolve and remove the original material, and all that is left is a **mold** or impression of the original. If a mold exists and then becomes filled by mud or sand, a **cast** is formed.

WHY ARE FOSSILS IMPORTANT?

Your class is examining the possible extinction of the African elephant. You pose the following question to the students: "If African elephants had become extinct last year, how would you know about them today?" A sampling of student replies might include the following: "I saw them in the circus," "I saw photographs of them in a book," "I read a book about people who studied them in Africa," "There was a television program that showed the problems the elephants were having in Africa," "I fed them peanuts at the zoo," "I saw the movie *Dumbo* six times," and "My mother told me about them."

Ask the following similar question about dinosaurs: "Dinosaurs became extinct more than 60 million years ago. How do we know about dinosaurs today?" A sampling of student replies might include these: "I saw them in the movies," "I watch the 'Flintstones'," "I read a book about dinosaurs," or "I saw a *Triceratops* skeleton in the museum." In the minds of the students, their responses to the two questions may be comparable. In terms of scientific observation, they are not.

Extinct animals are no longer available for first-hand observation. Animals that became extinct during the time modern man has existed on the planet (the dodo and passenger pigeon, for example) have been documented by paintings, photographs, detailed observation, and even stuffed specimens. Animals that became extinct before the appearance of man must necessarily document their own existence. That documentation comes in the form of fossils.

Scientists believe living organisms have existed on earth for more than 1 billion years. The earliest evidence of life recorded by man comes from cave paintings approximately 50,000 years old. The only evidence for the various life forms that existed on this planet during the preceding 999,950,000 years comes from fossils.

Fossils not only provide evidence for the existence of organisms, they also indicate how the organism changed through time, how it reproduced, how it lived, and how it died. Detailed study of fossils representing plants and animals that apparently lived together can also provide information about what earth was like millions, and even billions, of years ago. **Ecology** is the science of the relationship between organisms and their environments. Fossils allow scientists to explore **paleoecology**, that is, the study of environments and organisms that no longer exist. Such studies become important when investigating organism extinctions and could have even greater significance when applied to the changes man is making in his environment. And lastly, without fossils, this book would never have been written.

APPENDIX C
Geologic Time

For many years the geologic time scale was determined solely by whether an event or fossil in one area was younger or older than an event or fossil from some other area (relative age). The original age comparisons were made in Europe in the early 1800s, and the names used in the time scale reflected the geography of the area in which those events were originally described. Periods are named mostly for the areas in which certain rock sequences are located. For example, "Cambrian" for Cambria, the Roman name for Wales; "Jurassic" for the Jura Mountains of France and Switzerland. Other names of geologic periods describe the general type of rocks found: Cretaceous rocks are chalky and the Carboniferous (Mississippian and Pennsylvanian) rocks are coaly.

Although some fossil evidence of primitive life older than the Cambrian has been found (algae, bacteria, and primitive marine invertebrates), abundant fossil evidence does not appear until the Cambrian Period in the early Paleozoic. The eras—Paleozoic, Mesozoic, and Cenozoic—are designated based on the successions of life forms found, and they mean, successively, "old life," "middle life," and "recent life."

The ages and time intervals shown are not well defined. Sources disagree as to exact dates. The Cambrian is often given as starting 600 million years ago and the Cretaceous as ending 60 or 65 million years ago. The dates provided in this book are those recognized by the Geological Society of America. (The Geological Society of America has handy, inexpensive, pocket-size versions of the time scale available. They may be contacted at Box 9140, Boulder, CO 80301 or at [303] 447-2020.)

The earth is (again, depending upon your reference) approximately 4.5 billion years old, or 4,500 million years old. For most of that time, life (both plants and animals) apparently had only a minimal impact on the planet. Dinosaurs existed on earth only during the time indicated on the charts in figure C.1, page 226: 230 million to 66 million years ago. They were present on the earth for only 165 million of the earth's 4,500 million years, but while they were here, they dominated the land more than any other animal has ever dominated its environment. Man dominates the earth today, but our species has only been on earth for 1 to 2 million years. It would take another 163 million years of dominance before man could be considered a force comparable to the dinosaurs. Of course, at the rate man is now destroying the earth, it is frightening to imagine what the planet will be like 163 million years from now.

SUGGESTED READING

Benton, Michael. *On the Trail of the Dinosaurs*. New York: Crown, 1989.

Holmes, Arthur. *Principles of Physical Geology*. New York: Ronald Press, 1965.

Fig. C.1. The geologic time chart (modified from the Geological Society of America) showing the time span during which dinosaurs existed.

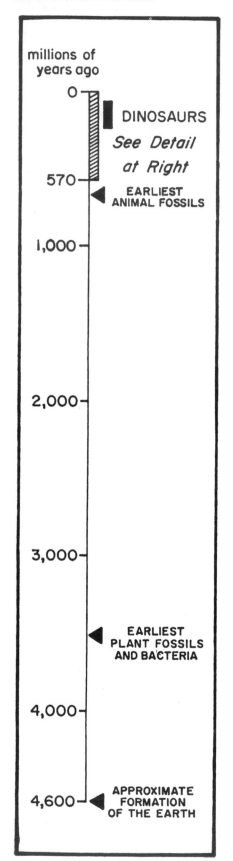

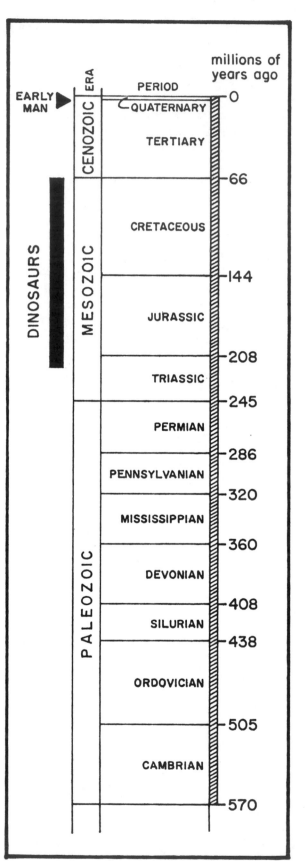

From *Investigating Science with Dinosaurs*, copyright 1993, Teacher Ideas Press, P.O. Box 6633, Englewood, CO 80155-6633

APPENDIX D
Pronunciation Guide to Extinct Animals Named in the Text

Name	Pronunciation
Albertosaurus	al-burr-tow-SOAR-us
Allosaurus	al-oh-SOAR-us
Ankylosaurus	ank-ih-low-SOAR-us
Apatosaur	a-PAT-o-soar
Archaeopteryx	ark-ee-OP-ter-ix
Arrhinoceratops	a-rhine-oh-SER-a-tops
Bactrosaurus	back-trow-SOAR-us
Brachiosaurus	brach-ee-oh-SOAR-us
Brontosaurus	bron-tow-SOAR-us
Camarasaurus	KAM-a-ra-SOAR-us
Camptosaurus	camp-tow-SOAR-us
Centrosaurus	sen-trow-SOAR-us
Ceratosaurus	ser-A-tow-SOAR-us
Coelurosaurus	see-lure-owe-SOAR-us
Compsognathus	komp-SOG-nay-thus
Corythosaurus	core-ih-thow-SOAR-us
Deinonychus	die-NON-ik-us
Dimetrodon	die-ME-trow-don
Dinosaur	DIE-no-soar
Diplodocus	dip-PLOD-oh-cuss
Edmontosaurus	ed-MONT-oh-soar-us
Elasmosaurus	ee-LAZ-mo-SOAR-us
Euoplocephalus	yoo-OP-low-SEF-al-us
Hadrosaurus	HAD-row-SOAR-us
Heterodontosaurus	HET-er-oh-DONT-oh-SOAR-us

Name	Pronunciation
Hypsilophodon	hip-sih-LOAF-oh-don
Iguanodon	ig-WAH-no-don
Lambeosaurus	LAM-bee-oh-SOAR-us
Lycorhinus	LYE-co-RHINE-us
Maiasaurus	MY-a-SOAR-us
Megalosaurus	MEG-a-low-SOAR-us
Mosasaur	MOW-zah-soar
Nemegtosaurus	ne-MEG-tow-SOAR-us
Ornitholestes	or-NITH-oh-LESS-teez
Ouranosaurus	oo-RAN-oh-SOAR-us
Pachycephalosaurus	PACK-ee-SEFF-uh-low-SOAR-us
Parasaurolophus	PAR-a-soar-AH-low-fuss
Plateosaurus	plate-ee-oh-SOAR-us
Plesiosaur	PLEE-zee-oh-soar
Procompsognathus	pro-komp-SOG-nay-thus
Protoavis	pro-tow-A-viss
Protoceratops	pro-tow-SER-a-tops
Sauropelta	SOAR-oh-PELL-tah
Spinosaurus	spy-no-SOAR-us
Stegosaurus	steg-oh-SOAR-us
Stegoceras	steg-oh-SER-as
Struthiomimus	STROOTH-ee-o-MIME-us
Styracosaurus	sty-RACK-oh-SOAR-us
Tenontosaurus	ten-ON-to-SOAR-us
Triceratops	try-SER-a-tops
Tyrannosaurus	tie-RAN-oh-SOAR-us
Ultrasaurus	ULL-tra-SOAR-us
Velociraptor	vell-AH-see-WRAP-tore
Zigongosaurus	zee-GON-go-SOAR-us

GLOSSARY

Absolute age — the age of something (fossil, rock layer) in years.

Adaptation — the modification of an organism in response to a change in its environment.

Annular — in the shape of concentric rings.

Articulated — as applied to a skeleton, one whose joints, segments, and limbs remain attached after burial and recovery.

Asteroid — a celestial body with a diameter between one and several hundred kilometers and an orbit usually between Mars and Jupiter.

Bipedal — the posture of walking or running on two legs, like man or birds.

Bivalves — mollusks with two calcareous shells, or valves, usually applied to clams.

Body fossil — a fossil composed of parts of the original organism: bones or teeth from dinosaurs, shells from marine organisms, or actual leaf material from plants.

Boyle's law — the law determined by Robert Boyle in the 1660s that states that at a constant temperature, the volume of a gas is inversely proportional to its temperature.

Carnivore — an animal whose diet consists of other animals.

Cast — the filling of the cavity left behind by an organism (*see* **Mold**).

Cold-blooded — an animal whose body temperature varies with its environment; cold-bloodedness is also called *ectothermy* or *poikilothermy*.

Coprolite — fossilized dung.

Correlation — the process by which rock layers in one area are related to those in another area.

Dendrochronology — the study of tree rings to examine and date past events.

Diurnal — occurring or active during the day.

Ecology — the study of the relationships between organisms and the environments in which they live.

Entropy — a measure of the natural tendency of systems to progress from order to disorder.

Extinct — no longer existing or living.

Fossil — any record of past life that has been preserved in rock.

Fossil assemblage — a collection of preserved past life that may or may not be indicative of the component organisms' association when living.

Fulcrum — the point of support of a lever.

Gastrolith — stones swallowed by dinosaurs, reptiles, and birds to help grind food during digestion.

Geologist — a scientist who studies the earth.

Geomorphic — having to do with the shape of the earth's surface.

229

Herbivore — an animal whose diet consists of plants.

Hypothesis — an explanation that accounts for a group of facts that can be tested by further investigation; an educated guess based upon the facts then known.

Index fossil — a fossil that provides precise correlations of time between diverse locations, having the features of recognizability, wide distribution, and limited time presence.

Law — the concept explaining the facts in which scientists have the most confidence, proven by the most observations and experimental data; almost equal to a fact.

Law of superposition — in a normal sequence of layered rocks, any layer is older than the layer immediately above it.

Mold — the impression made by an organism in rock as a result of burial (*see* **Cast**).

Newton's first law of motion — the law determined by Isaac Newton in the 1680s stating that an object at rest, or at motion in a straight line, continues until it is acted upon by a force.

Nocturnal — active mostly at night.

Paleoecology — the science of the relationships between ancient organisms and their environments.

Paleoichnologist — a specialized paleontologist who studies trace fossils.

Paleontologist — a scientist who studies the life of past geological ages.

Pelecypod — a class of mollusks with two calcareous shells (e.g., a clam) (*see* **Bivalve**).

Phytoplankton — minute, floating, aquatic plants.

Pore — a space in rock or soil not occupied by solid mineral matter.

Predator — an animal that lives by hunting others.

Prey — an animal hunted or caught for food.

Quadrupedal — walking or running primarily on four legs.

Radiometric — using radioactive decay to measure absolute age.

Relative age — the age of a rock layer or fossil as compared to another (e.g., younger or older).

Reptile — a cold-blooded vertebrate that uses lungs to breath, has an external covering of scales, and usually lays eggs.

Salinity — a measure of the total amount of solids dissolved in water.

Stereoscopic — a visual system in which, because of their slightly different positions, each eye has a slightly different view of an object. As the brain processes the slightly different signals from each eye, it generates a three-dimensional image of the original object and provides a sense of depth.

Taxonomy — the systematic classification of plants and animals according to their characteristics and evolutionary relationships.

Theory — a speculation that appears to be supported by all known facts and has no reasonable rival; a level of confidence above a hypothesis.

Trace fossil — a preserved feature resulting from the activities of organisms (e.g., burrows or footprints).

Vertebrae — the bones forming the spinal column.

Warm-blooded — having the ability to maintain a relatively constant body temperature independent of environmental conditions; also called *endothermy* or *homeothermy*.

BIBLIOGRAPHY

Alexander, R. McNeill. "Estimates of Speeds of Dinosaurs." *Nature* 261, no. 5,556 (1976): 129-130.

Alexander, R. McNeill. *Dynamics of Dinosaurs and Other Extinct Giants*. New York: Columbia University Press, 1989.

Alexander, R. McNeill. "How Dinosaurs Ran." *Scientific American* 264, no. 4 (1991): 130-136.

Aliki. *My Visit to the Dinosaurs*. New York: Thomas Y. Crowell, 1969.

Aliki. *Digging Up Dinosaurs*. New York: Thomas Y. Crowell, 1981.

Aliki. *Dinosaurs Are Different*. New York: Thomas Y. Crowell, 1985.

Aliki. *Dinosaur Bones*. New York: Thomas Y. Crowell, 1988.

Alvarez, Walter, and Frank Asaro. "An Extraterrestrial Impact." *Scientific American* 263, no. 4 (1990): 78-84.

American Geological Institute. *Dictionary of Geologic Terms*. Garden City, N.Y.: Dolphin Books, 1962.

American Heritage Dictionary, Second College Edition. Boston: Houghton Mifflin, 1982.

Andrews, J. T. "Recent and Fossil Growth Rates of Marine Bivalves, Canadian Arctic and Late Quaternary Arctic Marine Environments." *Paleogeography, Paleoclimatology, Paleoecology* 11 (1972): 157-176.

Andrews, Roy Chapman. *All About Dinosaurs*. New York: Random House, 1953.

Armour, Richard. *A Dozen Dinosaurs*. New York: McGraw-Hill, 1967.

Arnold, Caroline. *Dinosaur Mountain: Graveyard of the Past*. New York: Houghton Mifflin, 1988.

Asimov, Isaac. *How Did We Find Out About Dinosaurs?* New York: Walker, 1973.

Bakker, Robert T. *The Dinosaur Heresies*. New York: Zebra Books, 1986.

Batory, R. Dana, and William A. S. Sarjeant. "Sussex Iguanodon Footprints and the Writing of *The Lost World*." In *Dinosaur Tracks and Traces*, edited by David M. Gillette and Martin G. Lockley. Cambridge: Cambridge University Press, 1989.

Benton, Michael J. *The Dinosaur Encyclopedia*. New York: Simon & Schuster, 1984.

Benton, Michael J. *Do You Know How Dinosaurs Lived?* New York: Warwick Press, 1985.

Benton, Michael J. *On the Trail of the Dinosaurs*. New York: Crown, 1989.

Berenstain, Stan, and Jan Berenstain. *The Day of the Dinosaur*. New York: Random House, 1987.

Berenstein, Michael. *The Spike-Tailed Dinosaur: Stegosaurus*. Racine, Wis.: Western, 1989.

Bird, Roland T. *Bones for Barnum Brown*. Fort Worth, Tex.: Texas Christian University Press, 1985.

Black Hills Institute of Geological Research. *What Is a Dinosaur?* Hill City, S. Dak.: Black Hills Institute of Geological Research, 1990.

Booth, Jerry. *The Big Beast Book: Dinosaurs and How They Got That Way*. Boston: Little, Brown, 1988.

Borror, Donald J. *Dictionary of Word Roots and Combining Forms*. Palo Alto, Calif.: Mayfield, 1960.

Brown, Barnum. "Sinclair Dinosaur Expedition." *Natural History* 36 (1935): 3-15.

Burton, Jane, and Dougal Dixon. *Time Exposure: A Photographic Record of the Dinosaur Age*. New York: Beaufort Books, 1984.

Campbell, Neil A. *Biology*. Menlo Park, Calif.: Benjamin/Cummings, 1987.

Carroll, Susan. *How Big Is Brachiosaurus?: Fascinating Facts About Dinosaurs*. New York: Platt & Munk, 1986.

Casier, Edgar. *Les Iguanodons de Bernissart*. Brussels: Institut Royal des Sciences Naturelles de Belgique, 1960.

Charig, Alan. *A New Look at the Dinosaurs*. New York: Facts on File, 1983.

Chatterjee, Sankar. "Cranial Anatomy and Relationships of a New Triassic Bird from Texas." *Philosophical Transactions of the Royal Society of London*, Series B, 332, no. 1,265 (1991): 277-342.

Clarke, Adam. *Clarke's Commentary*. Nashville, Tenn.: Abingdon Press, 1977.

Cobb, Vicki. *The Monsters Who Died: A Mystery About Dinosaurs*. New York: Coward-McCann, 1983.

Cohen, Daniel. *What Really Happened to the Dinosaurs?* New York: E. P. Dutton, 1977.

Cohen, Daniel. *Dinosaurs*. New York: Doubleday, 1987.

Colbert, Edwin H. *Men and Dinosaurs*. New York: E. P. Dutton, 1968.

Colbert, Edwin H. *The Year of the Dinosaur*. New York: Charles Scribner's Sons, 1977.

Colbert, Edwin H. *Dinosaurs: An Illustrated History*. Maplewood, N.J.: Hammond, 1983.

Colbert, Edwin H., and William A. Burns. *Digging for Dinosaurs*. Chicago: Children's Press, 1967.

Cole, Joanna. *Dinosaur Story*. New York: William Morrow, 1974.

Collette, Alfred T., and Eugene L. Chiappetta. *Science Instruction in the Middle and Secondary Schools*. Columbus, Ohio: Merrill, 1989.

Courtillot, Vincent E. "A Volcanic Eruption." *Scientific American* 263, no. 4 (1990): 85-92.

Craig, M. Jean. *Dinosaurs and More Dinosaurs*. New York: Four Winds Press, 1965.

Crichton, Michael. *Jurassic Park*. New York: Ballantine Books, 1991.

Curtis, Will. *The Nature of Things*. New York: ECCO Press, 1984.

Czerkas, Sylvia J., and Stephen A. Czerkas. *Dinosaurs: A Global View*. New York: Mallard Press, 1991.

Czerkas, Sylvia J., and Everett C. Olson. *Dinosaurs Past and Present, Volumes I and II*. Los Angeles: Natural History Museum of Los Angeles County, 1987.

Daeschler, Ted. *The Dinosaur Hunter's Handbook*. Philadelphia: Running Press, 1990.

Demi. *Find Demi's Dinosaurs*. New York: Grosset & Dunlap, 1989.

dePaola, Tomie. *Little Grunt and the Big Egg*. New York: Holiday House, 1990.

Desmond, Adrian J. *The Hot-Blooded Dinosaurs*. New York: Dial Press, 1976.

Dixon, Dougal. *The First Dinosaurs*. Milwaukee, Wis.: Gareth Stevens, 1987.

Dixon, Dougal. *Hunting the Dinosaurs*. Milwaukee, Wis.: Gareth Stevens, 1987.

Dixon, Dougal. *The Jurassic Dinosaurs*. Milwaukee, Wis.: Gareth Stevens, 1987.

Dixon, Dougal. *The Last Dinosaurs*. Milwaukee, Wis.: Gareth Stevens, 1987.

Dixon, Dougal. *The Illustrated Dinosaur Encyclopedia*. New York: Gallery Books, 1988.

Dixon, Dougal. *The New Dinosaurs: An Alternative Evolution*. Topsfield, Mass.: Salem House, 1988.

Dixon, Dougal, Barry Cox, R. J. G. Savage, and Brian Gardiner. *The Macmillan Illustrated Encyclopedia of Dinosaurs and Prehistoric Animals*. New York: Macmillan, 1988.

Dunbar, Carl O., and John Rodgers. *Principles of Stratigraphy*. New York: John Wiley and Sons, 1957.

Erlich, Paul, and Ann Erlich. *The Causes and Consequences of the Disappearance of Species*. New York: Random House, 1981.

Eschmeyer, William N., Earl S. Herald, and Howard Hammann. *A Field Guide to Pacific Coast Fishes of North America*. Boston: Houghton Mifflin, 1983.

Farlow, James O. "Estimates of Dinosaur Speeds from a Trackway Site in Texas." *Nature* 294, no. 5,843 (1981): 747-748.

Farlow, James O. *On the Tracks of Dinosaurs*. New York: Franklin Watts, 1991.

Ferguson, C. W. "Concepts and Techniques of Dendrochronology." In *Scientific Methods in Medieval Archaeology*, edited by Rainer Berger. Berkeley, Calif.: University of California Press, 1970.

Funston, Sylvia. *The Dinosaur Question and Answer Book*. Boston: Little, Brown, 1992.

Geis, Darlene. *Dinosaurs and Other Prehistoric Animals*. New York: Grosset & Dunlap, 1959.

Geis, Darlene. *The How and Why Wonder Book of Dinosaurs*. New York: Grosset & Dunlap, 1960.

Gill, Shelley. *Thunderfeet: Alaska's Dinosaurs and Other Prehistoric Creatures*. Homer, AK: Paws IV, 1988.

Glut, Donald. *The Dinosaur Dictionary*. New York: Bonanza Books, 1972.

Glut, Donald. *The Complete Dinosaur Dictionary*. New York: Citadel Press, 1992.

Gore, Rick. "Extinctions." *National Geographic* 175, no. 6 (1989): 662-699.

Gould, Stephen J. *Bully for Brontosaurus*. New York: W. W. Norton, 1991.

Greene, Carla. *How to Know Dinosaurs*. Indianapolis, Ind.: Bobbs-Merrill, 1966.

Gurney, James. *Dinotopia*. Atlanta, Ga.: Turner, 1992.

Hanley, John. "Fossils and Time: Selected Books on Paleontology, Evolution and Earth History for Elementary Through College Students and Amateur Paleontologists." U.S.G.S. Open File Report 84-767. Lakewood, Colo.: U.S. Geological Survey, 1984.

Harris, Miles F., Dale T. Hesser, J. Allen Hynek, William H. Matthews, III, Chalmer J. Roy, James W. Skehan, S.J., and Robert E. Stevenson. *Investigating the Earth*. 4th ed. Boston: Houghton Mifflin, 1973.

Holmes, Arthur. *Principles of Physical Geology*. New York: Ronald Press, 1965.

Holsaert, Eunice, and Robert Gartland. *Dinosaurs: A Book to Begin On*. Chicago: Holt, Rinehart & Winston, 1959.

Horner, John R., and James Gorman. *Maia: A Dinosaur Grows Up*. Bozeman, Mont.: Museum of the Rockies, 1985.

Horner, John R., and James Gorman. *Digging Dinosaurs*. New York: Workman, 1988.

Howard, Robert. *The Dawnseekers*. New York: Harcourt Brace Jovanovich, 1975.

Hsu, Kenneth J. *The Great Dying*. San Diego, Calif.: Harcourt Brace Jovanovich, 1986.

Hurley, Patrick M. *How Old Is the Earth?* Garden City, N.Y.: Doubleday, 1959.

Hurley, Patrick M. "The Confirmation of Continental Drift." In *Continents Adrift, Readings from Scientific American*. San Francisco: W. H. Freeman, 1972.

Huxley, T. H. "On the Animals Which Are Most Nearly Intermediate Between Birds and Reptiles." *Geological Magazine* 5 (1868): 357-365.

Huxley, T. H. "Further Evidence of the Affinity Between the Dinosaurian Reptiles and Birds." *Quarterly Journal of the Geological Society of London* 26 (1870): 12-31.

Ipsen, D. C. *The Riddle of the Stegosaurus*. Reading, Mass.: Addison-Wesley, 1969.

Jaber, William. *Whatever Happened to the Dinosaurs?* New York: Julian Messner, 1978.

Jackson, Kathryn. *Dinosaurs*. Washington, D.C.: National Geographic Society, 1972.

Johnson, James H., Jr. *They Walked the Earth*. Cañon City, Colo.: P. Q. Publications, 1992.

Kaufman, Les, and Kenneth Mallory. *The Last Extinction*. Cambridge, Mass.: MIT, 1986.

Kerr, Richard A. "Origins and Extinctions: Paleontology in Chicago." *Science* 257, no. 5,069 (1992): 486-487.

Kerr, Richard A. "The Earliest Mass Extinction?" *Science* 257, no. 5,070 (1992): 612.

Kerr, Richard A. "Huge Impact Tied to Mass Extinction." *Science* 257, no. 5,072 (1992): 878-880.

Krishtalka, Leonard. *Dinosaur Plots and Other Intrigues in Natural History*. New York: Avon Books, 1989.

Lakes, Arthur. "The Dinosaurs of the Rocky Mountains." *Kansas City Review of Science* 2 (1879): 731-735.

Lambert, David. *Dinosaurs*. London: Franklin Watts, 1982.

Lambert, David. *Collins Guide to Dinosaurs*. London: William Collins and Sons, 1983.

Lambert, David. *The Dinosaur Data Book*. New York: Avon Books, 1990.

Lanham, Url. *The Bone Hunters*. New York: Columbia University Press, 1973.

Lasky, Kathryn. *Dinosaur Dig*. New York: Morrow Junior Books, 1990.

Lauber, Patricia. *Dinosaurs Walked Here*. New York: Bradbury Press, 1987.

Lawrence, Jerome, and Robert E. Lee. *Inherit the Wind*. New York: Bantam Books, 1955.

Leet, L. Don, and Sheldon Judson. *Physical Geology*. New York: Prentice Hall, 1971.

Lindsay, William. *The Great Dinosaur Atlas*. New York: Julian Messner, 1991.

Lockley, Martin. *Tracking Dinosaurs*. Cambridge: Cambridge University Press, 1991.

Lord, John. *Teaching About Energy*. Santa Monica, Calif.: Enterprise for Education, 1986.

Man, John. *The Natural History of the Dinosaur*. New York: Gallery Books, 1978.

Manetti, William. *Dinosaurs in Your Backyard*. New York: Atheneum, 1982.

Marsh, O. C. "A New Order of Extinct Reptilia (*Stegosauria*) from the Jurassic of the Rocky Mountains." *American Journal of Science*, 3d series, 14, no. 84 (1877): 513-514.

Marsh, O. C. "Notice of New Fossil Mammals." *American Journal of Science*, 3d series, 34 (1887): 323-324.

Matthews, William H., III. *Wonders of the Dinosaur World*. New York: Dodd, Mead, 1963.

May, Julian. *The Warm-Blooded Dinosaurs*. New York: Holiday House, 1978.

McAlester, A. Lee. *The History of Life*. Englewood Cliffs, N.J.: Prentice-Hall, 1968.

McGowen, Tom. *Album of Dinosaurs*. Chicago: Rand McNally, 1972.

McLoughlin, John C. *Archosauria: A New Look at the Dinosaur*. New York: Viking, 1979.

McMullen, Kate. *Dinosaur Hunters*. New York: Random House, 1989.

Milburn, Constance. *Let's Look at Dinosaurs*. New York: Bookwright Press, 1987.

Moody, Richard. *The World of Dinosaurs*. New York: Grosset & Dunlap, 1977.

Moore, Jo Ellen. *Dinosaurs and Other Prehistoric Animals, K-1*. Monterey, Calif.: Evan-Moore, 1991.

Moore, Raymond C., Cecil G. Lalicker, and Alfred G. Fischer. *Invertebrate Fossils*. New York: McGraw-Hill, 1952.

Most, Bernard. *The Littlest Dinosaurs*. San Diego, Calif.: Harcourt Brace Jovanovich, 1989.

Most, Bernard. *Four and Twenty Dinosaurs*. New York: Harper & Row, 1990.

Murphy, Jim. *The Last Dinosaur*. New York: Scholastic, 1988.

Newman, William L. *Geologic Time*. Denver, Colo.: U.S. Geological Survey, 1991.

Norman, David. *The Illustrated Encyclopedia of Dinosaurs*. New York: Crown, 1985.

Norman, David. *Dinosaur*. New York: Prentice Hall Press, 1991.

Norman, David, and Angela Milner. *Dinosaur: An Eyewitness Book*. New York: Alfred A. Knopf, 1989.

O'Neill, Mary. *A Family of Dinosaurs*. Mahwah, N.J.: Troll Associates, 1989.

Oram, Raymond F., Paul J. Hummer, and Robert C. Smoot. *Biology: Living Systems*. Columbus, Ohio: Charles E. Merrill, 1983.

Osborne, Henry Fairfield. "Fossil Wonders of the West." *Century Magazine* 46, no. 5 (1904): 680-694.

Ostrom, John H., and John S. McIntosh. *Marsh's Dinosaurs: The Collections from Como Bluff*. New Haven, Conn.: Yale University Press, 1966.

Owen, Richard. "Report on British Fossil Reptiles." *Report of the 11th Meeting of the British Association for the Advancement of Science* (1841): 142-143.

Panati, Charles. *Panati's Extraordinary Endings of Practically Everything and Everybody*. New York: Harper & Row, 1989.

Parker, Steve. *Dinosaurs and How They Lived*. New York: Dorling, Kindersley, 1991.

Paul, Gregory S. *Predatory Dinosaurs of the World*. New York: Simon & Schuster, 1988.

Pearce, Q. L. *All About Dinosaurs*. New York: Simon & Schuster, 1989.

Peters, David. *A Gallery of Dinosaurs and Other Early Reptiles*. New York: Alfred A. Knopf, 1989.

Peterson, Dave. *Apatosaurus*. Chicago: Children's Press, 1989.

Peterson, Roger Tory. *The Birds*. Life Nature Library. New York: Time Life, 1968.

Phipps, R. L., and J. McGowan. *Tree Rings: Timekeepers of the Past*. Washington, D.C.: U.S. Geological Survey, 1989.

Pittelman, Susan D., Joan E. Heimlich, Roberta L. Berglund, and Michael P. French. *Semantic Feature Analysis*. Newark, Del.: International Reading Association, 1991.

Plate, Robert. *The Dinosaur Hunters: Othniel C. Marsh and Edward D. Cope*. New York: David McKay, 1964.

Raup, David M., and J. John Sepkoski. "Mass Extinctions in the Marine Fossil Record." *Science* 215, no. 4,539 (1982): 1,501-1,502.

Romer, Alfred Sherwood. *Vertebrate Paleontology*. Chicago: University of Chicago Press, 1945.

Root-Bernstein, Robert Scott. *Discovering*. Cambridge, Mass.: First Harvard University Press, 1991.

Royston, Angela. *Eye Openers: Dinosaurs*. New York: Aladdin Books, 1991.

Russel, Dale A. *An Odyssey in Time: The Dinosaurs of North America*. Toronto: University of Toronto Press, 1989.

Sandell, Elizabeth J. *Seismosaurus, the Largest Dinosaur*. Marco, Fla.: Bancroft-Sage, 1988.

Sandell, Elizabeth J. *Stegosaurus, the Dinosaur with the Smallest Brain*. Marco, Fla.: Bancroft-Sage, 1988.

Sandell, Elizabeth J. *Triceratops, the Last Dinosaur*. Marco, Fla.: Bancroft-Sage, 1988.

Sandell, Elizabeth J. *Tyrannosaurus rex, the Fierce Dinosaur*. Marco, Fla.: Bancroft-Sage, 1988.

Sandell, Elizabeth J. *Ankylosaurus, the Armored Dinosaur*. Marco, Fla.: Bancroft-Sage, 1989.

Sandell, Elizabeth J. *Apatosaurus, the Deceptive Dinosaur*. Marco, Fla.: Bancroft-Sage, 1989.

Sandell, Elizabeth J. *Compsognathus, the Smallest Dinosaur*. Marco, Fla.: Bancroft-Sage, 1989.

Sandell, Elizabeth J. *Maiasaura, the Good Mother Dinosaur*. Marco, Fla.: Bancroft-Sage, 1989.

Sarton, George. *A History of Science*. New York: John Wiley and Sons, 1952.

Sattler, Helen Roney. *The Illustrated Dinosaur Dictionary*. New York: Lothrop, Lee & Shepard, 1983.

Sattler, Helen Roney. *Baby Dinosaurs*. New York: Lothrop, Lee & Shepard, 1984.

Sattler, Helen Roney. *Pterosaurs: The Flying Reptiles*. New York: Lothrop, Lee & Shepard, 1985.

Sattler, Helen Roney. *Stegosaurs: The Solar-Powered Dinosaurs*. New York: Lothrop, Lee & Shepard, 1992.

Schlein, Miriam. *Let's Go Dinosaur Tracking*. New York: HarperCollins, 1991.

Selsam, Millicent. *Tyrannosaurus rex*. New York: Harper & Row, 1978.

Sereno, Paul C. *How Tough Was a Tyrannosaurus?: More Fascinating Facts About Dinosaurs*. New York: Platt & Munk, 1989.

Sheehan, Angela. *Brontosaurus*. Windermere, Fla.: Ray Rourke, 1981.

Sheehan, Angela. *Dinosaurs*. Windermere, Fla.: Ray Rourke, 1981.

Sheehan, Angela. *Stegosaurus*. Windermere, Fla.: Ray Rourke, 1981.

Sheehan, Angela. *Triceratops*. Windermere, Fla.: Ray Rourke, 1981.

Sheehan, Angela. *Tyrannosaurus*. Windermere, Fla.: Ray Rourke, 1981.

Shuttlesworth, Dorothy E. *Dodos and Dinosaurs*. New York: Hastings House, 1968.

Shuttlesworth, Dorothy E. *To Find a Dinosaur*. Garden City, N.Y.: Doubleday, 1973.

Simon, Seymour. *The Largest Dinosaurs*. New York: Macmillan, 1986.

Simon, Seymour. *New Questions and Answers About Dinosaurs*. New York: Morrow Junior Books, 1990.

Smith, Kathie Billingston. *Dinosaurs*. New York: Simon & Schuster, 1987.

Stanek, V. J. *The Pictorial Encyclopedia of the Animal Kingdom*. New York: Crown, 1962.

Sternberg, Charles Hazelius. *Hunting Dinosaurs*. Edmonton, Canada: NeWest Press, 1985.

Stine, Megan, Craig Gillespie, Laurie Greenberg, Jamie Harms, Sharon Maves, Larry Malone, Carol Moroz-Henry, and Carol Stanbury, from the Smithsonian Institution. *Science Activity Book*. New York: GMG, 1987.

Storey, Kenneth B., and Janet M. Storey. "Frozen and Alive," *Science* 255, no. 9 (1990): 92-97.

Stout, William. *The Dinosaurs*. New York: Bantam Books, 1981.

Swinton, W. E. *Dinosaurs*. London: British Museum of Natural History, 1962.

Swisher, Carl C., III, Jose M. Grajales-Nishimura, Alessandro Montanari, Stanley V. Margolis, Phillipe Claeys, Walter Alvarez, Paul Renne, Estebán Cedillo-Pardo, Florentin J-M. R. Maurasse, Garniss H. Curtiss, Jan Smit, and Michael O. McWilliams. "Coeval 40Ar/39Ar Ages of 65.0 Million Years Ago from Chicxulub Crater Melt Rock and Cretaceous-Tertiary Boundary Tektites." *Science* 257, no. 5,072 (1992): 954-958.

Tarling, Don, and Maureen Tarling. *Continental Drift*. Garden City, N.Y.: Anchor Books, 1971.

Thulborn, Richard A. "Speeds and Gaits of Dinosaurs." *Paleogeography, Paleoclimatology, Paleoecology* 38 (1982): 227-256.

Thulborn, Richard A. "The Gaits of Dinosaurs." In *Dinosaur Tracks and Traces*, edited by David M. Gillette and Martin G. Lockley. Cambridge: Cambridge University Press, 1989.

Watson, Jane Werner. *Dinosaurs*. Racine, Wis.: Western, 1959.

West, Linda. *Dinosaurs and Dinosaur National Monument*. Jensen, Utah: Dinosaur Nature Association, 1985.

Whitaker, George O., and Joan Meyers. *Dinosaur Hunt*. New York: Harcourt, Brace & World, 1965.

Wilford, John Noble. *The Riddle of the Dinosaur*. New York: Vintage Books, 1985.

Williston, Samuel W. "American Jurassic Dinosaurs." *Transactions of the Kansas Academy of Science* 6 (1878): 42-46.

Wilson, Ron. *100 Dinosaurs from A to Z*. New York: Grosset & Dunlap, 1986.

Yorinks, Arthur. *Ugh*. New York: Farrar Straus & Giroux, 1990.

Zimmer, Carl. "Ruffled Feathers." *Discover* 13, no. 5 (1992): 44-54.

INDEX

ABOUT THE AUTHOR

Craig A. Munsart is a former energy industry geologist, educational programs manager at a children's museum, and middle school science curriculum writer. He has taught at the university, high school, junior high, and middle school levels and has lectured extensively to elementary schools. He holds a bachelor's and master's degree in geology from Queens College, City University of New York, and a bachelor's degree in architecture from Pratt Institute. He is presently an earth science educator in the Denver area and a secondary school physical science teacher in Jefferson County, Colorado public schools.